Anger Management Based Alcohol Treatment

Integrated Therapy for Anger and Alcohol Use Disorder

Anger Management Based Alcohol Treatment

Integrated Therapy for Anger and Alcohol Use Disorder

Kimberly S. Walitzer
Research Institute on Addictions at The University at Buffalo, Buffalo, New York, United States

Jerry L. Deffenbacher
Department of Psychology, Colorado State University, Fort Collins, Colorado, United States

Molly S. Rath
Research Institute on Addictions at The University at Buffalo, Buffalo, New York, United States

ELSEVIER

ACADEMIC PRESS
An imprint of Elsevier

Academic Press is an imprint of Elsevier
125 London Wall, London EC2Y 5AS, United Kingdom
525 B Street, Suite 1650, San Diego, CA 92101, United States
50 Hampshire Street, 5th Floor, Cambridge, MA 02139, United States
The Boulevard, Langford Lane, Kidlington, Oxford OX5 1GB, United Kingdom

Notices
Knowledge and best practice in this field are constantly changing. As new research and experience broaden our understanding, changes in research methods, professional practices, or medical treatment may become necessary.

Practitioners and researchers must always rely on their own experience and knowledge in evaluating and using any information, methods, compounds, or experiments described herein. In using such information or methods they should be mindful of their own safety and the safety of others, including parties for whom they have a professional responsibility.

To the fullest extent of the law, neither the Publisher nor the authors, contributors, or editors, assume any liability for any injury and/or damage to persons or property as a matter of products liability, negligence or otherwise, or from any use or operation of any methods, products, instructions, or ideas contained in the material herein.

British Library Cataloguing-in-Publication Data
A catalogue record for this book is available from the British Library

Library of Congress Cataloging-in-Publication Data
A catalog record for this book is available from the Library of Congress

ISBN: 978-0-12-812709-4

For Information on all Academic Press publications
visit our website at https://www.elsevier.com/books-and-journals

Publisher: Nikki Levy
Acquisition Editor: Nikki Levy
Editorial Project Manager: Karen Miller
Production Project Manager: Sujatha Thirugnana Sambandam
Cover Designer: Miles Hitchen

Typeset by MPS Limited, Chennai, India

Dedications

I dedicate this book to the many clients who participated in these research studies, shared their experiences and feedback with us, and provided important understandings and insights into why and how people become sober.

– Kimberly S. Walitzer

I would like to dedicate this book to Drs. Eugene Oetting, Ernest Chavez, Kimberly Walitzer, and Marv Moore, great mentors, colleagues, and, best of all, friends.

– Jerry L. Deffenbacher

I would like to dedicate this book to my incredible family and my brilliant co-authors.

– Molly S. Rath

Contents

Section III
Anger Management Based Alcohol Treatment Techniques

Section IV
Other Topics and Issues

About the Authors

Kimberly S. Walitzer, PhD, is deputy director and senior research scientist at the Research Institute on Addictions at the University at Buffalo, United States. She is a member of the American Psychologist Association and a licensed psychologist. Since 1990, she has conducted multiple randomized controlled research trials funded by the National Institutes of Health. This body of research has included foci on anger management based alcohol treatment, alcoholics anonymous facilitation treatment, motivational interviewing, life skills training, and spouse-involved alcohol treatment. She has developed standardized protocols for treatment delivery, implemented treatment with clients, and supervised clinicians in these treatment protocols. She lives in Kent, NY, on Lake Ontario, with her husband, Jim Heiler.

Jerry L. Deffenbacher, PhD, is professor emeritus, Department of Psychology, Colorado State University, United States, where he was a professor laureate and director of training. He is a fellow of the American Psychological Association, licensed psychologist, diplomate from the American Board of Professional Psychology, and distinguished diplomate from the North American Anger Management Association. Since the early 1980s, his scientific and professional interests have focused on basic research and theory testing regarding development of assessment instruments for and development and empirical validation of clinical interventions for general and driving anger. He also contributed to consideration of anger as an important clinical problem and potential diagnoses related thereto.

Molly Swart Rath is a Licensed Social Worker and Credentialed Alcohol and Substance Abuse Counselor at the Research Institute on Addictions at the University at Buffalo. She has worked on numerous grants funded by the National Institutes of Health, providing standardized treatment using evidence based therapies such as Cognitive Behavioral Therapy, Motivational Interviewing, Alcoholics Anonymous Facilitation, and Anger Management based Alcohol and Tobacco Treatment. She also has experience as a methadone clinic counselor, as a clinical supervisor for interns in training, and is a member of the Motivational Interviewing Network of Trainers (MINT). She lives in Hamburg, NY with her husband, Jim, and three magnificent teenagers, Eileen, Mac, and Charlie.

Acknowledgments

This work was supported by the NIH National Institute on Alcoholism and Alcohol Abuse grant award R01AA17603 entitled "Developing Anger Management (CRCS) for Use in Alcoholism Treatment." Appreciation is also due to the Project CATALYST team Sarah Pearson, Laura Slawiak, Aileen Tuohy, Mark Duerr, Diane Augustino and Kathleen Shyhalla. Pilot work was funded by the University at Buffalo's Research Institute on Addictions and was implemented by Carol Nottingham and Kathleen Skibicki. Kimberly Larkin, Robert Marczynski, and Lara Balawejder provided administrative and graphics assistance. Finally, we are grateful to Linda Paine-Hughes and Kelly Mercer who offered invaluable feedback on the penultimate draft of the book.

Section 1

FOUNDATIONS OF ANGER MANAGEMENT BASED ALCOHOL TREATMENT

Chapter 1

Introduction

Questions for Self-Reflection

- What is the attitude toward angry clients in your work setting?
- How often do you work with angry clients?

David's *Initial* Assessment

My name is David: *I'm an alcoholic. For most of my life, in fact. Looking back, I think I've been a problem drinker since I was 16 years old. Forty years later, and my family, my life, are a mess. I'm coming to treatment because my wife has "had it" with my drinking; I think that I've "had it" with my drinking too. I drink in the garage, away from her, away from the kids, and away from the pressure and conflict that is now my life. There, I drink my rum, every day, every evening. And then starts the arguing, the blaming, the tension, the guilt. I'm losing my wife and my kids and my life. I've been in treatment once before, after a drunk driving incident, and I was sober for four years. I don't know how it happened, but here I am, back at Square #1. I'm not sure how I got here, but I have to stop.*

Anger Management Based Alcohol Treatment. DOI: https://doi.org/10.1016/B978-0-12-812709-4.00001-9

David is not alone. He is one of over 32 million Americans who meet criteria for an alcohol use disorder according to the *Diagnostic and Statistical Manual of Mental Disorders, Fifth Edition* (DSM-V; American Psychiatric Association, 2013). He is presenting to treatment at this time because his wife has given him an ultimatum: "Stop drinking or get out."

The pretreatment assessment with David reveals that he is a daily heavy drinker with multiple negative consequences and a desire to stop drinking. David was raised by both parents. His father was a demanding man and a lifelong heavy drinker but without any clear negative consequences. His mom was an occasional drinker who took pride in caring for her family. David began experimenting with alcohol at 16 and was a regular drinker to intoxication by college. Nevertheless, he earned his degree and is now a mid-level supervisor in a large financial institution. Although he has missed some days at work due to his drinking—mostly Mondays, after an especially heavy drinking weekend—he is able to function well at work. His personal strengths include his dedication to his family and his career, his ability to organize and focus on detail-oriented tasks, and providing the financial comfort that his family enjoys.

His home life, however, is under severe stress. David leans toward arrogance when sober but is highly critical after drinking. He is a detailed-oriented person both at home and at work, and he is easily annoyed when things are not done "the right way." When he is frustrated and angry that things have not gone his way—such as dirty dishes in the sink or the garage door left open or other people having an opinion different than his own—he can become angry, ruminative, and passive aggressive (e.g., making snide comments and being uncooperative). David believes that his reactions are justified by the situational provocations and annoyances in his life. In his mind, the problems lie with the external stressors and annoyances in his environment, not in himself. His wife is disillusioned and believes that David can know no other life than drinking, drunkenness, and his angry frustrations. His three young adult children, two of whom live at home, both avoid and disrespect him. David has lost patience with his wife, his children, his job, and, importantly, with himself.

CASE STUDIES

We present three case studies to demonstrate anger management based alcohol treatment principles and techniques. We will follow the treatment course and outcomes of David, Stephan, and Tiffany throughout this book. These case studies will demonstrate clinical issues, therapy techniques, and common problems relevant to anger management based alcohol treatment. Loosely based on real clients, the names, demographics, and identifying details have been altered to maintain anonymity.

Overview

This volume is organized into four sections. Section 1 provides basic overviews of alcohol misuse, anger and anger management, and their intersection. Section 2 will discuss strategies to prepare a client (and therapist) for anger management based alcohol treatment, including comprehensive assessment of alcohol misuse, anger characteristics, and other important client factors. Section 3 will focus on the anger management based alcohol treatment skills and components, including self-monitoring, sobriety skills, relaxation coping skills, cognitive coping skills, coping skills rehearsal, and relapse prevention. Section 4 will describe several additional topics associated with anger management based alcohol treatment such as gender differences, client diversity, and application of anger-based treatments to smoking cessation and other negative moods. Materials in Appendices I and II provide public domain alcohol and anger assessment instruments, handouts, and worksheets to facilitate treatment delivery and evaluation.

MEET TIFFANY

My name is Tiffany: *I'm 32 years old and I swore I'd never become a drinker like my mom but here I am. When I was in my 20s drinking was just fun. I went out with my friends and only overdid it once in a while. And now, most nights I'm at home alone with my vodka and tea. Mornings have gotten rough. I'm miserable and it's getting worse. This is not how I pictured my life. I need help.*

Tiffany is a 32 years old, single, African-American female who was a social drinker until she had gastric bypass surgery, lost weight, and noticed a gradual increase in her drinking. She drinks vodka daily at home alone after work. Tiffany identifies numerous anger triggers and feels mad most of the time. She drinks both to calm herself down and to express her angry feelings to other people. Her anger and drinking have caused her to lose relationships, and she's concerned about potential consequences at her job. Tiffany is a stubborn and resilient person who wants a healthier life.

MEET STEPHAN

My name is Stephan: *I'm married, I'm gay, and I'm a drinker. In that order. I use pot a couple times a week, but that's beside the point. I'm here because of my drinking, not because I use pot occasionally. Is that going to be a problem for you?*

Stephan is a 43 years old, married, Caucasian male who drinks wine daily and uses alcohol to cope with frustration and resentment in his life. He is attached to his anger and sees it as a sign of strength. He sometimes acts out destructively when he's

(*Continued*)

(CONTINUED)

been drinking and regrets his actions the next day. He realizes both his drinking and his anger are causing problems in his marriage and putting him at risk for serious problems. He is funny and creative and knows he has the potential to have a better future.

Chapter 2

Brief Overview of Alcohol Use Disorder

Chapter Points

- Alcohol use disorder (AUD) is a chronic, widespread problem with significant consequences.
- The majority of people with AUD do not seek formal treatment.
- Craving for alcohol is a central component of AUD and can be easily triggered.
- A wide variety of treatment approaches are available and effective for treating AUD.
- Relapse to alcohol use after a period of sobriety is a common and challenging problem.

Questions for Self-Reflection

- What are some common stigmas about people with substance use disorders?
- Why do you think some people seek treatment while many others do not?

Stephan: *I've been drinking since middle school and I can still pretty much drink anyone under the table. I've always been the "life of the party", "class clown" kind of person. As you can imagine, I struggled a lot with my identity as a teenager so drinking and being the funny guy helped me get along. I learned to be sarcastic and attack first so I wouldn't be*

Anger Management Based Alcohol Treatment. DOI: https://doi.org/10.1016/B978-0-12-812709-4.00002-0

attacked. People respected me and I could always get a laugh, especially when I was drunk. Now that I'm in my 40's, it's not all fun and games anymore. Don't get me wrong, I enjoy a glass of good wine but honestly, I never have just one glass. I'm getting tired of the drinking and all the problems. I'm not completely sure I'm ready to give up on my 'good friend' alcohol but maybe it's time to grow up.

Alcohol use disorder (AUD) is a prevalent problem. According to the National Institute on Alcohol Abuse and Alcoholism "Alcohol Facts and Statistics" fact sheet (2017; see Fig. 2.1), about 15.1 million adults 18 and older had an AUD. Adult men are more likely to meet AUD criteria (8.4% of adult men) than women (4.2%). Unfortunately, only 6.7% of those with alcohol problems sought out formal treatment during the past year. Alcohol-related causes account for deaths of about 62,000 men and 26,000 women annually; this figure represents 31% of all driving fatalities. In addition to driving fatalities, alcohol misuse contributes to a wide variety of serious consequences, including liver problems; cancers; social, family, and work problems; and legal issues.

As delineated by the Diagnostic and Statistical Manual of Mental Disorders, Fifth Edition (APA, 2013), the diagnosis of AUD is made when an individual displays "a problematic pattern of alcohol use leading to clinically significant impairment or distress, as manifested by at least two of the following, occurring within a 12-month period..." (p. 490). This is followed by 11 symptoms including tolerance, withdrawal, craving, use in larger amounts than intended, persistent desire or unsuccessful efforts to cut down or control use, and continued use

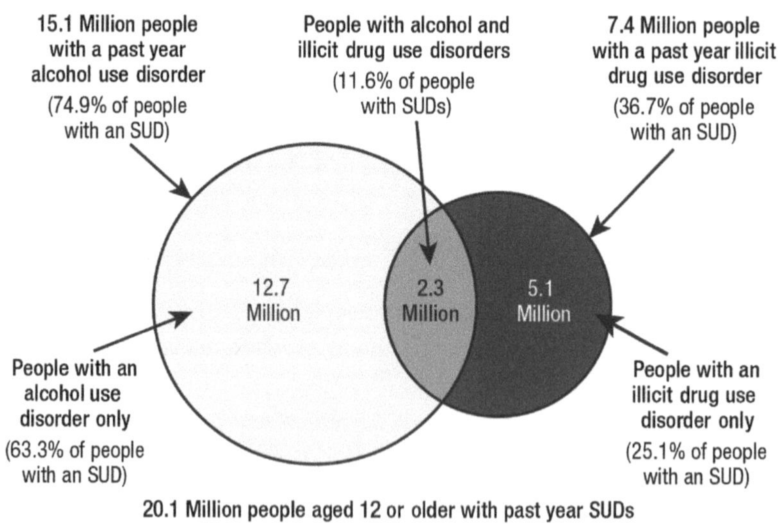

Figure 2.1 AUD and illicit drug use disorder in the past year among people aged 12 or older (SAMHSA, 2017).

despite recurrent problems. AUD is coded for severity as mild, moderate, or severe based on the number of symptoms endorsed.

Chronicity and Relapse

AUD is a chronic disease. Both "lapses" (i.e., relatively brief episode of drinking followed by a return to abstinence) and "relapse" (i.e., return to relatively heavy, consistent, and/or problematic drinking) typically characterize AUD during ongoing recovery. As such, returning to drinking following a period of abstinence is central to this disorder. For any individual person, the future possibility of relapse decreases as duration of abstinence lengthens. In other words, the longer individuals remain abstinent, the less likely they are to relapse in the future. Thus, maintaining a lengthening period of continuous abstinence is a critical predictor of long-term recovery and abstinence.

IT TAKES TIME...

Relapse to problematic drinking after a period of abstinence is a central issue in the treatment of AUD. Newly abstinent problem drinkers face the biggest probability of relapse during their first 70 days in recovery. However, if a former drinker is abstinent for 100 days, he or she has passed the time of greatest risk and the probability of relapse decreases dramatically (see Fig. 2.2). This 100-day mark, interestingly and probably not coincidently, roughly coincides with the oft-quoted advice of Alcoholics Anonymous (AA): 90 meetings in 90 days is emphasized for sobriety.

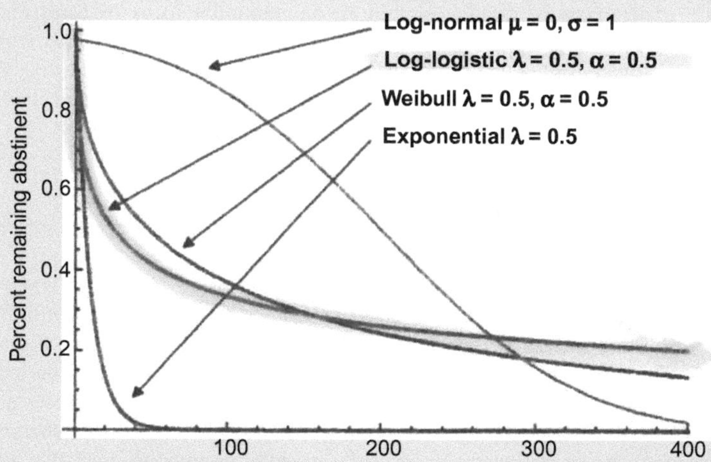

Figure 2.2 The relapse curve (Kirshenbaum, Olsen, & Bickel, 2009).

Craving

The experience of craving is a core experience for those with AUD and is deserving of additional consideration. Craving, the intense psychological and physiological sensations associated with a strong desire to drink, is a hallmark of AUD. Craving, a negative state itself, strongly predicts drinking in the short term (e.g., within 24 hours) and, to a lesser extent, in the longer term (e.g., within 1 week). As such, craving is an often identified precursor to relapse.

In the substance abuse treatment field, a "trigger" is something that initiates, or "triggers," craving for a client. A trigger may be a person, place, thing, mood, situation, memory, time of day, or thought. The link between the trigger and craving may be very automatic, occur with little to no warning, and outside of the client's awareness.

Craving is often a reaction to a drinking trigger. Further, craving is the intermediate step between a drinking trigger and a relapse (see Fig. 2.3). It is not uncommon, however, for problem drinkers to be unaware of this sequence and feel as though a slip or relapse to drinking is unpredictable and almost spontaneous. An important concept of the relapse prevention model is to understand and identify drinking triggers, recognize craving, and practice effective coping responses to break up the relatively automatic trigger–craving–drinking sequence.

THERAPIST TIP

A client's experiences of craving should be an important focus of assessment and treatment. It can be helpful to discuss how cravings are normal and also temporary (but perhaps frequent). In-session skills practice for coping with this aversive state may include approaches such as negative mood tolerance, distraction, and "urge surfing."

THERAPIST TIP

Cravings and urges to drink are like ocean waves. "Urge Surfing" is a mindfulness-based strategy that recognizes craving but does not act on it. Instead of fighting the craving or trying to push it away, the goal is to step back and "watch" the urge as it starts, peaks, and subsides. Silently and with eyes closed, the client focuses attention on the place in the body experiencing the urge. With guidance from the therapist, the client describes the sensations as specifically as possible (quality, intensity, location, shape, etc.) and how these sensations change during the exercise. With practice, the client learns to "ride out" urges like a surfer on an ocean wave.

Figure 2.3 Craving mediates the relationship between drinking triggers and drinking lapses.

Relapse Prevention Model

Relapse is a highly individual and complex process. A dynamic model of relapse was proposed by Witkiewitz and Marlatt (2004, 2007) that intertwines associations and chains of events between risk factors, cognitive processes, physical withdrawal symptoms, coping behaviors, and affect. Importantly, Witkiewitz and Marlatt put forth that this model of relapse follows the principles of catastrophe theory. Briefly put, catastrophe theory proposes that minor, and possibly perceived as insignificant, changes in early phases of a process (e.g., in a client's self-esteem) can lead to a sequence of events ultimately causing major changes in behavior (e.g., in this case relapse to drinking). This notion that a small change early on in the model can lead to a sequence of events to cause a major behavioral change helps to explain why relapses can be difficult to predict and why it is often challenging to identify the trigger.

In order to decrease the likelihood of slips and relapse during recovery, it is critical to identify an individual's triggers for drinking, that is, their high-risk situations for relapse. Although the specific details of a particular client's high-risk situations are unique, there are two important domains: interpersonal and intrapersonal drinking triggers. Common examples of interpersonal triggers include conflicts with family and friends, celebratory situations, and negatively charged interactions. Examples of common intrapersonal triggers include negative mood states (e.g., anxiety, depression, and anger), positive mood states, low self-esteem, and low self-efficacy.

Treatment Approaches

A variety of treatment modalities, philosophies, and approaches are found in the AUD treatment field. Modalities include outpatient, inpatient, residential, and hospital-based detoxification; it is not unusual for individuals to experience more than one modality during a treatment experience. A common treatment philosophy in the United States is based on AA, and many treatment programs and agencies are AA-based or AA intensive. A disease model and abstinence-based mutual-help group organization, AA is frequently a component of an individual's recovery from AUD. AA philosophy includes the belief in and reliance on a Higher Power, surrendering control over one's addiction, and acceptance of the disease of alcoholism. Additional treatment philosophies and associated approaches include enhancing intrinsic motivation for change (e.g., motivational enhancement treatment), family systems theory (e.g., behavioral couples therapy), and behavioral theory (e.g., community reinforcement approach). These approaches are each efficacious and play important roles in the AUD treatment field.

Most relevant to this volume is a group of interventions under the rubric of Cognitive Behavior Therapy (CBT). CBT is based on principles of learning and behavior change. In brief, the first goal of CBT strategies involves uncovering and understanding the client's functional analysis of drinking. This process involves identifying the client's triggers for craving and drinking and the factors maintaining the drinking problem. These triggers and factors may be situational, environmental, emotional, and cognitive and are often a complex combination of such. Identifying these high-risk triggers is an important foundation for identifying a client's individual skills deficits that are associated with these triggers and factors. The skills-based approaches selected for the individual's therapeutic protocol, both cognitive and behavioral in nature, are based on this functional analysis of drinking. Principles and strategies of skills training and relapse prevention are then incorporated in into the client's skill set for addressing AUD.

Tiffany's Psychosocial Assessment

When I was in my 20's drinking was just fun. I went out with my friends and only overdid it once in a while. Then I had gastric bypass surgery and things changed. I lost over 100 pounds in a year, and that's great... but also disappointing because my skin is so stretched out and I still look awful. I thought losing weight would help my social life but I've actually lost friends, including my boyfriend who said he was fed up with my complaining and my drinking. Most nights I drink my vodka on the couch in my apartment... at least I'm not eating too much... And I hate my job. I come home so mad and tired, all I want to do is drink and fall asleep. Mornings at work are really rough now. I usually have a headache and I think people avoid me on purpose. I'm miserable and it's getting worse. This is not how I pictured my life. I need help.

During the psychosocial assessment, Tiffany states that her mother was a daily drinker who often passed out after dinner, leaving Tiffany to take care of her younger brothers. Her father, a weekend drinker, worked long hours to support the family. When he was home, he was critical, especially of Tiffany as she steadily gained weight. Tiffany revealed that she was sexually abused by a cousin when she was a young teenager but never told her parents. She left home at 18 to start college but dropped out because she could not afford it. She works as a customer service representative and has always had positive performance reviews. However, she is not sure if the next review will be as good. She says she wants to go back to school and find a better job, maybe working with computers. Tiffany is intelligent, responsible, assertive, and resilient.

Tiffany is drinking close to a pint of vodka daily. She likes vodka because it is lower in calories and because her stomach cannot handle carbonated beverages like beer anymore. She has had some blackouts, which scare her. Her morning headaches and irritation have become so frequent that a supervisor cautioned her about her attitude toward certain coworkers; it was this caution and advice from her supervisor that motivated Tiffany to seek help at this time. Tiffany says she should be saving her money for skin removal surgery instead of drinking. She says she would like to get married and have kids someday and definitely does not want to be like her mom—drunk and neglectful.

Tiffany reports feeling angry all the time and consistently overreacts to other people and situations. She gets mad at bad drivers, her mom, waiting in line, her ex-boyfriend, her lazy brothers, her friends, and especially at herself. She says she is also frequently angry at people who make unfair judgments about her because she is black. She says drinking sometimes calms her down and makes her feel less angry. She also frequently calls people on the phone while drinking when she has the courage to tell them what she really thinks. She feels assertive and powerful when she is angry and drunk, and questions the negative impact her anger has on others. Interestingly, she deals with angry customers regularly in her job but never loses her temper with them.

Summary

This chapter has provided a brief overview of AUD, its diagnostic characteristics, its chronic course, and a broad look at efficacious treatments. We have discussed the phenomenon of craving, how it can be triggered by characteristics of the environment, and its relationship to alcohol consumption. We turn next to an in-depth consideration of the nature of anger-related emotions, their formation and triggers, and their many forms of expression and consequences.

Suggested Readings

Grant, B. F., Goldstein, R. B., Saha, T. D., et al. (2015). Epidemiology of DSM-V alcohol use disorder results from the National Epidemiologic Survey on alcohol and related conditions III. *JAMA Psychiatry 72*, 757–766.

This national survey of over 36,000 US individuals demonstrates the current prevalence of AUD, its comorbidity with other mental health disorders, and the low rates of treatment among those affected.

Kirshenbaum, A. P., Olsen, D. M., & Bickel, W. K. (2009). A quantitative review of the ubiquitous relapse curve. *Journal of Substance Abuse Treatment, 36*, 8–17.

This article combines results from 20 previously published research papers to study the basic shape and uniformity of the relapse curve. This review concludes that, across studies and over 15,000 subjects, the shape of the relapse curve is similar and follows a log-logistic distribution. Importantly, the amount of sober time that a client accumulates predicts his or her likelihood of future relapse (see our Fig. 2.2). Our clients may be reassured that the longer they are abstinent, the less likelihood they will relapse.

McHugh, R. K., Fitzmaurice, G. M., Griffin, M. L., Anton, R. F., & Weiss, R. D. (2016). Association between a brief alcohol caving measure and drinking in the following week. *Addiction, 111*, 1004–1010.

Research literature has been unclear with regard to whether craving predicts a client's risk for future drinking and relapse. This research helps to clear this confusion. Although the degree to which a client is craving is not a strong predictor of relapse over the long term (in the following several months), strong craving does indeed put a client at risk for drinking in the short term (in the following week). This conclusion underscores the importance of strengthening a client's skills for managing the craving experience.

Witkiewitz, K., & Marlatt, G. A. (2007). Modeling the complexity of post-treatment drinking: It's a rocky road to relapse. *Clinical Psychology Review, 27*, 724–738.

This important article presents the dynamic process of relapse as including components of a client's cognitive processes, affective state, and effective coping behaviors as contributory to relapse (see our Fig. 2.2). Incorporating catastrophe theory, this model recognizes that very minor changes in a client's functioning early in the model (e.g., thinking or affect) may have a profound impact further in the model (e.g., drinking and relapse). Thus, although important to gain insight into relapse, triggers for relapse may be difficult to determine.

Chapter 3

Overview of Anger-Related Emotions

Chapter Points

- Anger is a fundamental human emotion characterized by the experience of unpleasant feelings and strong physiological reactions.
- Anger-producing triggers are filtered and affect how a person will react at any given time.
- The intensity of anger does not predict the behavioral expression of anger.
- The experience and expression of anger can be both productive and destructive based on intensity, frequency, duration, and consequences.

Questions for Self-Reflection

- What are your thoughts on justified anger?
- What are some common stereotypes about angry people?

David: *I know I drink too much but I don't think my anger is really a problem. I've never been in jail, hell, I've never been arrested, and other than my DWI, I've never even gotten a freaking ticket! My wife's been telling me for years that I have a bad temper but I've never laid a hand on her or*

Anger Management Based Alcohol Treatment. DOI: https://doi.org/10.1016/B978-0-12-812709-4.00003-2

the kids and I get so pissed off when she tells me to just calm down. She has no idea the amount of stress and bullshit I put up with every day. Sure I lose it once in a while when I get home to a mess, any sane person would! I work hard all day, I drive an hour each way in traffic; is it too much to ask to come home to a clean kitchen? Seriously—it's not me; it's the lazy, inconsiderate, rude jerks at work, on the road, in the stores, on the phone, and in my own house. I swear it's getting worse all the time and I'm fed up. But that doesn't mean I'm out there getting in fights or beating my wife! I'm not like that at all.

A Brief Overview of Anger Emotions

Although there are many theories of emotions and their development and expression, Russell (1980) suggests that emotions may be described by two dimensions. One is the degree of valence along a continuum from unpleasant to pleasant. The other describes the arousal intensity from mild to intense. As seen in Fig. 3.1, anger is an aroused, unpleasant emotion. Other anger-related emotions (i.e., frustration and annoyance) differ somewhat in arousal and pleasantness, but they lie in the same quadrant and share the features of being arousing, negative emotions. Collectively, we refer to these as anger-related emotions (e.g., feeling angry, mad, furious, enraged, frustrated, irritated, and annoyed).

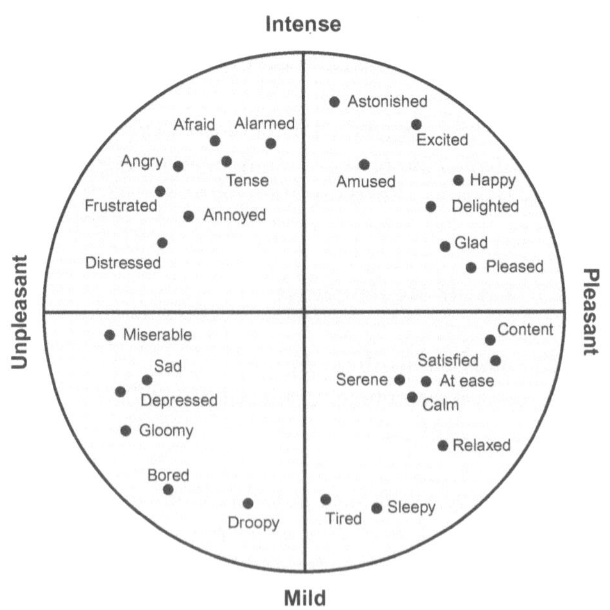

Figure 3.1 A circumplex view of emotion.

Nomenclature of Anger-Related Emotions

Anger-related words, most notably anger, hostility, and aggression, are often used interchangeably. However, these three concepts have distinct meanings. First, anger is an emotion and can be described as a "state" or a "trait." As a state, anger is experienced at a moment in time, marked both with physiological arousal (e.g., elevated heart rate and perspiration) and emotional arousal (e.g., ranging from mild annoyance to extreme rage). Trait anger, in contrast, is the general predisposition of an individual to experience anger-related emotions over the course of time and in a variety of situations. Higher trait anger individuals are angered easily, frequently, and intensely; lower trait anger individuals are angered rarely and mildly. Second, hostility refers to a cognitive mind-set. Hostility reflects an individual's interpretations of other peoples' motivations, life situations, and the world in general. Suspiciousness and the tendency to attribute malevolent and harmful interpretations to others' behaviors characterize an individual high in hostility. As would be expected, high hostility is associated with greater experience of anger-related emotions. Finally, aggression is a behavior. Expressed verbally, physically, or passive-aggressively, aggression is behavior with the intent to harm, hurt, or communicate displeasure toward others, objects, or social systems.

ANGER: AN UNHEALTHY EMOTION

The experience of anger is linked to a variety of health concerns and disorders. Anger is associated with cardiovascular problems, chronic pain, a variety of mental health disorders, and insomnia. In addition, anger, hostility, and aggression often play a causal role in contributing to family, work, and legal problems.

ANGER: A CONSTRUCTIVE EMOTION

Anger-related emotions, even when strong, may indicate that a circumstance is not right and needs attention. For example, the anger an employee feels about being overlooked for a promotion at work may motivate him or her to talk to the boss or consider a job change. A woman angry at her partner may use the emotion as a signal that the relationship needs attention or that she should break off the relationship. Anger can signal a problem and lead to constructive problem-solving.

A Brief Look at Anger-Management Therapies

Given the risk for medical and psychosocial problems associated with the experience and expression of problematic anger, hostility, and aggression, it is not surprising that several therapeutic approaches have been developed to address problematic anger. Three primary techniques for managing and controlling problematic anger are cognitive therapy, relaxation skills, and cognitive–behavioral therapy. Cognitive therapy includes techniques that focus on thinking and thoughts, such as cognitive restructuring. Relaxation skills refer to strategies such as progressive muscle relaxation, positive imagery, and other relaxation exercises. Cognitive–behavioral therapy refers to techniques that combine cognitive therapy with a behavioral component such as relaxation skills. These therapies are effective in managing and reducing the experience of anger-related emotions and their behavioral consequences.

The Nature of Anger

The above overview suggests that anger is a fundamental human emotion. Anger appears to be part of the basic fight or flight reaction and, therefore, the capacity for anger seems to be hardwired into the human nervous system. We will devote more time here describing anger because clinicians tend to be less familiar with the anatomy of anger than with other common clinically relevant emotions such as anxiety, fear, and depression. Hopefully, this detailed breakdown of anger will facilitate a better understanding and provide a framework for identifying important aspects of anger reactions, the anger experience, and anger expression that may be targeted for intervention.

THE CYCLE OF ANGER

Anger is an emotional–physiological–cognitive experience. Although the physiological and emotional elements may appear in just moments before the cognitive aspects, the client tends to experience these simultaneously with the elements co-occurring, cycling, reinforcing, and stimulating one another. Conceptually, these elements may be separated, but for the client experiencing them, they blend together as anger.

Emotionally, anger is experienced along of continuum of valence. At the low end, there is no or minimal anger. Emotional intensity increases from mild states such as irritation and annoyance, to moderate states such as being angry or very frustrated, to very intense states such as fury and rage. Although some anger is experienced as cold (e.g., icy fury), most anger is experienced as a hot emotion, consistent with concomitant physiological arousal.

Anger includes significant physiological arousal. The cardiovascular system reacts with elevated heart rate and increased blood pressure (e.g., heart racing or beating very hard). As large amounts of warm blood are redirected from internal organs to the external musculature, the person may experience a flushing and reddening of the skin and areas of warmth or heat (e.g., reddening of the neck and face, a warm flush across the chest and upper arms). Sweating may also ensue as that system activates to cool the body. Muscle tension increases in specific areas (e.g., tense shoulders, tightened jaw, and clenched fists) or more generally. Adrenaline is released both peripherally and from the adrenal glands leading to things like feeling restless, agitation, pacing, and a sense of being hyper. The gastrointestinal system may also react (e.g., upset stomach, a tense stomach and abdomen, increased lower bowel activity). Breathing may show changes as well (e.g., shallow, rapid breathing, shortness of breath, or a sense of not being able to catch a breath). Although an individual may not experience all of these, he/she often experiences several of them in a pattern that is fairly typical for him/her. Identifying personal aspects of arousal helps the individual understand his/her anger, but also these internal physical cues can become important signals for the person to initiate different elements of intervention.

When angry, the person's cognitive processes change in focus and content. The person often becomes highly sensitized to angering themes (e.g., cues of disrespect, rejection, denigration, threat, and attack), perhaps focusing on these issues to the exclusion of other important input. Attributions, especially when cues are open to a variety of interpretations, may shift toward seeing others as malevolent, manipulative, and attacking. This is referred to as a "hostile attributional bias," and the person responds to the internally construed reality whether accurate or not. The individual's running self-talk tends to be filled with anger-engendering and anger-supportive thoughts. These tend to include things such as (1) broad, overgeneralized, often obscene labels or conclusions (e.g., "He is a total jerk!" or "What a bitch!"); (2) catastrophizing or overly negative thinking (e.g., things are awful, terrible, or the end of the world); (3) dichotomous, either/or thinking (e.g., "He always does that." or "She hates me."); (4) violation of rigid rules (e.g., "He shouldn't do that." or "Nobody should be treated like that."); and (5) personalization (e.g., "I know he is doing this to me on purpose."). Thoughts and images often include a sense of being violated and victimized, of retribution, revenge and retaliation, of blame and punishment for perceived wrong doing, and of verbal (e.g., yelling at people) or physical aggression (e.g., threatening to "kick the crap out of them"). Attentional processes may become narrowed as the person perseverates on an issue and ruminates about an injustice or perceived wrong, replaying it over and over. Positive resources in the person's environment and internal coping resources may receive lessened attention, only furthering the cycle of anger.

Triggers for Anger

For a few individuals with significant brain injuries or problems of neural dysregulation, anger may appear unprompted. Anger seems to well up within or simply explode without cause. However, for most people in most situations, anger appears to be elicited by one or more triggers. As with triggers for drinking, triggers for anger may be external or internal to the person.

External Triggers

Many triggers are external. Individuals can often quickly identify the condition that angers them (e.g., "When she disrespects me, I'm instantly pissed." or "Rude drivers annoy the hell out of me."). Moreover, there is the perception that the trigger causes the anger. In addition, from the person's perspective, changes in anger level often seem appropriate and proportional to the circumstances. In other words, although the person may not like the anger, anger in response to the situation makes sense. Triggers vary widely and may include specific situations (e.g., being the recipient of an obscene gesture), events that share a common theme (e.g., a sense of being disrespected or put down), objects (e.g., a car not starting, a drawer that is stuck), behavior of self (e.g., missing an important meeting, saying something inappropriate to another person), behavior of others (e.g., a coworker not doing his work, a spouse being sarcastic), and general negative conditions (e.g., bad weather, politics, job layoffs at work).

External Triggers Plus Associated Memories and Images

Other triggers appear external but include additional internal associations and memories. That is, anger is elicited by the external situation plus the negative memories and images associated with the external trigger. For example, an individual may be sensitive and overreactive to teasing or loud arguments because of being teased as a child or exposed to nasty parental arguments. In situations like these, the individual may be unaware or partially aware of the relationship between the external trigger and prior anger-related experience.

WHY ARE YOU SO MAD?

Kashdan, Goodman, Mallard, and DeWall (2015) studied anger triggers in the daily life events of 173 college students over the course of 3 weeks, yielding a total of 2342 anger episodes. Five general categories of anger triggers emerged: other people, psychological/physical distress, intrapersonal demands, environment, and undifferentiated. When "other people" was the predominant trigger, anger was more intense. Further, anger reactions from an "undifferentiated" or unclear source were the most intense and difficult to regulate.

Internal Triggers

Some anger is triggered primarily from internal sources. Rumination is a common internal trigger. The person gets focused on past injustices, injuries, disrespect, slights, or losses. Anger escalates as the individual turns these events over and over in his/her mind, often focusing on key anger-increasing elements and in some cases embellishing or revising the recall of events. Anger arises not from the initial event(s) but from the continued and ongoing mental recycling of those events. For example, when Stephan got married several years ago, his parents and brother refused to come to the wedding or even acknowledge his relationship with Michael. Stephan continued to ruminate on this slight almost daily and especially while he was drinking. As he got drunk, he would think about how vindictive and small-minded his family was and imagined the things he would say to their faces someday. Sometimes, anger is triggered primarily by other feelings and emotions (e.g., feelings of guilt, shame, anxiety, or depression). That is, a client becomes angry in reaction to one of these feelings. To understand the client's anger, the therapist needs to understand the connection to the emotions that preceded it. For example, Tiffany became very angry when she received any negative feedback at work. She acknowledged that her anger was way out of proportion to the actual feedback. However, for her, even slightly negative feedback elicited a deep sense of embarrassment and failure and her anger stemmed from these feelings. Essentially, some anger is primarily triggered by internal thoughts, images, and feelings rather than external events.

STUCK ON REPLAY...

Denson, Moulds, and Grisham (2012) studied different types of cognitive appraisals on anger resulting from recollections of an anger-inducing memory. College students were randomly assigned to engage in either rumination, cognitive reappraisal, or distraction. As expected, reappraisal was the effective anger regulation strategy; students who engaged in reappraisal reported lower levels of anger following the intervention. In contrast, rumination maintained the experience of anger.

Pre-Anger State

Triggers for anger are filtered through certain conditions at the time they are experienced. Some of these are transitory; others are more enduring characteristics. Individuals may not be aware of how these transitory states and conditions influence their anger. Enhanced awareness of and targeting these conditions for intervention may be important to assist in anger reduction. For example, couples may not want to discuss potentially conflict-laden issues when tired and stressed on a Friday evening after a long, hard week. The issues may well need attention but not under these conditions.

Momentary Emotional and Physical State

The probability and intensity of anger is influenced by the immediate emotional and physical state of the person at the time. If the person is happy and feeling positive, anger is less likely to happen or to be as intense. Positive feelings seem to buffer anger; negative feelings seem to have the opposite effect. One especially negative emotional condition is prior anger. Prior anger seems to facilitate anger in response to subsequent provocations. That is, anger seems to have a carry-over effect, even if the subsequent events are unrelated to the initial anger. For example, when David has an angry interaction with his wife over breakfast, he is likely to be angered more easily and intensely on the commute to work. Conversely, if angered on the commute home, he is more likely to be angered by his wife and children upon arriving home.

ONE THING LEADS TO ANOTHER. . .

Nearly any negative emotional state (e.g., stressed, anxious, depressed, ashamed) or physical state (e.g., in pain, fatigued, jet lagged, hungry, cold, sick) increases the chances of subsequent anger. Such conditions appear to increase the presence and saliency of negative imagery, thoughts, and feelings, which lower the threshold for anger.

Culture and Socialization Influences

Every culture and group around the world has norms for what one can and should become angry about, how intense one's anger should be, and how that anger should and should not be expressed. These norms guide emotional and behavioral responses and facilitate social functioning. Sometimes, socialization processes (e.g., specific family dynamics, certain adolescent peer groups) set dysfunctional norms for how much anger is to be experienced, in response to what triggers, and how the anger is to be expressed. For example, one's family of origin may condone a great deal of experienced anger and sanctioned aggressive, abrasive, and interpersonal exchanges. Family members may regularly scream and yell and possibly even throw things at each other. These behaviors are "normal" in this family context, but dysfunctional and disruptive in adult relationships governed by a general set of cultural rules for appropriate experiences and displays of anger. Moreover, sometimes anger-related norms may clash with norms for other groups or contexts which the person inhabits. For example, the norms for angry language at a sporting event are different than at a professional staff meeting.

Enduring Psychological Characteristics

A person's psychological development includes establishing habitual ways of processing, making sense of, and finding meaning in the world. These include the person's expectations for how others will behave, the person's sense of right and wrong, beliefs about what should and should not happen, personal rules and guidelines for living, and a sense of important and valued tasks to be achieved. These psychological characteristics are what Lazarus (1991) called "ego identity" and Beck (1976) "the personal domain." Anger ensues from a perceived attack on or affront to ego identity or trespass on the personal domain. Anger develops from challenges to or violations of expectancies and personal rules for living and the blocking or interfering with important goal-directed behavior. When elements of ego identity or personal domain are permeable and flexible, anger is likely mild to moderate. However, as these become more inflexible, dogmatic, and dictatorial, anger is likely to escalate and aggression is more likely to follow. It is important to understand these personally valued dimensions and, in some cases, change their rigidity in order to lower anger.

Anger-Related Appraisal Processes

Emotional and physiological aspects of anger quickly trigger cognitive reactions and interpretations. A useful way of organizing this appraisal process is primary then secondary appraisal (Lazarus, 1991). Cognitive appraisal has two processes. Primary appraisals involve assessment of outside, triggering events. Secondary appraisals involve an evaluation of the person's capacity to cope with the event. Different cognitive appraisals are associated with the likelihood of anger being experienced, the degree of anger experienced, and the probability of expressing that anger in specific ways.

WHAT NOW?

An appraisal is a person's cognitive interpretation and evaluation of an event or situation. The primary appraisal is the person's initial cognitive assessment of a negative event ("Wait a minute! What just happened here?"). The secondary appraisal is the person's cognitive assessment of possible reactions, resources, and options ("Ok; so now what am I going to do about this?").

Primary Appraisals

Anger often stems from a person perceiving a blameworthy attack on his or her personal domain. The person's values, rules for living, expectations for how she is to be treated and important goal-directed behavior are thwarted or under threat. Anger is an emotional–physiological–cognitive activation to address this perceived threat for which someone or something is responsible and should be punished.

Four primary appraisals influence the likelihood and intensity of anger. One is controllability or preventability (i.e., beliefs that other people could have controlled or prevented the event). Anger tends to increase when we believe that a preventable event has been experienced. That is, from our perspective, the event need not have happened, and we are angry because it did. For example, David firmly believed that if the people he worked with would just follow the rules and get the job done right the first time, he would not need to get so upset. If these people were more careful and diligent, they could absolutely prevent the situations that provoked his anger. He also replayed this scenario at home on a regular basis with his family and the chores. If they simply had the chores done before he came home, he would not need to overreact and get so angry.

Anger is usually lower in intensity if the situation is seen as something that could not be completely prevented, or even thinking that other people are often doing the best they can, even if it is not objectively very good. In the example above, if David was able to accept the chaos and inevitable mistakes of others, his reactions may have been different.

Another anger-enhancing appraisal is that of intentionality (i.e., beliefs that others initiated the event on purpose). Our anger is likely to increase significantly if a negative event is viewed as a function of another's conscious desires and intentions. Anger is thus seen as stemming from a personal and intentional attack. For example, Stephan got a call from his sister over the weekend. He usually looked forward to her calls, but this time, all she talked about was their parents, some new health issues, and how tired she was of driving them to doctor visits. Stephan got angry, feeling that she was intentionally blaming him for not helping with their care. He felt attacked, accused, and betrayed. He made some sarcastic comments and hung up on her.

Anger is oftenless intense if the trigger is perceived as unintended, uncontrollable, a function of a mistake, or due to ignorance or emotional distress. In the example above, if Stephan had decided to hear his sister's complaints as merely her need to tell someone how exhausted and overwhelmed she was feeling, he would have been less angry and reactive.

A third anger-engendering appraisal is that of the trigger being unfair or unjustified. That is, our anger goes up because we did not deserve to experience the triggering event. The event is viewed as unfair and unreasonable. For example, Stephan was in line to check out at the supermarket, when he realized he forgot Michael's favorite crackers. He left his cart in line and ran to grab the crackers. When he came back, his cart had been moved and a woman with two small children and an overflowing cart had taken his spot in line. He could not believe she had the audacity to move his cart and make him wait even longer to check out. He spent the rest of the day complaining about the woman and his unfair treatment in the grocery store to anyone who would listen.

Anger tends to be lower if the situation is interpreted as reasonable, fair, or justified. Even if we do not like the event, we believe that it fits the circumstances and is a reasonable outcome. Perhaps, if Stephan had decided that the woman with her small, wiggly children, and overflowing cart needed get home more quickly than he did, he would have been more understanding and less angry.

A fourth anger-enhancing set of appraisals involve blame and punishment (i.e., the trigger is responsible for the anger and also deserving of blame and retribution). Anger and potentially aggressive and punishing behavior are seen as appropriate and justified, because the source is blamed. For example, Tiffany and her ex-boyfriend had been together for 5 years when he decided to end their relationship. Tiffany was furious that he abandoned her after all that time and especially after her surgery. She thought they'd be married by now. She blamed him for taking advantage of her and she frequently entertained thoughts of retribution. She was hoping the universe would punish him somehow and she never missed an opportunity to bad-mouth him on social media and to others.

Anger tends to be lower if we perceive multiple contributing sources to provocation, see ourselves as part of the problem, and/or if responsibility for problems is separated from the need to blame and punish. There was a part of Tiffany that wanted to blame her ex-boyfriend completely for leaving her. Another part of her knew that the breakup was directly related to her increased drinking and negativity. She did not like thinking about that part; it was easier to blame him. However, had she included her responsibility as well as his, she would have experienced less anger and helplessness.

Secondary Appraisal

Secondary appraisals -- the perceived ability to cope with or successfully react to angering situations -- also influence the nature and course of anger. Anger increases and positive coping decreases when people feel overwhelmed, out of control, or unable to cope (e.g., "I just couldn't take it. I totally lost it, raging uncontrollably."). For example, when describing a recent disagreement with his son, David said, "I tried but I just couldn't take another minute so I let him have it."

Another secondary appraisal appears somewhat unique to anger. Here, people believe that they should not have to deal with or put up with events which they are confronting (e.g., "I shouldn't have to wait on hold this long!" or "My wife shouldn't be so damn demanding and unreasonable."). That is, people hold a narcissistic rule or belief that exempts them from hassles, injustices, slights, disrespect, and frustrations that nearly everyone encounters. From this perspective, anger seems normal and reasonable because it stems from outside and from something they should not have to experience. For example, David, as a father and breadwinner, firmly believed that he deserved more respect from his son and that he should never have to put up with any attitude or insolence. He often said, "I shouldn't have to put up with this crap! I never disrespected my father like this."

A third type of secondary appraisal involves the sense that anger is a reasonable response to the situation (e.g., "I was pissed, but they had it coming." or "Do that to me and you are going to catch hell."). That is, anger and aggression are seen as fitting the circumstances and justified. For example, David believed that it was his job as a parent to keep his son in line. He never hit his son but he also never hesitated to criticize and yell at him anytime he fell short of David's high expectations. David believed that his son was "asking for it" with his lazy attitude.

A fourth type of secondary coping appraisal, of particular relevance to this book, is how people see alcohol consumption as an anger coping strategy. Many angry individuals use alcohol in an attempt to cope with their anger (and other negative emotions). They think (appraise) that alcohol will help them calm down and cope with their anger (positive alcohol coping appraisals). They think thoughts like, "I'm going to stop off and have a couple of beers and then I won't be so pissed at my boss," or "A drink will help me chill and get out of this angry mood." For example, David saw drinking as the primary way for him to calm down and relax after his hectic work day, long commute, and family stress. He believed that having a couple of drinks or more after work helped him chill out and cope with his life.

Under some circumstances, this is correct for some people some of the time. If, while having a drink or two, they disengage from antagonistic or frustrating environments, calm down, and think about how to handle the situation constructively, then the drink may help to lower anger and cope effectively. However, in spite of positive alcohol–anger coping expectancies, outcomes are often not nearly so positive. For example, if people either stay in the angering environment or quickly reengage with it, the disinhibiting effect of alcohol may contribute to an angry, potentially aggressive situation. Individuals may not think and plan constructively. Instead, they may drink and ruminate about the anger-provoking situation. Angry feelings and hostile thinking increase along with the probability of aggression or other dysfunctional behavior. Such anger-enhancing rumination under the influence of alcohol is a particular problem if people soon encounter the provocative situation again. They are primed with angry emotions, hostile thinking, and aggressive and dysfunctional coping strategies, all with alcohol onboard.

These are but a few of the negative alcohol–anger outcomes that can occur. It should be noted that individuals often do not revise their alcohol–anger coping appraisals and decrease their use of alcohol to cope with anger based on their negative experiences. That is, they often do not learn from their mistakes. When anger inevitably reappears, alcohol is consumed again, often with repeated negative outcomes. Alcohol–anger coping appraisals are important to address clinically to help individuals assess whether alcohol is an effective coping strategy. If alcohol consumption is not positive or benign, then changing the secondary coping appraisals and related behaviors are important targets of change.

Anger Expression

The intensity of anger does not determine how that anger is expressed. For example, three drivers might be cut off rudely by another driver and be equally angry. The first might explode with shouts and cursing punctuated by a series of obscene gestures. A second driver might boil on the inside and entertain thoughts and images of revenge and retaliation, but externally demonstrate nothing unusual. The third driver might experience the anger, but shift to positive coping and problem-solving (e.g., backing away from the offending driver, engaging in relaxing or distracting behavior such as listening to music on the radio), and engage in more benign coping thinking (e.g., "Maybe he didn't see me," "Maybe he's just having a bad day," or "Maybe he did that on purpose. Some people just push their way through life. I'm not going to waste my time on him."). In these examples, the situation and the intensity degree of anger are identical, but how anger is expressed differs substantially.

Like the third example above, not all forms of anger expression are negative or dysfunctional. To the contrary, especially when anger is mild to moderate in intensity, anger may facilitate identifying and addressing personal and social injustices and standing up for one's rights and those of others. Anger may motivate positive problem-solving (e.g., anger in a work situation may lead workers to identify better ways of handling issues at work). Anger at one's self may push important changes in things such as diet and exercise. Such examples are supported by research (e.g., Deffenbacher, Oetting, Lynch, & Morris, 1996; Deffenbacher, Oetting, Thwaits, et al., 1996; Spielberger, Sydeman, Owen, & Marsh, 1999). For example, when angered, some individuals reduce and regulate their emotional arousal. They reduce negative behaviors and address events in a calmer, more problem-oriented manner.

They become more cognitively reflective, slowing their thought processes and considering possible behaviors and consequences before acting. Others attempt to distance themselves from provocative events and develop alternative ways of addressing the situation. Others shift into an open, assertive way of communicating. They listen supportively to others and try to take their thoughts and feelings into account, while not giving up their own thoughts and preferences. They engage in respectful communication and attempt to problem-solve and find options that are mutually acceptable. Mutually acceptable outcomes are not always possible, but this form of communication tends to reduce anger, support relationships, and build good will for future interactions.

However, as anger intensity increases, so does the chance of more negative, dysfunctional ways of expressing anger. Some people, like the second driver, experience intense anger but hold it in. While they may not show much outwardly, they are seething on the inside. They tend to be fairly critical and judgmental, to entertain quite hostile, aggressive thoughts, images and fantasies, and to harbor resentments and grudges. Generally, what they do not show is much outward expression. On occasion, however, they may "lose it" or "blow up," dramatically overreacting explosively.

Other people handle their anger more like the first driver and engage in maladaptive, often aggressive forms of anger expression. Some forms of expression are verbal in nature. For example, some people become very loud and intimidating by turning up the volume (e.g., shouting, yelling). Others change the content of their communication and become verbally assaultive (e.g., engage in sarcasm, make hostile cutting remarks, belittle and put others down, call others names or negative labels, curse and employ culturally negative epithets, etc.).

Other forms of anger expression are less verbal and more physical. For example, some express their anger physically toward people through things such as hitting, punching, kicking, shoving, slapping, and using weapons. Other physical forms of expression do not make contact but are physically directed toward others (e.g., gestures such as giving the other person "the finger," shaking a fist at them, slapping their own forehead in disbelief, etc.). Still other people express their anger physically, but assault the physical rather than social environment. They hit, slam, throw, break, and smash things rather than people. Other forms of anger expression are less physical but no less communicative. For example, angry individuals may use their eyes and face to express anger (e.g., intense, hostile glares, cold intimidating stares, rolling their eyes, giving them "the look that could kill," or shaking one's head accompanied by a stern, disapproving look). Other negative forms of anger expression through body language are more from the neck down (e.g., a hand gesture cutting across the throat, hands on hips, and a menacing finger pointed at another).

While these are but some of the ways in which anger may be expressed, they capture the range, from the positive, prosocial through to the negative, dysfunctional forms of expression. People, especially those who are frequently angered, report engaging in a variety of forms of anger expression. That is, they report employing a variety of positive forms of expression on some occasions and variety of negative forms in other circumstances. Research (e.g., Deffenbacher & Sabadell, 1992) supports this suggestion. People low in general anger report expressing anger in ways that reduce emotional arousal and address issues in a constructive manner. They also report using much less anger suppression and outward, negative anger expression. Overall, positive constructive anger expression and control predominate for low-anger individuals. They appear to have rich repertories of positive coping strategies for expressing and dealing with anger. In contrast, high general anger individuals report more suppression, more outward negative expression, and less emotional and behavioral control. However, high-anger individuals do report equal tendencies to cope with anger in constructive ways. That is, they report trying to manage and control their emotions and behavioral expressions; sometimes it works and often it does not. High-anger individuals thus appear to have fewer and/or less effective coping skills and to be more vulnerable to reverting to anger suppression and more aggressive forms of expression.

THERAPIST TIP

Be careful to avoid the assumption that any given client responds to anger-provoking cues with either all positive reactions or with all maladaptive reactions; in truth, every client engages in both. Assessing each client's complexity of responding will offer insight into how anger is embedded in the client's world, what coping strategies the client already uses, and may help identify positive forms of anger expression.

Anger Consequences

Anger does not inevitably lead to negative consequences. However, as the frequency and intensity of anger increase and anger is expressed maladaptively, the chances of adverse consequences, sometimes very negative, rise. Some negative consequences are emotional in nature. People may feel guilty, ashamed, embarrassed, and/or depressed for how they expressed anger. They may feel angry with themselves and afraid that they may do it again and experience other negative outcomes. All of these tend to lower self-esteem and self-efficacy.

Anger may also influence personal health. Some health consequences result from personal injury (e.g., a cut or broken appendage from slugging or kicking something). Other health consequences are more the result of chronic anger (e.g., headaches, bruxism and dental damage, essential hypertension, and coronary artery disease). Other physical problems are the outcome of the ways anger is expressed (e.g., a broken nose in an altercation or death or serious injury in a road rage incident).

Verbal and physical anger expressions often lead to significant disruptions in close interpersonal and family relationships. Dysfunctional anger expression often spills over into the work place (e.g., a shouting match with a coworker or a rude interaction with a customer). These not only have the direct effects from the events but also can result in indirect effects (e.g., being fired, demoted, or put on probation). Inappropriate anger expression can have serious educational consequences as well (e.g., an adolescent being suspended from school for cursing at a teacher or a college student being put on disciplinary probation or terminated from school because of a fight with another student). Other adverse anger-related outcomes may be legal (e.g., arrest for assault and disorderly conduct or a citation for insulting a police officer) or formal/disciplinary in nature (e.g., being written up at work for a negative interaction with a supervisor).

Anger can also prompt other impulsive or unsafe behaviors and consequences such as reckless driving, unprotected sex, and use of alcohol and other drugs. In turn, many of these behaviors may lower inhibitions and impair judgment, which intensifies the cycles of anger, aggression, and other outcomes. Anger can also prompt other dysfunctional but less impulsive behavior (e.g., inappropriate avoidance or withdrawal).

In summary, intense anger and dysfunctional anger expression are often associated with more frequent and severe negative consequences. Further, multiple negative consequences may stem from the same anger episode (e.g., emotional, interpersonal, vocational, and financial outcomes stemming from one significant anger episode at work).

Defining Problematic Anger

Anger can be associated with positive and beneficial outcomes or anger can eventuate in negative consequences. So, when does anger become problematic or dysfunctional? As with many clinical conditions, this is a judgment call. There are no clear lines of demarcation. Moreover, there are no diagnostic guidelines to help, because the DSM-V contains no identifiable anger disorders and related criteria. The following dimensions may be helpful in making a judgment, especially if several of these cluster together in the same person's experience.

Anger Frequency

Infrequent anger which is not associated with aggressive (e.g., violent outburst) or nonaggressive (e.g., binge drinking), behaviors is likely to be of minimal consequence. However, as the frequency of anger episodes increases, so does the opportunity for negative anger expression and adverse consequences. Some anger consequences can be severe, whereas others may be relatively minor. Even if the consequences tend to be relatively minor, the high frequency reduces the quality of life, drains the overall coping resources, and increases vulnerability to stress.

Anger Duration

Mild-to-moderate anger is often fairly short lived. However, some individuals are angry for long periods of time, with approximately 25% of the people reporting anger that lasts for a day or more (Tafrate, Kassinove, & Dundin, 2002). Sometimes, this is a result of existing in a toxic environment with chronic provocation and frustration. Often, however, long periods of anger result from ruminating and obsessing about angering events. For example, Stephan was angry for several hours most evenings and much of weekend days because he ruminated intensively about how his parents and his brother "ruined his wedding day" by refusing to show up and thought about "what complete assholes" they are. These anger episodes were lengthy (2–10 hours), fairly intense, and often associated with heavy consumption of alcohol. Anger stemmed not from a current situation, because the wedding had taken place almost 6 years earlier but from his continued review and imagery about the events and his family. Prolonged exposure like this affords greater opportunities for negative anger expression, negative anger consequences, and other dysfunctional behavior. Moreover, chronic prolonged anger increases chances of anger-related health consequences, of anger facilitating additional anger, and of reduced quality of life and overall positive tone of life.

Anger Intensity

Anger is experienced along a continuum from little or no anger to very intense states such as fury and rage. Most individuals can rate their anger experience on 0–10 or 0–100 scales, with ratings around 45–50 on the latter scale being seen as starting to become problematic. More intense anger is often associated with verbal and physical aggression and risky behavior, which, in turn, are associated with more frequent and severe negative consequences. Intense anger also often results in feeling out of control or about to lose control which is a negative internal state for most people. Some health consequences such as heart attacks are also associated with recent intense anger episodes.

Anger Expression and Consequences

One of the most important elements of determining problem anger is the form of anger expression and the resulting outcomes. Many forms of anger expression lead directly (e.g., punching a wall leading to broken bones in the hand) or indirectly (e.g., a verbal argument with a coworker eventuating in a negative performance review at work) to negative consequences. Research (e.g., Deffenbacher, Oetting, Lynch, & Morris, 1996; Deffenbacher, Oetting, Thwaites, et al., 1996; Leibsohn, Oetting, & Deffenbacher, 1994; Tafrate et al., 2002) supports this conclusion. Compared to low-anger individuals, high-anger individuals have anger leading things such as greater disruption or termination of interpersonal and family relations, physical injury to self and others, property damage, interference with work and school performance, legal and quasi-legal outcomes, financial costs, alcohol/drug use and related negative consequences, and risky behaviors. They also experience more anger-related guilt, anxiety, depression, lowered self-esteem, and greater physiological arousal. Adverse consequences tend to occur more often, to be more severe in nature, and to have a wide variety of anger consequences associated with any given episode.

HOW DO I KNOW FOR SURE?

Although there are no uniform guidelines by which to judge whether anger is problematic, in general anger is more likely to be a problem if it is

- More frequent
- Lengthier
- More intense
- Expressed in impulsive, aggressive ways
- Expressed in dysfunctional but nonaggressive ways
- Associated with more frequent and/or severe negative consequences

A final factor is that of people's *own perception* of anger as a problem. As with most mental health conditions, individuals can assess their own anger as an issue. However, many individuals may not see their anger as a problem until others (e.g., spouses, partners, family members, employers, school systems, and legal systems) urge or force them to seek help. Therefore, anger is more likely to be a problem if important others who may deliver significant negative consequences define that anger as problematic or if individuals self-define anger as a concern.

DEALING WITH JUSTIFIED ANGER

When:

- an adult is physically or sexually assaulted;
- a child is subjected to physical, sexual, or psychological abuse;
- a person is a victim of violent or other crimes;
- a person is discriminated against due to their gender, religious, racial, sexual orientation, etc.;
- a spouse/partner unilaterally terminates a relationship, has an affair, depletes financial resources, or has alcohol/drug problems;
- a person experiences significant health issues unrelated to personal choices (e.g., degenerative spine disease or amyotrophic lateral sclerosis [ALS])....

Unfair, unjust, negative events are part of the human experience. Events can be unfair, unjust, or wrong at the individual level and also at the societal level. Children should not be abused. Groups should not be denigrated and discriminated against. Should I/we/they not be angry about such conditions? Is not such anger appropriate and justified?

Our response is a tentative, compassionate "Yes, but..." Yes, but how long and strong is the anger? Yes, but what is the anger leading to or associated with? Yes, but is the anger facilitating the addressing and potential resolution of issues or is anger immobilizing the individual or group from taking constructive action? Yes, but is the person or group who was once victimized by an event now being victimized again by ongoing anger that prevents growth for the person or group? Bad, unfair, unjust, unreasonable events happen to good people. These are painful existential realities at the individual and sometimes group level. Anger and how it is expressed is not always helpful in such situations. Our approach is to help individuals identify whether anger is working for them and helping them meet their goals. If not, we help them explore strategies to lower their anger and develop ways to function effectively and not be bound or defined by past injustices. As anger is lowered, they are free to pursue meaningful life goals, including justice reform (individually or socially defined), if they so choose.

WHAT IS TRAUMA-INFORMED CARE?

Trauma can be defined as a person's emotional response to an extremely disturbing negative experience. According to SAMHSA (2015), a trauma-informed approach is a framework that involves the following:

- Realizing the widespread impact of trauma and understanding the paths to recovery.
- Recognizing the various signs and symptoms of trauma.
- Responding to the effects of all forms of trauma, including the resulting coping mechanisms, by fully integrating knowledge about trauma.
- Actively resisting re-traumatization.

(*Continued*)

(CONTINUED)

These *Six Key Principles* of a trauma-informed approach are designed to inform practice, policy, and procedures as well as to promote the linkage to recovery and resilience for those individuals and families impacted by trauma.

1. Safety;
2. Trustworthiness and transparency;
3. Peer support;
4. Collaboration and mutuality;
5. Empowerment, voice, and choice; and
6. Cultural, historical, and gender issues.

Summary

Anger is a clinically meaningful emotion. Our conceptual and diagnostic systems such as DSM-V, however, provide clinicians with little help in identifying patterns of problematic anger experience and expression. Anger is associated with triggers, both internal and external, or their combination. These triggers are processed through various filters or appraisals such as the immediate physical and emotional state of the person; the cultural and family belief systems regarding anger; the person's unique history of important goals, rules, values, and beliefs; and the person's appraisal of the threat value of the trigger and their ability to cope with it. Anger is the cognitive, emotional, and physiological outcome. It varies in terms of frequency, intensity, duration, and the breadth of things that trigger it. Anger can be expressed in many different ways, some adaptive and functional, and others destructive and damaging. Identifying problematic anger is a judgment call. In general, anger that is more frequent, more intense, lengthier in duration, expressed in aggressive or other dysfunctional ways, and leads to negative consequences is more likely to be seen as a problem. Next, we turn to the associations between drinking and anger and how the presence of these links can inform treatment.

Suggested Readings

Deffenbacher, J. L., Oetting, E. R., Thwaites, G. A., Lynch, R. S., Baker, D. A., Stark, R. S., … Eiswerth-Cox, L. (1996). State-trait anger theory and the utility of the Trait Anger Scale. *Journal of Counseling Psychology*, *43*, 131–148.

This research presented eight studies that showed characteristics and correlates of high general anger. High-anger individuals were marked by more frequent and intense anger, more frequent anger at a problem intensity, greater anger suppression and outward, negative expression and less controlled anger expression, and more frequent and more severe adverse anger consequences.

Deffenbacher, J. L., Petrilli, R. T., Lynch, R. S., Oetting, E. R., & Swaim, R. C. (2003). The Driver's Angry Thoughts Questionnaire: A measure of angry cognitions when driving. *Cognitive Therapy and Research*, *27*, 383–402.

This research addressed the cognitive element of anger. Five different but correlated types of cognitions were elucidated for driving anger: (1) judgmental/disbelieving (i.e., identifying a problem and mildly negative judgments about the problem), (2) pejorative labeling/verbally aggressive (i.e., name calling, denigration, and thinking about telling others off), (3) physically aggressive (i.e., thinking about being physically aggressive and the behaviors to execute said aggression), (4) revenge/retaliatory (i.e., thinking about revenge and the behaviors to extract revenge), and (5) coping self-instruction (i.e., thinking about ways to cope positively with the frustration and provocation). Forms of thinking tended to correlate more with specific forms of anger expression behind the wheel, the leading authors to suggest targeting cognitive–behavioral linkages together.

Denson, T. F., Moulds, M. L., & Grisham, J. R. (2012). The effects of analytical rumination, reappraisal, and distraction on anger experience. *Behavior Therapy*, *43*, 355–364.

One hundred and twenty one college students were randomly assigned to engage in rumination (i.e., repetition of negative thoughts), cognitive reappraisal (i.e., modify the negative evaluation of the situation), or distraction (i.e., focusing attention on a neutral topic). As expected, reappraisal was the effective anger regulation strategy; in contrast, rumination maintained the experience of anger (but did not increase it). These findings underscore the importance of teaching and implementing cognitive therapy strategies for anger regulation.

Kashdan, T. B., Goodman, F. R., Mallard, T. T., & DeWall, C. N. (2015). What triggers anger in everyday life? Links to the intensity, control and regulation of these emotions and personality traits. *Journal of Personality*, *84*, 737–749.

This study followed 173 college students over the course of 3 weeks to identify anger triggers experienced in daily life. The participants kept daily diaries and described each day's most intense anger emotion, its intensity and the trigger. Findings include that the intensity of anger was influenced by the nature of the trigger, with "other people" triggers yielding greater anger intensity. Also, undifferentiated anger, with no clear trigger, was the most intense and difficult to regulate. These findings suggest that anger-management efforts should include understanding and clarifying anger triggers when the source of the anger is unclear or unknown.

Substance Abuse and Mental Health Services Administration. *Trauma-informed approach and trauma-specific interventions*. (2015). Downloaded from: https://www.samhsa.gov/nctic/trauma-interventions (accessed on April 16, 2018).

Chapter 4

The Anger–Alcohol Connection

Chapter Points

- Anger and alcohol have three important associations: anger can trigger drinking or relapse to drinking, drinking can trigger anger, and drinking can unleash aggressive behavior.
- An early-treatment therapeutic task is to assess the client's alcohol–anger associations and, when present, increase the client's recognition and insight into these relationships.

Questions for Self-Reflection

- What connections do you see between alcohol and anger in your clients?
- How often do you work with clients who have Alcohol Use Disorder (AUD) and are angry?
- Is anger more often an antecedent or consequence of alcohol use in your opinion?

Stephan's *Initial Assessment*

You ask me about my drinking? I work evenings so I sneak a few drinks at work to help me get through. Some nights I have a couple glasses of wine

Anger Management Based Alcohol Treatment. DOI: https://doi.org/10.1016/B978-0-12-812709-4.00004-4

with Michael, my husband, if he's awake when I get home. Not a problem. It's good wine and helps me chill out. The problem is the couple, or three even, bottles of wine I drink on my days off. Those days I'm drunk most of the time. Alcohol's been a faithful companion since I was 14 but it's really starting to cause problems. I've had blackouts, the neighbors called the police, I'm getting fat, and my doctor says my blood pressure's too high. AA? Yes, I've tested it out a few times. I like the ideas, but the stories are so depressing. And I don't fit in; I'm gay and I'm not a down-and-out drunk.

Anger? Yes, you could say I'm an angry person. I have a lot to be stressed about; my dead-end job, all the idiots I deal with on a daily basis, my marriage that's falling apart.... So many things in my life piss me off. I usually keep a lid on it but sometimes, when I'm drinking, I lose control. I've yelled, I've screamed, I've thrown a plate full of food, and last month I put my fist through the kitchen wall and smashed some dishes. Broke two fingers. But, understand, my anger is important to me. I'm not going to accept disrespect. My boss, the stupid drivers on the road, Michael's complaining ... I won't be a doormat, not to anyone. I have the right to express myself.

During psychosocial assessment, Stephan reports being the middle of three children raised in a "typical" two-parent family. Although his father was a good provider, Stephan says that his dad was often away for work, and when he was home, he was impatient and distant. His mom, a part-time school nurse, was loving but sometimes withdrawn; looking back, Stephan realizes that she was probably depressed when he was young. Stephan says both his parents were shocked and disappointed when they found out he was gay so he rarely sees them anymore. Only his younger sister came to his wedding; his parents and his brother refused to attend. He has been with his husband Michael for almost 10 years and believes alcohol both helps them connect and causes arguments. He is feeling unhappy in his marriage and has lately been considering a separation.

Stephan says he started drinking heavily and smoking pot in high school and dropped out during his senior year, another disappointment for his parents. He eventually earned his high school diploma and has worked in restaurants most of his adult life. He says his current job is stressful and he hates his boss and coworkers. He is frustrated with what he believes to be menial, substandard work. He thinks he should be doing more with his life and feels stuck. His personal strengths include his tenacity, his friendly personality (when sober), creativity, and sense of humor.

Stephan admits that he has been aggressive and violent when intoxicated. About a month ago, during an argument with Michael, he destroyed their kitchen, punching through the wall, smashing plates, and throwing other objects. Neighbors heard the angry commotion and called the police; no arrest was made. It was this event that lead him to seek treatment now. On further questioning, Stephan denies any interpersonal violence or physical altercations with others. Stephan provides a list of anger triggers, including other drivers, his boss and coworkers, stupidity, incompetence, dishonesty, his husband's complaining, and his lack of success in life. He acknowledges that he is attached to his anger; anger expression is important to feel in control of his life.

Stephan's drinking is intertwined with his experience and expression of anger-related emotions. During the periods of "lighter" drinking, Stephan reports that the alcohol quiets his daily ruminations and generally relaxes him. His heavier drinking days, however, seem to trigger the expression of anger emotions. It is during these times that his drinking and angry expressions are most intense. Stephan is not sure if he is ready to get rid of his "old friend" alcohol, but he knows that it is causing serious problems in his life.

The Intersection of Anger and Alcohol

Anger-related emotions, hostility, and aggression have strong linkages with drinking behavior, drinking problems, and AUD. Anger is associated with AUD in at least three important ways. First, anger-related emotions are powerful antecedents for drinking behavior. For both problem and nonproblem drinkers, anger-related emotions can trigger drinking because these negative emotions are, at least initially, generally calmed by alcohol. Light-to-moderate alcohol consumption reduces tension and stress, both emotionally and physiologically. Thus, the experience of anger-related tension and stress is an important trigger for drinking. Second, in individuals vulnerable to anger (i.e., those high on trait anger), alcohol consumption may unleash impulsive, aggressive behavior. Described colloquially as the "angry drunk," heavier drinking and problem drinking may trigger the experience and expression of anger-related emotions, hostility, and verbal and physical aggression. Third, during AUD recovery, elevated state anger can be a powerful trigger for relapse to drinking. That is, anger triggers drinking and is often used to justify drinking (e.g., "I was so pissed I had to have a drink to calm down."). Additionally, high trait anger and hostility are associated with relapse. In sum, alcohol consumption is often associated with some reduction of stress, tension, and anger during active drinking periods. During recovery and

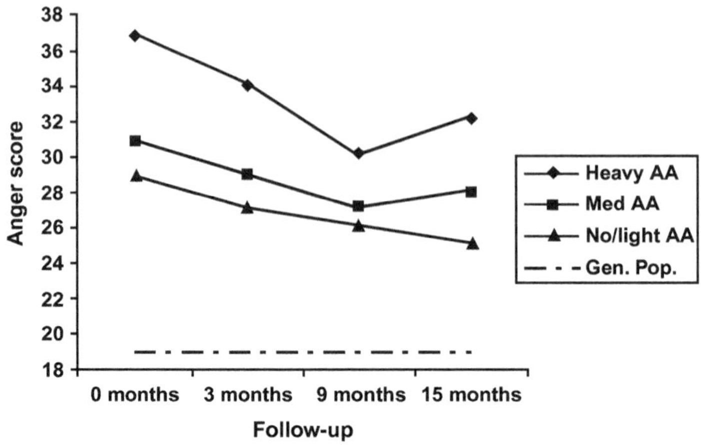

Figure 4.1 Anger as a function of Alcoholics Anonymous attendance and time (Kelly, Stout, Tonigan, Magill, & Pagano, 2010).

abstinence, this linkage remains present and the experience of anger-related emotions can trigger craving for alcohol and relapse to drinking.

Research by Kelly, Stout, Tonigan, Magill, and Pagano (2010) examined whether frequency of Alcoholics Anonymous (AA) attendance, changes in anger, and changes in alcohol consumption covary during treatment and the year following treatment. As demonstrated in Fig. 4.1, alcohol-dependent individuals reported substantially higher levels of anger relative to the general population. Although anger declined over time, their level of anger remained higher than the general population throughout the study. Second, the individuals who attended AA more frequently reported higher anger during the study relative to the individuals who reported attending AA less frequently. Finally, and most importantly, alcohol-dependent individuals reported similar changes in anger levels and in drinking levels over time. It could not be statistically confirmed whether anger affected drinking or drinking affected anger. However, the fact that anger and drinking covaried over time strongly links anger and drinking together. Kelly concludes "anger appears to be a serious and enduring problem among those suffering from alcohol dependence and is consistently related to heavy alcohol consumption" (p. 443).

ANGER AND AA

Anger and resentments have an important role in recovery in AA's philosophy. In Step 4, members must address their anger and resentments during recovery from alcoholism. In fact, this topic has a specific worksheet in AA materials to facilitate

(Continued)

(CONTINUED)

Resentment Work Sheet									
Column 1 Resentments	Column 2 The Cause?	Column 3-Affects My? (Seven Parts of Self) Check all That Apply!							Column 4 Where Was I to Blame
		Self-Esteem	Pride	Pocket Book	Emotional Security	Ambitions	Personal Relations	Sex Relations	

Figure 4.2 An example of the Alcoholics Anonymous worksheet on resentments.

addressing angry thoughts and feelings (see Fig. 4.2). Failure to address resentments, honestly and deeply, according to AA, will lead to a return to drinking and failure to achieve full sobriety.

ANGRY FACES AND ALCOHOL

Electrophysiological and behavioral research conducted by Maurage et al. (2008) indicate that the recognition of anger in facial expressions is abnormal in problem drinkers. Difficulty in recognizing anger may contribute to problem drinkers incorrectly reacting to others' emotional expressions and thus increase risks for personal problems and consequences. Moreover, consuming alcohol may exacerbate tendencies to misread or misconstrue interpersonal cues.

Anger Management Based Alcohol Treatment

The anger management therapy presented in this volume is based on cognitive and behavioral learning principles. The client's recognition of anger-related emotions as both triggers for and consequences of alcohol consumption is key. The client's functional analysis of drinking may indicate that these negative emotions trigger drinking to cope. The psychosocial assessment may indicate that drinking and intoxication are followed by problematic expression of anger-related emotions. Once sober, the experience of anger-related emotions may again trigger drinking and relapse. The key to breaking this sequence of events is the development and enhancement of the client's coping strategies for anger-related emotions and reduction of hostile cognitions. Consistent with Cognitive Behavior Therapy (CBT) learning theory principles, the client's effective engagement of anger management coping techniques—both cognitive and behavioral—makes the engagement of a nondrinking positive coping response more likely.

Research conducted by the authors of this volume tested anger management based alcohol treatment in a randomized controlled trial (Walitzer, Deffenbacher, & Shyhalla, 2015); 76 high-anger alcohol-dependent drinkers were randomly assigned to receive either anger management based alcohol treatment or AA facilitation therapy. Both were delivered in 12 outpatient sessions. These clients were then interviewed 3 and 6 months after treatment to gather information about their alcohol use, consequences, and anger-related emotions. Findings included that, first, drinkers in both treatments reported decreased drinking and anger-related emotions during the 6 months following the end of treatment. Second, changes in anger predicted alcohol outcomes after both treatments; individuals with greater reductions in anger after treatment were, on average, the clients to have better alcohol outcomes. Third, change in trait anger was a stronger predictor of outcome among treated clients with anger management based alcohol treatment, relative to clients receiving AA facilitation. Individuals in the anger management based alcohol treatment had, on average, a stronger relationship between improvements in anger and alcohol problems.

RCT?

A randomized clinical trial (RCT) is an important research design for evaluating the efficacy of an experimental treatment protocol. Research clients are randomly (i.e., by chance alone) assigned to either the experimental treatment protocol or a control comparison protocol. Typically, research data are gathered before, during, and after treatment to characterize the clients' clinical outcomes. The use of randomization and the presence of a control comparison allows researchers to make stronger statements regarding the efficacy (or lack thereof) of an experimental treatment.

Who is Appropriate for Anger Management Based Alcohol Treatment?

We ask, "Is my client ready for AUD treatment? If so, is my client appropriate for anger management based alcohol treatment? If so, is my high-anger client ready for anger management based alcohol treatment?"

The first question—"is my client ready for AUD treatment?"—is complex and multifaceted, to say the least. There are many opinions regarding methods to assess readiness in clients presenting with AUD. In the language of Prochaska and DiClemente's Transtheoretical Model of behavior change, we are asking whether the client is in the "contemplation," "preparation," or "action" stage within the process of change. In the language of AA, we are asking whether the client has "hit bottom" and is ready to work Step 1 and admit powerlessness. In the language of Miller and Rollnick's Motivational Interviewing (2013), the therapist will guide an ambivalent client to enhance and express intrinsic motivations for change. Each of these "readiness" definitions are valid.

The second question—"is my AUD client appropriate for anger management based alcohol treatment"—is more straightforward. In the RCT on anger management based alcohol treatment conducted by the authors with high-anger problem drinking clients, high anger was defined as responding "moderately," "quite a bit," or "extremely" to being distressed in the past week by annoyances and frustrations. (Individuals who responded "not at all" or "a little bit" were not eligible for the anger management based alcohol treatment RCT.) This question was asked at the beginning of outpatient treatment. This eligibility criterion was used to select clients for whom the anger management based alcohol treatment would likely have personal relevance. We recommend this relatively simple criterion to evaluate whether a client is potentially appropriate for anger management based alcohol treatment therapy.

THERAPIST TIP

Some clients may not recognize their anger or may use different words to describe their experiences. In this case, anger issues may emerge over the course of other AUD interventions. As appropriate, anger management based alcohol treatment may be added later on into a client's course of treatment.

Finally, "Is my high-anger client ready for anger management based alcohol treatment?" is, again, a complex but critical question. Two primary criteria of readiness are awareness of anger-related emotions and insight into the connection between anger and drinking. It is not uncommon, however, for clients to need preparatory work to gain this awareness and insight. During the initial psychosocial assessment, the therapist assesses anger-related emotions and consequences and listens for and asks about anger and alcohol linkages. If and when these issues surface, the therapist begins to draw the client's attention to these linkages using reflections. Examples of such an assessment are described in Chapter 5, Assessment Instruments and Considerations.

There are a number of considerations in answering this question; some of these considerations can be addressed by the therapist while others pose more of challenge. Based on Deffenbacher and McKay (2000), we describe several of these hindrances to anger management based alcohol treatment readiness, and possible therapeutic response, below:

- Some high-anger clients may be out of touch with their anger and thus do not see anger management as relevant to AUD treatment. In order to address this hindrance, the therapist must guide clients to a greater awareness of their experience and expression of anger-related emotions.
- High-anger clients may be aware of their anger but have minimal insight into its risk for potential or actual negative consequences. As such, clients, like the Tiffany case study, do not "own" their anger as a problem because they fail to fully appreciate the negative impact it has on others. Again, the therapist must work with clients to help them understand and appreciate the effect their anger has on others.
- Certain high-anger clients may believe that anger is a fundamental characteristic of who they are. These clients, such as the Stephan case study, may see their anger as justified and appropriate in multiple roles in their lives. This may signal that extra therapeutic effort should target increasing the clients' insight into the negative consequences of anger, followed by discussion of less detrimental strategies for expressing anger-related emotions.
- Some high-anger clients minimize their own responsibility for and contribution to their anger. Instead, these individuals attribute their anger to external sources, such that outside situations and people are responsible. These clients, such as the David case study, are challenging candidates for anger management based alcohol treatment because their strongly held interpretation is that their anger is entirely out of their control. The therapist must work with these clients to help them own some of the experience and expression of anger in order for anger management based alcohol treatment to be successful.
- Certain high-anger clients may experience anger as a symptom of another mental health disorder. Anger and alcohol problems may be dually diagnosed with posttraumatic stress disorder or a mood disorder. In these complex cases, the clients' comprehensive treatment plan must address both the AUD as well as the additional mental health disorder. Although anger management based alcohol treatment may have a place in the overall treatment plan, it may not be appropriate as the first intervention provided.

THERAPIST TIP

Although we, as clinicians, typically have a favorite or primary therapeutic approach, we recognize that no single therapy is appropriate for all clients. We do propose that anger management based alcohol treatment is a treatment protocol that is relevant and appropriate for a significant proportion of problem drinkers. However, a therapist's training and clinical insight into a client's situation should ultimately guide the selection of treatment components for any given client.

Summary

In order to determine whether a client may be appropriate for anger management based alcohol treatment, a comprehensive psychosocial assessment should be completed. Our next chapter discusses effective assessment of AUD, experience and expression of anger-related emotions, and their interaction.

Suggested Readings

Deffenbacher, J. L., & McKay, M. (2000). *Overcoming situational and general anger: A protocol for the treatment of anger based on relaxation, cognitive restructuring and coping skills training (therapist protocol).* Oakland, CA: New Harbinger Publications, Inc.

This book is the basis for the anger management protocol in anger management based alcohol therapy. Comprehensive in scope, it includes extensive background and rationale, therapist material, client handouts, and worksheets and in-session exercises for implementing this cognitive–behavioral approach to anger management.

Kelly, J. F., Stout, R. L., Tonigan, J. S., Magill, M., & Pagano, M. E. (2010). Negative affect, relapse, and Alcoholics Anonymous (AA): Does AA work by reducing anger? *Journal of Studies on Alcohol and Drugs*, *71*, 434–444.

This important journal article examines the relationships between AA attendance, anger, and alcohol use in alcohol-dependent individuals over the course of 15 months. Findings include that (1) clients' initial anger scores were substantially higher than the general population, (2) clients with higher anger were more likely to attend AA with greater frequency, and (3) changes in alcohol use and changes in anger levels covaried over time. The authors suggest that, although levels of anger appeared unaffected by AA attendance, AA goers may improve their ability to manage and tolerate anger.

Maurage, P., Campanella, S., Philippot, P., Vermeulen, N., Constant, E., Luminet, O., et al. (2008). Electrophysiological correlates of the disrupted processing of anger in alcoholism. *International Journal of Psychophysiology*, *70*(1), 50–62.

Electrophysiology—the examination of the timing and shape of electrical brain waves—is useful for understanding the functions and dysfunctions of the brain. In this journal article, researchers examined the processing of emotional facial expressions, including anger, among problem drinkers and healthy matched controls. Evidence indicates the disturbed processing of anger specifically in problem drinkers at both behavioral and electrophysiological levels. This dysfunction may be associated with the attentional level (N2b/P3a) of the information processing stream.

Miller, W. R., & Rollnick, S. (2013). *Motivational interviewing: Helping people change* (3rd ed.). New York, NY: Guilford Press.

This most recent third edition provides and enhances the foundation of motivational interviewing (MI), a powerful and effective approach to helping people change, which originated in addiction treatment and continues to spread to other disciplines. MI is defined by the authors as a "collaborative conversation style for strengthening a person's own motivation and commitment to change" (p. 12) and can be useful on its own or in conjunction with other treatment approaches, including anger management based alcohol treatment. This book is an accessible and essential resource for anyone interested in learning about MI.

Walitzer, K. S., Deffenbacher, J. L., & Shyhalla, K. (2015). Alcohol-adapted anger management treatment: A randomized controlled trial of an innovative therapy for alcohol dependence. *Journal of Substance Abuse Treatment, 59*, 83–93.

In this study, researchers randomly assigned 76 high-anger individuals with alcohol dependence to receive 12 outpatient sessions of either alcohol-adapted anger management treatment (AM) or Alcoholics Anonymous facilitation (AAF) therapy. Clients were then followed for 6 months after the end of treatment. On average, clients in AM and in AAF reported decreased drinking and decreased anger after treatment. Interestingly, individuals' changes in trait anger were a stronger predictor of posttreatment drinking consequences within AM relative to those in the AAF.

Section II

ASSESSMENT AND PREPARATION

Chapter 5

Assessment Instruments and Considerations

Chapter Points

- In addition to the open-ended assessments, standardized questionnaires provide a quantitative assessment of functioning and can be used throughout treatment to monitor progress.
- In-depth assessment can assist in evaluating a client's suitability and readiness for anger management based alcohol treatment.
- We describe several relevant, brief, and available assessment measures and explain how they can be used in treatment.
- Case examples are used to demonstrate the use of the Initial Anger Assessment.

Questions for Self-Reflection

- How do you feel about using assessment tools and sharing results with clients?
- How do you know your interventions are working?

Therapist: *I know a lot about assessing clients for alcohol and drug use disorders and I'm comfortable asking about things like anxiety and depression. But I'm not as confident talking about anger emotions. This client*

Anger Management Based Alcohol Treatment. DOI: https://doi.org/10.1016/B978-0-12-812709-4.00005-6

seemed kind of irritated during our session and talked about being mad at several things in her life. I think anger may be related to some of her drinking and consequences. I'd like to assess her for anger management treatment too? But where do I start?

Assessment of a client's functioning is critical to individualizing treatment goals, monitoring treatment progress, and measuring treatment outcomes. Although a comprehensive discussion of assessment methods is not included in this volume, we will describe several tools that are particularly relevant for clients in anger management based alcohol treatment. Our model, the biopsychosocial assessment model of alcohol use disorder (AUD), seeks to understand a client's biological (e.g., medical and physiology domains), psychological (e.g., intrapersonal domains), and social (e.g., interpersonal domains) of functioning. This model appreciates that AUD risk and onset, active drinking phase, and recovery are complex and multifaceted. We will focus on three content domains: alcohol involvement, anger, and satisfaction with treatment. We will then present our case studies, the results of their pretreatment assessments and how these assessment findings inform individualized treatment decisions.

ASSESSMENT INSTRUMENTS

Standardized assessment tools, that is, questionnaires and interviews, are administered the same way, with the same wording, each time they are given. Use of standardized assessments can reveal client change in alcohol involvement and in anger-related emotions over the course of treatment. In this chapter, we discuss both more informal open-ended assessments as well as standardized assessments that we have found useful (and in the public domain) in tracking pre- to posttreatment change.

Pretreatment Assessment: Alcohol Involvement

Alcohol involvement can be assessed through a combination of open-ended interviews, standardized questionnaires, and biological markers. We describe each of these methods next.

Initial Screening for Alcohol Use Disorder Treatment

An oft-necessary eligibility criterion for alcohol treatment is that the presenting individual meets AUD diagnosis. As is the case for many treatment providers, making a diagnosis is accomplished through review of each of the 11 DSM-V (APA, 2013) criteria for AUD. Based on these 11 criteria, a score of 2 and 3 indicates a mild AUD, 4 and 5 indicates a moderate AUD, and 6 or more indicates a severe AUD. The 11 criteria are based on symptoms occurring in the past

12 months. Because the diagnostic criteria wording does not easily lend itself to an interview format, we slightly modify some of the questions to make them more client friendly:

1. Have you often had times when you ended up drinking more, or for longer, than you intended?
2. Have you persistently wanted or tried to cut down or stop drinking but couldn't?
3. Have you spent a lot of time getting or using alcohol, or recovering from drinking?
4. Have you had cravings for alcohol or had strong urges to drink alcohol?
5. Have you found that drinking—or being sick from drinking—often interfered with taking care of your family or your house? Or it often caused problems at work or school?
6. Have you continued to drink despite persistent problems, or worsened problems, with family or friends?
7. Have you given up or cut back on activities that were important or interesting to you in order to drink?
8. Have you more than once gotten into situations during or after drinking that put you at more risk of getting hurt (such as driving, swimming, using machinery, walking in a dangerous area, or having unsafe sex)?
9. Have you continued to drink even though it was making you feel anxious, depressed, making a health problem worse, or after having a memory blackout?
10a. Have you had to drink much more than you used to in order to get the effect you want?
10b. Or have you found that your usual number of drinks had much less of an effect than before?
11a. Have you found that when the effects of alcohol were wearing off, you had withdrawal symptoms, like sleep trouble, shakiness, restlessness, nausea, sweating, or a racing heart?
11b. Have you taken a drink to avoid these withdrawal symptoms?
(Based on DSM-V, APA, 2013)

ALCOHOL WITHDRAWAL—DIAGNOSTIC CRITERIA

Withdrawal from alcohol can be not only uncomfortable, but life threatening. When someone has quit or reduced heavy, prolonged alcohol use, the following symptoms should be evaluated within the first few days:

Sweating
Pulse rate over 100 bpm

(*Continued*)

(CONTINUED)

Hand tremors (shakes)
Insomnia (trouble sleeping)
Nausea or vomiting
Visual, tactile, or auditory hallucinations
Psychomotor agitation (can't sit still)
Anxiety
Seizures

These symptoms are especially concerning if any of them are causing clinically significant distress or impairment in the person's life. Medical intervention is sometimes necessary to help a person safely detox from alcohol.

I CAN DRINK 'EM ALL UNDER THE TABLE!

The word for this is tolerance. Essentially, tolerance is the ability to consume large qualities of alcohol without showing or feeling effects. A person may be "intoxicated" but may not appear "drunk." As tolerance increases over time, a person may need to drink more and more alcohol in order to feel the effects. A high tolerance increases the risk of developing an AUD, and it can lead to dangerous consequences including health problems, risky behaviors, and legal troubles. Some people are proud that they can "hold their liquor," and yet it's this high tolerance that increases the likelihood of problems. This scenario is similar to a person who cannot feel pain and therefore does not know their hand is burning on a stove until they see it. People with high alcohol tolerance are missing the essential warning system telling them to slow down or stop. Tolerance is therefore an important factor to consider in the diagnosis of AUD.

A diagnosis of AUD is a necessary eligibility criterion for treatment entry. We do not, however, require that strong motivational factors be present, such as firm commitment to an abstinence goal. It is not unusual for individuals seeking treatment to present with doubt regarding their commitment to life-long abstinence. When an individual gives voice to this uncertainty, we interpret this as naturally occurring ambivalence that can be explored and addressed in early treatment sessions and not as a contraindication to treatment.

Open-Ended Assessment

Agencies that treat people for AUD will have their own versions of substance use assessment tools. In our work, we begin with the Initial Alcohol Assessment which includes a series of open-ended questions. We cover topics including past and current drinking patterns, triggers and consequences of drinking, other substance use, medical issues related to drinking, treatment and self-help history, periods of abstinence, success in making other behavior changes, and strength of the support system. We also ask about the importance of changing, client's confidence level in making changes, and what needs to happen right now to make that change more likely to happen.

THERAPIST TIP

The initial questions we ask in this early session set the tone for the assessment and treatment process. We open with "Tell me about why you've come here." or "How can we help you?" In this way, we give the client time to explain what brought them to treatment. Our questions, when possible, intentionally avoid closed, yes/no queries in order to encourage the client to give fuller explanations.

THERAPIST TIP

Reflective listening is a common technique used by therapists regardless of theoretical orientation. Reflective listening involves hearing and understanding what is being said by the client and then reflecting that understanding back to the client. In essence, when using reflective listening, the therapist is taking a guess at what the client means. More powerful than "Yes, I see," or a series of questions, reflective listening can emphasize a message originally voiced by the client and encourage the client to expand and explore it in more detail. But perhaps most importantly, reflective listening demonstrates empathy, understanding, and presence which are essential in establishing a strong therapeutic alliance.

Alcohol Consumption

Standardized assessment of alcohol consumption is central to describing the client's presenting picture. The Quick Drinking Screen (QDS; Roy et al., 2008) is a brief and reliable interview for quantifying a client's drinking along multiple dimensions. The QDS includes questions regarding the: (1) frequency of drinking, (2) average quantity consumed, and (3) frequency of heavy drinking [defined as five for men or four for women standard drinks in a single occasion]. An additional question regarding the frequency of abstinent days may be added to the interview. The specific questions for the QDS are found in the Appendix I. The time frame of the QDS may be adjusted according to need. One time frame used for assessing drinking at pretreatment is the 30-day period prior to, and inclusive of, the client's most recent drink. A time frame helpful to capture posttreatment drinking is to use the most recent 30 days.

WHAT'S A STANDARD DRINK?

Alcoholic beverages vary considerably in their ethanol (pure alcohol) content. In order to use a shared language to describe drinking amounts, we explain the measurement unit of a "standard drink" to the client. In brief, a standard drink is equivalent to 13.6 g absolute ethanol. Thus, one standard drink is equivalent to (approximately) a 12 oz beer, 5 oz of wine, 1.5 oz of hard liquor, and so forth.

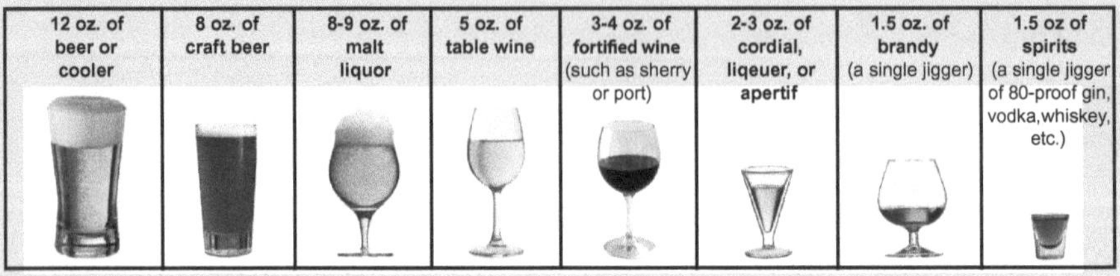

WHAT IS BINGE DRINKING? WHAT IS HEAVY ALCOHOL USE?

National Institute on Alcohol Abuse and Alcoholism defines binge drinking as a pattern of drinking that brings the blood alcohol concentration (BAC) levels to 0.08 g/dL. This typically occurs after four drinks for women and five drinks for men—over the course of 2 hours. Substance Abuse and Mental Health Services Administration defines heavy alcohol use as binge drinking on 5 or more days in the past month. Drinking at this level or above puts people at greater risk for developing AUD.

DRINKING CONSEQUENCES

In addition to quantifying the client's recent alcohol use, it is also critical to use a standardized method to quantify the client's recent history of problems associated with drinking. To this end, we recommend the Short Inventory of Problems (SIP; Kiluck, Dreifuss, Weiss, Morgenstern, & Carroll, 2013). The SIP questionnaire assesses five domains of drinking problems: impulse control, interpersonal, intrapersonal, physical, and social problems. We include an anger domain to further connect the anger and alcohol consequences. In addition to these six subscales, a single total score may be used to quantify drinking problems across domains. As with the QDS, the time frame for the questionnaire may be adapted for specific purposes. We recommend use of a 3-month reporting window to capture pretreatment drinking problems and 30-day window for posttreatment problems.

THE FOUR ANGER ITEMS ADDED TO SIP INCLUDE:

- I have felt irritable or angry as a result of my drinking
- When drinking, I have broken or smashed something
- I have gotten into a physical fight while drinking
- While drinking, I have said harsh or cruel things to someone

Craving for Alcohol

Cravings for and urges to drink alcohol are a key experience in AUD and certainly worthy of inclusion in an assessment. Kavanagh et al. (2013) reviewed the many questionnaires available that assess craving for alcohol. One of the briefer measures recommended is the Penn Alcohol Craving Scale (PACS; Flannery et al., 1999), a five-item questionnaire that assesses frequency, intensity, and duration of craving experiences, average craving level during the past week, and difficulty resisting drinking if alcohol were to be available; (see Appendix I). The PACS is psychometrically sound, has concurrent validity, and predicts relapse to drinking.

Biological Markers

Biological markers of AUD provide another important source of information to complement the above-described self-report measures. First, and most common, is the blood alcohol concentration (BAC). Typically, expired air is blown into a hand-held unit (e.g., a breathalyzer) that determines the amount of alcohol in the breath, which corresponds to the amount of alcohol in the blood. This highly valid biological marker of intoxication is typically used by the legal system with regard to intoxicated driving.

Next, biomarkers of alcohol use and abuse may be categorized as indirect state markers and direct state markers. Indirect state markers assess chronic alcohol consumption indirectly via, for example, the activity of particular liver enzymes. For example, the activity of gamma-glutamyltransferace (GGT), aspartate aminotransferace (AST), and alanine aminotransferace (ALT) will be elevated with chronic heavy alcohol use. Although medically important in their own right, combinations of liver enzyme activity, and trends in these enzymes, may be used to track chronic alcohol abuse and longer term treatment outcome. A caveat, however, is that although these indirect state markers are sensitive to chronic abuse, they are also influenced by gender, age, and non-alcohol-related medical illnesses. Further, these indirect measures are not sensitive to acute and recent alcohol consumption.

Direct state markers measure alcohol consumption via ethanol metabolites formed after drinking and are thus timely and rapidly sensitive to recent consumption. These direct ethanol metabolites are advantageous in that they have higher sensitivity and specificity relative to indirect state markers. Ethanol metabolites are detectable in serum, whole blood, urine, and hair samples and can measure light to heavy amounts of consumption over the course of hours to several months. Ethyl glucuronide is the most frequently used marker and is sensitive to low amounts of alcohol consumption in urine samples. Phosphatidylethanol, alternatively, differentiates moderate alcohol consumption from heavy alcohol use in whole blood samples.

In sum, both indirect and direct state markers of alcohol consumption have utility in detection of recent and chronic alcohol consumption, liver dysfunction, and treatment outcomes. Use of multiple markers can provide a broad picture of alcohol involvement, independent from self-report.

Additional Assessment Tools

We have recommended a variety of domains for a brief alcohol involvement assessment including DSM-V diagnosis, alcohol consumption and consequences, craving, and biological markers. Our instrument selections above represent only one of the measures available for each domain, and our coverage of domains is not exhaustive. Just to name a few, additional constructs of interest could include physical dependence on alcohol, alcohol-related cognitions (e.g., self-efficacy for abstinence, alcohol effect expectancies), family history of alcohol problems, social drinking network, past experiences with treatment and mutual-help groups, and drinking triggers and situations. Assessment of alcohol involvement should be both broad and deep; the domains of focus should be selected on the particular interest of the clinician and agency.

Pretreatment Assessment: Anger-Related Emotions

Open-Ended Anger Assessment

Anger emotions are rarely assessed out of context. They may be included as part of a discussion of general negative affect (NA) or possibly as a trigger for or a consequence of drinking. Our Initial Anger Assessment (see Appendix I) uses an open-ended question format and shares elements of a Cognitive Behavior Therapy functional analysis (antecedents–behaviors–consequences). We start by asking what makes clients feel angry (triggers—internal, external, situational). We make sure to

Figure 5.1 The anger (Celsius) thermometer.

include the range of anger-related emotions such as frustration, irritation, annoyance etc. We ask about the frequency of the anger emotions (how often angry emotions happen) and ask the clients to rate the intensity of their anger on a 0–100 scale (like a Celsius thermometer where 0 is cool and 100 is boiling; see Fig. 5.1). We ask clients to describe what happens in their bodies (physiological reactions like muscle tension or face turning red) when angry. We ask what other emotions they notice along with the anger (depression, guilt, fear). We are especially interested in the thoughts and even images that run through their minds when they're angry or frustrated (self-talk, rumination). We spend time exploring behaviors that result from these angry feelings (yelling, silence, swearing), and then we consider both the positive and the negative consequences of those behaviors and the angry feelings in general. We ask about how important people in their lives (family and friends) react to their anger. We also want to know about strategies they already use to calm down when they're angry or frustrated (drink, count to 10). At the end, we ask them to describe how anger and alcohol may be connected for them (e.g., anger leads to drinking, alcohol increases anger, alcohol use becomes a source of conflict and anger with others). Throughout this assessment, we use reflective listening and encourage clients to explore the often complex connections between anger and alcohol use.

THERAPIST TIP

Sometimes clients begin this process by announcing that they are not angry people, often equating anger with abuse and aggression. There is a perception that people who need "anger management treatment" are necessarily abusers. Other clients have come to see their anger as part of their identity and need extra support in exploring their experience of anger. Open questions, nonjudgmental listening, and gentle reflections can help clients understand their experiences with anger emotions and alcohol in a new way.

Another brief, useful anger measure is the Dimensions of Anger Reaction (DAR; Forbes et al., 2014). Respondents report on a five-point scale (0 = none/almost none of the time, 4 = all/almost all of the time) how often reactions/consequences happened in the last 4 weeks (see Appendix I). Three items assess how often anger occurred (frequency), how strong reactions were (intensity), and how long anger lasted (duration). The fourth item addresses the person's desire to hit others when angry (physical aggression propensity), while the fifth measures how anger interferes with social relations (social consequences). The DAR possesses good reliability, evidence of convergent and divergent validity, and an upper quartile cut score (i.e., a score of 12 or higher) that provides a reasonable index of when anger tends to be a problem. Moreover, the 4-week time frame provides insight into recent functioning with regard to anger.

DAR +2

Clinicians may want to add two items to the DAR as prompts to explore two other areas. Items would be rated on the same scale, but not included in the score. One could inquire how often the person wanted to hit, break, throw, or smash things (physical aggression toward the physical environment) and how often they wanted to do things like yell at, curse out, put down, name call, others (verbal assault).

The DAR can be useful in at least four ways. First, it can be included as a brief screening measure addressing anger among other relevant clinical issues. It is short and simple to use. Items and response choices are easy to read and understand. These features reduce the fatigue, confusion, and resistance that longer instruments and more complex ratings may engender. Second, it provides for normative self-comparisons; a score of 12 (or more) indicates "a level of anger that is associated with psychological distress and functional impairment" (p. 170). Helping angry clients understand how their DAR score compares to others, both generally and in terms of a score level that suggests problematic anger, may help them see anger issues in a new light and perhaps increase motivation for change. Third, going over responses provides leads from which to expand open-ended interviews. For example, *What kind of situations make you angry?* (making reference to the frequency item); *What do you typically do when you are really angry?* (reference to the intensity and physical aggression items); *What kinds of thoughts and images go through your mind when you are angry for a long time?* (reference to duration item); and *You mentioned your anger impacts your social relationships. Could you give some recent examples?* (reference to social consequences item). Fourth, the DAR can assist in assessing treatment outcome. That is, giving it before and after treatment can provide a measure of treatment-related change. If it is used in this fashion, clinicians must remember that the range of scores (0–20) is relatively low such that a change of a few points may reflect meaningful change.

The Positive and Negative Affect Schedule (PANAS: Watson, Clark, & Tellegen, 1988; Serafini, Malin-Mayor, Nich, Hunkele, & Carroll, 2016) is a brief and valid assessment of both positive and negative emotions. The scale presents 20 affect words to which the client responds "very slightly" to "extremely" on a five-point scale (see Appendix I). Two of the words are anger related ("irritable" and "hostile"); we recommend the addition of four more anger-related words to broaden the six-item anger subscale ("angry," "scornful," "disgusted," and "loathing"). As with the scales described earlier, the time frame for reporting can be modified to the situation; we recommend the previous (one) week reporting window. The three resulting subscales of the PANAS—Positive Affect Scale (PA) (10 items), Negative Affect Scale (NA) (10 items), and anger emotion affect (6 items)—each are important in describing a client's affect status. Too often, as clinicians, we focus primarily on negative affect and its experience and consequences; positive affect and its benefits are overlooked as a source of client strength or resilience factor. We recommend including positive affect and its triggers and consequences in the context of anger management based alcohol treatment.

PANAS SCORING

Our scoring method is to calculate the numeric average (i.e., the mean) of the items in each subscale (see Appendix I). Each score (ranging from 0 to 4) can then be understood in words such as "Not at all," "Moderately," or "Extremely" which often have more clinical relevance.

Additional Anger Assessment Tools

As described above, the combination of a broad open-ended assessment, the DAR, and the PANAS will provide a basic understanding of the client's anger frequency, intensity, triggers, and consequences. Additional assessment tools exist that capture alternative anger dimensions and more narrowly defined aspects of anger emotions. Spielberger et al.'s (1999) State-Trait Anger Expression Inventory (STAXI; also see Lievaart, Franken, & Hovens, 2016) assesses anger-related emotions both as an emotional state (State Anger) as well as a personality dimension (Trait Anger). The STAXI also describes the experience, expression, and control of anger. Deffenbacher et al. (1996) describe a questionnaire focused on dimensions of anger expression including subscales for physical assault on people/objects, direct expression, noisy arguing, and verbal assault. Derogotis et al.'s (1983) Brief Symptom Inventory (BSI) includes a hostility subscale that describes the psychiatric nature of anger-related emotions. Although the PANAS and the DAR were selected for this volume based on their brevity, psychometrics, and public domain status, these additional scales are also highly useful.

Satisfaction With Treatment

Using a standardized Client Satisfaction Questionnaire adapted from Attikisson et al. (1982), we gather information about how clients perceived their treatment experience. Client responses to these closed-ended and open-ended questions allow the clinic staff to identify the strengths and relative weakness of their clinic and the treatment they offer. The questionnaire purposely does not request feedback on specific therapists or counselors by name and, instead, focuses on the nature of treatment and the clinic. Clients rate the quality of treatment services received, whether they received the services they sought, whether the program met their needs, and their degree of satisfaction with treatment.

Summary

A combination of open-ended assessment interviews and standardized questionnaires are highly useful for describing a client's pretreatment presentation, assessing appropriateness and readiness for anger management based alcohol treatment, determining the specific goals of treatment, and tracking changes throughout the course of treatment. The next chapter discusses readiness and strategies to prepare the client—and therapist—for anger management based alcohol treatment. The remainder of this chapter demonstrates the use of the assessment process with our case study clients.

David's *Initial Anger Assessment*

Therapist: *If it's okay with you, I'd like to switch gears now and talk more about your own experience with anger and how it may connect with your drinking.*

David: *Sure, I know my drinking is a problem but honestly I'm surprised that we're even talking about anger. I've never hit anyone, I've never even been in a real fight, and I don't think most people who know me would think I need anger management.*

Therapist: *It sounds like you don't think of yourself as an angry person because you've never hit anyone. Physical violence is definitely a way some people express anger but it's one of the more extreme examples. I guess what I'd like to figure out with you are other ways that anger emotions, including annoyance, irritation, frustration are affecting your daily life even if you're not acting out in a physically violent way. Does that make sense to you?*

David: *Yeah that's fine.*

Therapist: *Thanks. Hopefully this will become clearer as we talk today and over the rest of our time together. So first of all I'm wondering if you can tell me what situations make you feel frustrated and/or angry.*

David: *Well, I can't stand cheaters, liars, and people who always cut corners and take the easy way out. These kids coming out of college now are so damn lazy! I'm seriously worried about the future of this country. And I'm fed up with people who can't follow simple rules—I see that a lot at work and especially when I'm driving. The left lane is not the Sunday driving lane for God's sake!*

Therapist: *Ok, you're noticing things at work and on the road. What else?*

David: *I hate when people waste my time and my money. I'm sick of inconsiderate, disrespectful people and that includes my family. Is it really that hard to get the dishes done, turn down the heat, and close the stupid cabinets in the kitchen at night? Seriously? I work hard all day to pay the bills and they can't even walk the frickin' dog.*

Therapist: *You seem to have a lot of different situations that frustrate you. How often would you say you feel frustrated or angry?*

David: *I never gave it much thought but I guess it happens pretty often. You have to understand, I deal with way too many incompetent people in my life.*

Therapist: *So you're feeling this way pretty often. Anger is an emotion that can have an especially strong effect on our bodies. For example, some people tense their jaw, some see red, some feel hot, some get headaches or stomachaches. What do you notice in your body when you're angry?*

David: *If I had to pick one I'd say stomachache.*

Therapist: *You think anger may be affecting your stomach and that can be unpleasant. Anger can also show up with other emotions. For example, some people when they're angry also feel sadness, shame, helplessness, or anxiety. What other emotions do you think might be there when you're angry?*

David: *I've never really noticed any other emotions except being mad.*

Therapist: *Sometimes those other emotions aren't there and sometimes they're hard to recognize. We'll have more time over the next few weeks to figure out what's going on for you. I'm also interested in how intense your anger emotions are for you. If you were to rate your anger on a 100 point scale, like a Celsius thermometer or the speedometer on a car, where 0 is not angry at all and 100 is the most angry you've ever been, where do you think you are most days?*

David: *I do like putting numbers to things but that's a tough one because it changes. If I had to pick one overall number, I'd say 70. I'm at 60 at work most days and close to 80 at home. But again, it depends on what other people are doing.*

Therapist: *You're right, it's not easy to put one number to it so thanks for giving it a try now. I'm glad you like numbers because we'll be using them to get a better understanding of your anger emotions each time we meet. There are also a lot of different words people use when they're angry. What words do you tend to use most often?*

David: *I can get pretty foul at times if that's what you mean.*

Therapist: *So you definitely use some choice words when you're angry. I'm also wondering how you describe yourself when you're angry. Some people say they're irritated, annoyed, some say pissed off, some say furious.*

David: *I think irritated and pissed depending on who's doing what.*

Therapist: *I'm also curious about the thoughts and maybe even images or pictures that run through your mind when you're feeling angry. If there was a small microphone or camera in your head, what would it hear you saying to yourself when you're mad?*

David: *Huh. That's different. I think that people should know better and just do things the right way the first time. I think that if people would show respect and do what they're supposed to do, I wouldn't get so mad. I think this world is full of rude, ignorant, lazy people and it's getting worse. I don't know if I have any images, I'm more of a rational thinker than a dreamer.*

Therapist: *It is different and I appreciate your willingness to describe some of your thoughts. That's also something we'll spend more time on throughout this program. I know you said you don't lash out physically when you're angry so I'm wondering how you do act when you're mad?*

David: *At work, I'm known as a no-nonsense guy who's a stickler for details. If anything, I get real quiet and stare people down. They get the message loud and clear. At home I might stomp around, I can be real sarcastic, I'm good at the cold shoulder, and sometimes I'll slam a door or a cupboard to make a point. I get mad enough to yell sometimes and even the dog runs and hides.*

Therapist: *You have different reactions at work and at home and you're mainly concerned about what happens at home. I'm wondering what good and bad things happen when you're angry?*

David: *Well, I think my high standards have helped me at work and I get respect because people are afraid of me. At home, it's not like that at all. My wife is fed up with my temper and my kids avoid me and act even more disrespectful. I'm also now wondering if my stomach problems are related; I take way too many antacids every day.*

Therapist: *You're worried that your anger may affecting your family relationships and your stomach. What other reactions from the important people in your life do you notice when you're angry?*

David: *Sometimes my wife tells me I'm impatient and mean and not the man she married. Sometimes the kids don't include me in family plans. That hurts.*

Therapist: *Your family is really important to you.*

David: *Yeah—that's the main reason I'm here. I'll lose them if something doesn't change.*

Therapist: *I'm glad you're here and serious about changing. I truly think this program can help you. When you're angry, what do you do to calm down?*

David: *At work I just get busy and get things done. At home I drink and I also tinker in the garage.*

Therapist: *Tell me more about the connection between your anger and your drinking.*

David: *I never really thought about it much. Sometimes I just drink. It's become a daily habit. Lots of people I know have some drinks after work to relax. I drink to wind down at the end of the day, especially after work and if I come home to a mess in my house. But I also think my family would say I'm much more impatient and crabby when I'm drinking. It's confusing.*

Therapist: *You're confused; sometimes you drink to calm down and sometimes drinking makes you feel and act even more angry.*

David: *Exactly! I can't keep drinking like this and my wife and kids don't take me seriously anymore when I'm drunk.*

Therapist: *I really appreciate your honesty today. I know talking about drinking and anger emotions isn't easy. Hopefully together we can work toward finding new ways for you to make changes to both. How does that sound?*

David: *I'm here because I need help. I know my drinking is a huge problem and I'm starting to think my anger might be more of a problem than I thought. I'm open to whatever you have to help me to save my marriage and live a better life.*

David's Pretreatment Assessment Measures

David answered yes to all 11 DSM-V symptoms, the highest possible score, indicating a Severe AUD. On the QDS, he reported drinking daily with an average of 11 standard drinks per day. His greatest number of drinks in 1 day was 17; he reported 30/30 heavy drinking days and no days without alcohol use over the past month. His average craving score on the PACS was 4.4 out of 6. On the SIP, he had an overall score of 26 out of a possible 57 with highest numbers on the intrapersonal and interpersonal subscales. His SIP anger score was 5 out of 12. His PANAS results showed an average PA score of 2.1 and a NA score of 3.0. His average PANAS anger score was 2.5. His score on the DAR was 14 out of 25 with scores of 3 or more on anger frequency, intensity, duration, and social consequences.

Interpretations

David's assessment results confirmed that he was a heavy daily drinker with both high tolerance and high craving levels who was experiencing significant problems as a result of his drinking. His responses on the SIP revealed especially noteworthy issues with his family and his self-image. Relatedly, on the PANAS, his average NA score was relatively high while he seemed to struggle to identify with positive emotions. His scores on the PANAS anger scale averaged out to 2.5 which falls between "Moderately" and "Quite a bit" in terms of how he had been recently affected by anger emotions. His score on the DAR suggested a level of anger that is associated with psychological distress and functional impairment. The alcohol results were consistent with his self-report during the open-ended assessments of drinking; the results of the anger emotions came as more of a surprise to him since he originally did not consider himself to be an "angry person."

Therapist Thoughts (Alcohol)

Can this client be safely treated on an outpatient basis? When a client has been drinking at potentially dangerous levels with no days of abstinence, the initial concern is appropriate level of care. The therapist needs to assess the client carefully and involve medical staff to determine if there is a need for detox services to help the client quit drinking and avoid life-threatening withdrawal symptoms. In this case, the therapist explained these concerns to David who asked for the chance to try it on his own and cut down his drinking gradually. He said he had done it this way in the past and never had any problems. He was instructed to call his Primary Care Provider and seek medical attention immediately if he noticed any withdrawal symptoms and he agreed. The therapist also spent adequate time each week checking in with David about his progress in cutting down his alcohol use and would have referred him for medical services if needed. David expressed no doubt about the seriousness of his alcohol use and the consequences for his family and his health.

Therapist Thoughts (Anger)

David seemed to lack insight into the extent of his anger emotions and the consequences in his life. David took pride in the fact that people at work feared him; at the same time, his anger was alienating him from his family. David frequently externalized his anger, believing that his angry reactions were justified by the behavior of others. He also appeared to be unaware of the strong connection between his drinking and anger. All these factors indicated that more effort was needed to help him understand the consequences of his anger, the connection between his anger and his drinking, and the role he played in his angry reactions and behaviors. David benefitted from the therapist sharing some of the anger assessment measure results especially since he seemed to appreciate numbers. It was essential that the therapist demonstrated respect for David's view of his situation while also taking extra time up front to help him better understand these issues as well as the potential usefulness of this treatment. David was very motivated by his dedication to his family and he seemed willing to try anything that could help. He was bright, organized, and had a strong support system.

Tiffany's *Initial Anger Assessment*

Therapist: *If it's okay with you, I'd like to spend some time talking more about your experience with anger and also how it might be related to your drinking.*

Tiffany: *I get pretty mad but I have a right to be!*

Therapist: *You get pretty mad—I want to hear more about that. First of all I'm wondering if you can tell me what makes you feel frustrated or angry.*

Tiffany: *How much time do we got? I hate my job, my mom's a drunk, my brothers are lazy, my boyfriend dumped me, people are stupid and racist, my friends are selfish, I hate my body because of all the loose skin, I've had shit done to me and I've done shit I'm not proud of and that keeps me up at night.*

Therapist: *Thanks for sharing all that. Is there anything else?*

Tiffany: *That's enough for now.*

Therapist: *It is. There's a lot that makes you feel angry.*

Tiffany: *Uh-huh. I got a lot going on and sometimes all I have to do is look in the mirror and I can't even stand myself.*

Therapist: *It sounds like some of your anger comes from the outside and some of it comes from inside you. How often would you say you feel angry?*

Tiffany: *I feel like I'm some kind of mad like all the time.*

Therapist: *So you're feeling mad almost all the time. For most people, feeling that much anger can have an especially strong effect on your body.*

For example, some people tense their jaw, some see red, some feel hot, some get headaches or stomachaches. What do you notice happening in your body when you're angry?

Tiffany: *I sometimes get kind of dizzy when I'm real mad.*

Therapist: *When you're feeling really angry you get dizzy and you don't like that. Anger can also happen at the same time as other emotions. For example, some people when they're angry also feel sad, ashamed, helpless, scared, or anxious. What other emotions do you think might be there when you're angry?*

Tiffany: *I don't know. I'm afraid I'll be alone forever so does that count?*

Therapist: *Being afraid is certainly an emotion that can happen with anger. We'll have more time over the next few weeks to figure out more about what's going on for you with other emotions. I'm also interested in getting a better idea of just how intense your anger emotions usually are. If you were to give your anger a score on a 100 point scale, like a Celsius thermometer, where 0 is not angry at all and 100 is the angriest you've ever been, where do you think you are on most days?*

Tiffany: *I don't know how to answer that. It's not 0 and it's not 100. Something in between. I don't know.*

Therapist: *Don't worry, it's not easy choose one number. We'll get more practice using numbers to talk about your anger as we go along. There are also a lot of different words people use to show how angry they feel. I'm wondering how you describe yourself when you're angry. For example, some people say they're annoyed, some say irritated, some say pissed off, some say furious.*

Tiffany: *Pissed off.*

Therapist: *Thanks. I'm also curious about the thoughts and maybe even pictures that run through your mind when you're angry. If there was a tiny microphone or camera in your head, what would it hear you saying to yourself when you're mad?*

Tiffany: *When I'm really pissed off I think "I can't f-ing stand this." When I look in the mirror I tell myself I'm an ugly f-ing bitch who deserves to be alone. I picture people laughing and talking about my ugly body too. Sometimes I think about all the things I could've done and said to people but didn't. I'm getting' mad just talking about this—how's that helpful? I thought this therapy shit was supposed to make you feel better, not worse.*

Therapist: *You have some pretty powerful thoughts and images in your mind when you're angry and it can be upsetting to talk about. I appreciate your honesty; you're really helping me get a better idea of what's going on for you. I feel confident that we can work together in this program to help you feel better. I have a few more things I want to find out more about. Do you want to take a short break or keep going?*

Tiffany: *Let's just get this over with.*

Therapist: *Thanks for hanging in there. So when you're feeling angry like that, what do you do? How do you act?*

Tiffany: *It depends. At work, when a caller pisses me off, I stay calm on the outside because if I didn't, I'd lose my job. I get paid to deal with jerks. At home, I yell, I punch my pillows, and I call up people to tell them off. That feels good. If I'm super mad at myself and my body, or thinking too much about the past, I sometimes cry but never in front of anyone else.*

Therapist: *You have different reactions to anger at work and in your personal life and it sounds like you're mostly concerned about what's going on personally. I'm wondering what kinds of things happen for you, both good and bad, when you're angry.*

Tiffany: *Well, I'm good at my job so that's good. At home, getting really pissed off gives me the guts to tell people how I really feel but I'm starting to think they're avoiding my phone calls.*

Therapist: *You're worried your angry phone calls are messing up your friendships. What other not-so-good things do you notice about your anger?*

Tiffany: *When I get all caught up thinking about the past stuff, I can get pretty pissed off, I feel depressed, then I can't sleep.*

Therapist: *So things that happened in the past can make you pretty angry and depressed when you think about them now. What does your depression feel like?*

Tiffany: *Well, don't go thinking I'm going to kill myself—I'm too vain for that. I just feel really sad and like life is so unfair to me, and I just want to run away.*

Therapist: *So the anger and sadness are all tied up together and drinking is a way you try to run away when you feel like that.*

Tiffany: *Yep. It kind of works but I never really get away.*

Therapist: *I'm hopeful that some of the work we'll do together in this treatment will help you think differently about all these things, anger, sadness, drinking, especially since they seem really connected.*

Tiffany: *Ok. I'm here for help.*

Therapist: *I'm glad you're here and I truly believe this can help you. So I'm wondering how important people in your life react when you're angry?*

Tiffany: *My ex-boyfriend blocked me totally—what an asshole! My friends hang up on me when I'm in a mood. Or they pretend they don't see my number come up. That's bullshit—I know they're always on their phones so I just text and say what I got to say. They can't ignore me all the time!*

Therapist: *You want to be honest with people but you don't want to lose your friends.*

Tiffany: *Like I said, I'm afraid to be alone forever.*

Therapist: *Being alone is a scary thought for you. Is there anything else about your anger that worries you?*

Tiffany: *I love her, but I don't want to end up a bitter, miserable, old drunk like my mom.*

Therapist: *You want more out of life.*

Tiffany: *Damn right I do.*

Therapist: *It sounds like you'll do just about anything to get the life you want and deserve. I admire your determination. So when you're feeling angry, what do you already do to calm yourself down both at work and at home?*

Tiffany: *At work they train us how to handle the pain-in-the-ass calls and if someone just won't shut up, I send them to my supervisor. I drink at home to calm me down and I like to pet my cat. I go to the gym after work a couple days a week but that's more to get in shape. My boyfriend used to rub my back when I was upset but now he's gone too.*

Therapist: *Tell me more about the connection between your anger and your drinking.*

Tiffany: I feel strong when I'm drunk and angry. I drink to chill out but sometimes I get mad at myself for drinking.

Therapist: *Let me see if I got this. Sometimes you drink to chill out, sometimes drinking makes you more angry, and sometimes being drunk and angry together makes you feel powerful.*

Tiffany: *That's all true but it sounds really messed up when you say it like that.*

Therapist: *Thinking about anger and alcohol together can be pretty confusing. You're definitely not alone in that. I really appreciate your honesty today. I know talking about this stuff hasn't been easy for you and I can tell you're pretty brave. Hopefully together we can work at finding new ways for you to make changes to both your anger and your drinking. How does that sound?*

Tiffany: *I'm still not sure about all this but I'm here.*

Tiffany's Pretreatment Assessment Measures

Tiffany's 7 DSM-V symptoms, while less than David's, indicated that she also had an AUD in the Severe range. On the QDS, she reported drinking 6 days per week with an average of 6 standard drinks per day. Her greatest number of drinks in 1 day was 8.5; she reported 20/30 heavy drinking days and 3 days without alcohol over the past month. Her PACS average craving score was 3 out of 6. On the SIP, she had an overall score of 27 out of 57 with highest numbers on the intrapersonal and anger subscales. Her SIP anger score was 6 out of 12. Her PANAS results showed an average PA score of 1.6 and an average NA score of 3.4. Her average PANAS anger score was 3.7. Her score on the DAR was 16 out of 25 with highest numbers on the frequency, intensity, duration, and social consequences of anger.

Interpretations

Tiffany's assessment confirmed moderate cravings, regular heavy drinking, and related life problems, especially in the areas of self-esteem and anger. Her PANAS NA score was more than twice as high as her PA score indicating that she also struggled to identify with many positive emotions. Her average of 3.7 was close to "Extremely" on the PANAS anger scale. Her high DAR score put her at greater risk for psychological distress from anger. These results were consistent with her self-report on both of the open-ended interviews.

Therapist Thoughts (Alcohol)

Tiffany's heavy drinking, especially in light of her recent gastric bypass surgery, presented a concern for the therapist with regard to potential medical issues.

In discussing this with Tiffany, the therapist learned that Tiffany had no history of withdrawal symptoms and said she "feels fine" on days that she does not consume any alcohol. Nevertheless, Tiffany was encouraged to seek medical attention if needed and therapist continued monitoring her throughout the treatment program. The therapist also checked in with Tiffany to explore what she already knew about heavy drinking after bariatric surgery and provided information to fill in any gaps. Tiffany's problems with alcohol had developed relatively recently despite growing up with parents who drank heavily. Therefore, the therapist guessed that Tiffany had sober coping skills already and would spend time exploring what worked for her as well as suggesting new skills.

Therapist Thoughts (Anger)

Tiffany's intense experience with anger emotions was notable. Her assessment numbers were high and she described a wide variety of triggers that involved herself, her relationships, society, and her profession. Tiffany's strong self-directed anger and poor body image posed a unique challenge. She both externalized and internalized her anger. Tiffany seemed to have a limited awareness of the consequences of her angry reactions and the connections with her emotions and alcohol use. Tiffany briefly disclosed past sexual abuse which seemingly had never been addressed. At the initial assessment visit, the therapist began to contemplate the need for a mental health referral for Tiffany to be evaluated for possible PTSD. Tiffany may have been experiencing secondary trauma which may require more intervention. The therapist also planned to spend time helping Tiffany understand the potential benefits of this treatment since she felt strong and powerful when drunk and angry and feared becoming weak. On the flip side, it was obvious that Tiffany had anger-management skills that she had been using successfully at her job for years. She seemed to lack the confidence to translate those skills to her personal life, so supporting her strengths and increasing her confidence became another key focus for the therapist. Tiffany was resilient, responsible, and determined.

Stephan's *Open-ended Anger Assessment*

Therapist: *If you don't mind, I'd like to spend some time talking more about your experience with anger and how it may connect with your drinking.*

Stephan: *Sure—you're the boss!*

Therapist: *Honestly I hope we can share that title in here. You're the boss of you and I'm here to work with you and offer some ideas. To start with, can you tell me what makes you feel frustrated or angry?*

Stephan: *Yeah sure—I was just kidding about the boss stuff. I like to joke around. But seriously, just about anything can piss me off: my bogus, dead-end job, my incompetent co-workers, my disrespectful boss who uses me, people who mistreat animals, most drivers, dishonest people, my judgmental parents, my idiotic brother, and my whiny husband, who I love but sometimes I wish he would just cut the shit.*

Therapist: *Thanks for sharing all that. Is there anything else?*

Stephan: *Yeah, I'm just getting started—I can't stand people with no sense of humor, those idiots who get in the less than 10 item lines with a full cart, customer service reps who don't speak English, ignorant homophobes, customers who treat you like a servant, dirty politicians... I feel like I could go on all day!*

Therapist: *You seem to have a lot of different situations that make you angry. How often would you say you feel like that?*

Stephan: *It happens a lot but I don't think I always would call it angry.*

Therapist: *That's a good point. In this program, what we're calling anger emotions also includes things like frustration, annoyance, and irritation. Does that sound more like what you mean?*

Stephan: *Absolutely. Sometimes I'm totally pissed off and other times I'm just really annoyed.*

Therapist: *Thanks for clarifying; that'll come in handy. So basically you notice yourself feeling anger-type emotions pretty frequently. For most people, those kind of emotions can have especially strong effects on the body. For example, some people tense their jaw or neck, some see red, some feel hot, some get headaches or stomachaches. What do you notice happening in your body when you're angry?*

Stephan: *I can literally feel my blood pressure go up, I know I clench my fists, which scares Michael, and probably my jaw too because it hurts a lot and I get headaches. By the way, I would never hit Michael and he knows it. He's just so dramatic sometimes.*

Therapist: *So you're feeling a variety of things in your body when you're mad and it sounds uncomfortable for you and for Michael.*

Stephan: *Yeah. I might get mad and break stuff but I never have and never will hurt anyone physically. I'm a lover, not a fighter!*

Therapist: *You sometimes get angry enough to break things but you've never gotten to the point of hurting someone physically and you want to keep it that way. For many people, there are other emotions that can happen at the same time as anger-type emotions. For example, some people also feel depressed, guilty, afraid, or anxious when they're angry. What other emotions do you think might be there for you?*

Stephan: *Tough question. If I had to guess, it'd probably be disappointment. I'm not even close to where I want to be in life and I'm just spinning my wheels at this point. That sucks.*

Therapist: *Disappointment is certainly an emotion that can happen with anger. We'll have more time over the next several weeks to figure out more about that and the other emotions that might be connected for you.*

Stephan: *Great—you've certainly got your work cut out for you putting up with me! I'm complicated.*

Therapist: *Then I'm even more glad we're a team working together on this! I'm curious about the intensity of the anger-type emotions you feel. So, if you were to rate your anger on a 100 point scale, like a Celsius thermometer, where 0 is not angry at all and 100 is the most angry you've ever been, where do you think you are most days?*

Stephan: *65*

Therapist: *Thanks. We'll be using numbers like that to talk about your anger in more detail throughout the program. There are also a lot of different words people use when they're angry. I'm wondering how you typically describe yourself when you're angry. For example, some people say they're annoyed, irritated, pissed off, furious...*

Stephan: *Mad or pissed off. Annoyed too.*

Therapist: *Thanks. I'm also curious about the thoughts and maybe even pictures that run through your mind when you're angry. If there was a tiny microphone or camera in your head, what would it hear you saying to yourself when you're mad?*

Stephan: *I'd hate to have to listen to that recording! My head is so f-ed up most of the time! It would make a pretty sick reality show though, ha-ha! Anyway, I can hear myself saying "I can't put up with this shit anymore." I also picture how I would teach all the stupid morons in the world a lesson, especially when I'm driving or stuck in line.*

Therapist: *I appreciate your willingness to be honest about this. You have some pretty powerful thoughts and images when you're angry. We'll spend more time talking about those kinds of thoughts each week. When you're feeling angry like that, what do you do? How do you act?*

Stephan: *As you've probably guessed already, I am the king of sarcasm. I'm also an aggressive driver and I swear a lot under my breath. I'm not afraid to speak my mind when I have to but there are also times I just bite my tongue and roll my eyes. I've also been told I have a very haughty sigh if you can believe it.*

Therapist: *You have a few different reactions when you're feeling anger emotions. I'm wondering what good and bad things happen when you're angry?*

Stephan: *Honestly, getting angry keeps me from being a doormat. That's another thing that pisses me off about Michael. He never loses his temper so people just walk all over him. I never want to be like that.*

Therapist: *You see your anger as a sign of strength. That's also something we'll talk more about in upcoming sessions. Are there things about your anger that are not so good?*

Stephan: *I do know that my anger gets me in trouble once in a while. I've almost been a few car accidents, it's expensive to replace dishes, and I've lost friends after nasty arguments.*

Therapist: *You're worried that your anger may cause an accident, you break stuff, and it's affected your relationships. What other reactions from the important people in your life do you notice when you're angry?*

Stephan: *Michael won't even fight with me anymore. He can't keep up with my sarcasm. He just leaves.*

Therapist: *You're worried about your marriage.*

Stephan: *Hell yeah. We're hanging on by a thread.*

Therapist: *That really bothers you and I truly think this program can help you. When you're angry, I'm wondering what you do to calm down.*

Stephan: *I drink wine and I listen to jazz music. It helps unless I drink too much.*

Therapist: *Tell me more about the connection between your anger and your drinking.*

Stephan: *I drink to relax and it's usually fine except once in a while I overdo it and I do stupid shit like last month when I wrecked the kitchen. I'm not a destructive person but drinking sometimes brings out the worst in me.*

Therapist: *Let me see if I got this. Sometimes you drink to calm down and sometimes drinking makes you more angry and even destructive.*

Stephan: *Yep. That that's me. Kind of like the Incredible Hulk but not as green, ha-ha!*

Therapist: *A less green Hulk—that's an interesting image! I really appreciate your honesty today. I know talking about drinking and anger isn't easy. Hopefully together we can work toward finding new ways for you to make changes to both. How does that sound?*

Stephan: *I know I need to quit drinking for now but I am NOT interested in becoming a milquetoast doormat and I will always be an angry driver so I'm not totally sold on this anger management stuff. I'll keep an open mind as long as you understand where I'm coming from. Deal?*

Stephan's Pretreatment Assessment Measures

Stephan's 8 DSM-V symptoms indicated a Severe AUD. On the QDS, he reported drinking 7 days per week with an average of 5 standard drinks per day. His greatest number of drinks in 1 day was 13; he reported 23/30 heavy drinking days, and 1 day without alcohol over the past month. His PACS average craving level was 2.2 out of a possible 6. He also reported using cannabis almost daily but denied any concerns about his use. On the SIP, he had an overall score of 22 out of 57 with highest numbers on the anger and interpersonal subscales. His SIP anger score was 6 out of 12. His PANAS showed a PA score of 2.7 and a NA score of 2.9. His average PANAS anger score was 3 and his DAR number was 12 out of 25, with scores of 3 on frequency, duration, and social consequences of anger.

Interpretations

Stephan's results showed a pattern of relatively low craving, daily heavy drinking, weekend binges, and related problems especially in the areas of anger and conflict with others. His average NA scores were slightly higher than his PA scores, indicating that he may be more aware of his positive emotions while still experiencing significant negative emotions. His average of "3" or "Quite a bit" on the PANAS anger scale and his DAR score put him right at the cutoff point for experiencing a distressing level of anger. Stephan described a strong attachment to his anger and a fear of appearing weak without it. His results were consistent with his self-report during the open-ended assessments.

Therapist Thoughts (Alcohol)

Stephan reported no concerns about withdrawal symptoms. He was confident he could easily stop drinking during the program but he was unsure about long-term abstinence. Stephan's craving score was relatively low in relation to his alcohol consumption. This may have been because his daily drinking made him unaware of the cravings even if they were present. It could also be explained by his regular use of cannabis which could mask the experience of craving. (At other times, clients are reluctant to acknowledge cravings because of a stigma, a dislike of the word, or they may not have a solid understanding of the craving experience which can be quite subjective.)

Therapist Thoughts (Anger)

Stephan seemed to justify his anger by focusing on the bad behavior and imperfections of others. Past resentments, especially with his family, and self-directed anger would be explored further in treatment. Stephan had some degree of awareness of the consequences of his anger and seemed to clearly recognize the link with his drinking. At the same time, he felt strongly attached to his identity as an angry person and to the energy he feels when angry. Challenging Stephan about his belief that his anger prevents him from being a doormat would have been ineffective and possibly damaging to the therapeutic relationship. Instead the therapist gently explained the rationale and potential benefits of the anger-management treatment with a long-term goal of helping Stephan decide for himself if the skills would have the ability to improve his life. Stephan's use of humor also stood out. Sometimes he used it sarcastically to express his anger, sometimes he used it to avoid painful topics, other times he was just plain funny. Helping Stephan recognize how he was using his humor was valuable in treatment and offered another a great tool for managing anger and coping with certain anger triggering situations. And finally, Stephan's awareness of his positive emotions was relatively high, suggesting an area of strength to affirm and reinforce.

Suggested Readings

Forbes, D., Alkemade, N., Mitchell, D., Elhai, J. D., McHugh, T., Bates, G., ... Lewis, V. (2014). Utility of the dimensions of anger reactions-5 (DAR-5) scale as a brief anger measure. *Depression and Anxiety*, *31*, 166–173.

The DAR is a brief, reliable, and valid measure of multiple aspects of the anger experience. Scores of 12 and above are interpreted as a level of anger associated with distress and impairment.

Kiluck, B. D., Dreifuss, J. A., Weiss, R. D., Morgenstern, J., & Carroll, K. M. (2013). The Short Inventory of Problems-Revised (SIP-R): Psychometric properties within a large, diverse sample of substance use disorder treatment seekers. *Psychology of Addictive Behaviors*, *27*, 307–314.

The SIP is a 15-item scale that quantifies the occurrence and frequency of adverse consequences associated with substance use. This article describes the internal reliability and convergent validity of the SIP. This research demonstrates that SIP scores predict treatment retention; higher scores (i.e., greater problems) predict poorer retention.

Miller, W. R., & Rollnick, S. (2013). *Motivational interviewing: Helping people change* (3rd ed.). New York, NY: Guilford Press.

This most recent third edition provides and enhances the foundation of Motivational Interviewing (MI), a powerful and effective approach to helping people change, which originated in addiction treatment and continues to spread to other disciplines. MI is defined by the authors as a "collaborative conversation style for strengthening a person's own motivation and commitment to change" (p. 12) and can be useful on its own or in conjunction with other treatment approaches, including anger management based alcohol treatment. This book is an accessible and essential resource for anyone interested in learning about MI.

Roy, M., Dum, M., Sobell, L. C., Sobell, M. B., Simco, E. R., Manor, H., & Palmerio, R. (2008). Comparison of the quick drinking screen and the alcohol timeline followback with outpatient alcohol abusers. *Substance Use & Misuse*, *43*, 2116–2123.

This study demonstrated the psychometrics of the QDS, an interview to assess alcohol consumption in problem drinkers. Although more extensive instruments are available to assess alcohol use, the QDS has the advantage of being brief (three questions), reliable and valid. It has become an oft-used measure to assess alcohol use rapidly and accurately.

Serafini, K., Malin-Mayor, B., Nich, C., Hunkele, K., & Carroll, K. M. (2016). Psychometric properties of the positive and negative affect schedule (PANAS) in a heterogeneous sample of substance users. *American Journal of Drug and Alcohol Abuse*, *42*, 203–212.

Substance Abuse and Mental Health Services Administration, Key substance use and mental health indicators in the United States: Results from the 2016 National Survey on Drug Use and Health. In *HHS publication no. SMA 17-5044, NSDUH series H-52*. Rockville, MD: Center for Behavioral Health Statistics and Quality, Substance Abuse and Mental Health Services Administration; 2017. Retrieved from: https://www.samhsa.gov/data/.

The PANAS is a widely used assessment of positive and negative affect. This journal article demonstrates that the PA and the NA scales are valid and reliable for individuals who use substances. Positive affect and negative affect are separate, but correlated, domains.

Wurst, F. M., Thon, N., Yegles, M., Schrück, A., Preuss, U. W., & Weinmann, W. (2015). Ethanol metabolites: Their role in the assessment of alcohol intake. *Alcoholism: Clinical and Experimental Research*, *39*, 2060–2072.

This review article describes four direct ethanol metabolites that have high sensitivity and specificity for alcohol consumption. Relative to indirect state markers (e.g., liver enzyme activity) which assess chronic alcohol abuse over longer periods of time, these direct ethanol metabolites detect alcohol consumption and abuse over the course of days to several months.

Chapter 6

Preparation for Anger Management Based Alcohol Treatment

Chapter Points

- Understanding factors that influence readiness for change on the client's part, the therapist's part, and on the part of the client–therapist team is necessary for good alcohol and anger outcomes.
- A variety of strategies are proposed to prepare the client and therapist for anger management based alcohol treatment.
- Assessment of dangerous and life-threatening situations is essential throughout treatment.

Questions for Self-Reflection

- What angry words upset you the most?
- What swear words offend you most easily?
- How comfortable are you with anger emotions in your own life?
- Do you believe anger can be a productive and helpful emotion?

Stephan: *In my opinion, anger management means you've given up and you're practically begging the f-ing world to walk all over you. It's like*

Anger Management Based Alcohol Treatment. DOI: https://doi.org/10.1016/B978-0-12-812709-4.00006-8

putting a big red "S" on your chest but instead of S for Superman, it's an S for Sucker! If I didn't get mad, I'd be nothing more than a pathetic f-ing doormat. Anger buys me respect; I want people to fear me, or at least think twice before they try to take advantage of me. Who would intentionally choose to be the wounded zebra in a lion's den?

Several conditions need to converge to obtain positive outcomes of anger management based alcohol treatment. First, the client must understand and accept that anger and anger–alcohol issues are causing significant problems and therefore be motivated to change the anger and anger–alcohol connection. That is, the person must own and accept the anger–alcohol problems and want help with them. Second, the therapist must be able to listen openly and respectfully to the client's concerns and be skilled in assisting the client to reduce anger and the anger–alcohol connection (the focus of this book). Finally, the client and therapist need to share the same understanding of problems and the approach to resolving them.

Client Factors Interfering With Treatment

There are multiple client issues which may interfere with or prevent establishing a therapeutic environment for anger management based alcohol treatment. The following are common challenges to treatment implementation.

Anger and Anger-Alcohol Are Part of Another Disorder

Anger alone or mixed with alcohol is sometimes best conceptualized as part of another disorder. For example, anger is a symptom of disorders such as posttraumatic stress disorder (PTSD), dysthymia, major depression, bipolar disorder, and personality disorders (e.g., antisocial, borderline, narcissistic, and paranoid personality disorders). If the anger and alcohol link is an element of such disorders, then conceptualization and treatment planning may need to be broadened and anger and alcohol treated within that expanded framework. The approach described in this book may be less helpful as a comprehensive treatment but still appropriate as a component of the overall treatment plan.

Anger and Alcohol Are Embedded in High Levels of Violence

Anger and alcohol can be mixed with high levels of violence. Intimate partner violence, child abuse, and frequent altercations and physical assault should always be assessed. Anger reduction may still be relevant at some point, but not initially. The first priority is to protect the lives and safety of those involved. Therapists need to assess the potential for violence and, when necessary, initiate ethically and legally appropriate interventions.

We suggest that therapists attend to the following issues. First, at the beginning of initial contact with a client, therapists need to inform clients regarding the limits of confidentiality, including danger to self or others, child neglect, abuse and grave impairment, and the steps the therapist will take to address these issues, should they arise. Therapists need to anticipate the potential for violence and know the legal and system procedures for addressing violent threats and behaviors. If therapists practice in a service delivery system, we suggest that the procedures be periodically updated with in-service training on how to assess and address potential violence. Roleplaying and behavioral enactment training are strongly encouraged so that therapists feel comfortable and efficacious in executing interventions for client violence.

Anger and Anger-Alcohol Are the Result of an Abusive, Coercive, or Highly Toxic Environment

An individual may report high levels of anger and alcohol use as a result of a very negative current environment, such as spouse or child abuse, sexually harassing or abusive interactions, bullying, or abusive work environments. Anger management based alcohol treatment may be relevant at some point in time, but the client is not in a present place to benefit from this treatment. The first goal is remove the client from or otherwise address the effects of the negative environment. Strategies might include crisis intervention, empowering the client to leave or establish strong boundaries, or referral to legal and other social services.

Client Factors Interfering with Readiness to Change

Several common issues associated with low readiness are outlined here along with potential interventions to raise awareness and readiness. Throughout treatment, the therapist explores these issues in an open, nonjudgmental way with regard to the client's relationship with anger and alcohol. In nearly all situations, the costs and benefits of anger and alcohol will be explored.

Increasing Awareness of Anger and Anger–Alcohol Connections

Some clients are emotionally disengaged and have limited insight into how they feel, think, and react. Rarely do they appear for therapy on their own. They are often referred by others—spouses, employers, and schools—because of the impact of their anger and alcohol use on others.

Readiness enhancement activities focus on the clients becoming more aware of how they feel, think, and express themselves when angry and how alcohol is interlaced in this fabric. For example, clients may be encouraged to self-monitor anger and anger expression. Clients might keep track of the situations that elicit anger, the thoughts, and feelings experienced, along with how anger was expressed. Over time, they might add monitoring the immediate and delayed consequences to themselves and others.

In addition, clients might be encouraged to ask others in their immediate environment for feedback on their anger. Others frequently notice very specific things of which clients are unaware. These might include changes in level or tone of voice, type of language used, body language like frowning or dirty looks and glares, or certain types of behavior such as stomping off, clenching teeth, or slamming doors. Once such behaviors are identified, then they can be added to self-monitoring.

In session, the therapist may create a strong anger experience by having the client visualize or reenact some angering event. When anger is experienced, the therapist and client explore the feelings, thoughts, images, urges, and real behavior involved. Doing this several times increases the client's immediate experience and awareness of anger and how this may relate to alcohol use.

Standardized psychological assessment instruments (see Chapter 5: Assessment Instruments and Considerations) may be used in at least two ways. First, clients' scores may be compared normatively to others. Clients can then be asked to explore how their scores compare to other people and why. Second, clients can be asked to explain why they marked specific items the way that they did. Since items tend to be somewhat general, clients can be asked for specific examples and how they think, feel, and express anger-related emotions in those situations.

THERAPIST TIP

Therapists should monitor their surprise when clients have low insight and understanding of their emotions and behaviors. Therapists as a group tend to be emotionally oriented and self-aware. Some clients are not. These clients often need frequent, gentle, repeated exposure to become more self-aware.

Increasing Awareness of the Impact of Anger

Some clients are aware of their experience and expression of anger, but not necessarily the consequences to themselves and others. Often, the clients' experiences have led them to think that many consequences are normal and to be expected. For example, if raised in a loud, argumentative family, a client may not recognize the impact of loud curse-filled arguments on others. Other consequences may start more internally. For example, a woman experienced high levels of anger while driving 45 minutes each way to and from work. Initially, she was unaware that the pain and tension in her jaw and headaches were associated with the anger. After further exploration, she became aware that in addition to the headaches, she tended to withdraw from her husband and daughters after angry commutes, drink extra glasses of wine, and experienced a lethargy such that she often missed events with her family.

Readiness enhancement with these individuals focuses on increasing awareness of internal and external consequences of their anger. For example, early therapy may focus on an exploration of positive and negative consequences of anger. It is important to recognize that some anger consequences may be experienced as positive. The person may feel strong, empowered, not pushed around, run over by, or taken advantage of by others. Certain forms of anger expression (e.g., verbal abuse or sullen withdrawal) may achieve important goals (e.g., get others to do what we want, get others to leave us alone, leave some topic or issue undiscussed that we do not want to face). Such positive outcomes should be acknowledged. However, the negative consequences also need to be explored. Some open-ended questions for such exploration might include the following: *What are the positive outcomes of your anger? What are the negative consequences of your anger? Is your anger getting you all of what you want? If you were going to change your anger, what would you have to give up? If you were to change your anger, what would you get? How is alcohol use related to your anger? What are the positive and negative outcomes of how alcohol is mixed with your anger?*

Often it is helpful to create a two (positive/negative consequences) by two (short- and intermediate/long-term consequences) table and process the nature of the consequences in each quadrant (see Fig. 6.1). Working through several examples on this grid may help clients understand the short- and long-term consequences of their anger. Moreover, going over several examples typically increases another insight: specifically, the long-term, positive consequence quadrant is usually empty or includes very few positive consequences. Observing this allows for an exploration of both the price the clients are paying in terms of negative consequences and how they might achieve some of the short-term positive consequences without paying the negative consequences.

Self-monitoring (see Chapter 7: Self-Monitoring and Self-Awareness) can be adapted to emphasize tracking the consequences. For example, when clients are angry, they record the internal consequences to self (e.g., thoughts and feelings like strong, tough, guilty, out of control, or stupid) and external consequences (e.g., others fought back, others withdrew, or supervisor expressed disapproval).

Some negative anger consequences are delayed and result from an accumulation of negative events over time. For example, anger-related health consequences such as coronary artery occlusion can be a result of a long period of angry, hostile experiences. Spouses/partners often do not terminate relationships because of a single anger episode, but rather long series of such events. Likewise at work, being fired or demoted often results from many poorly handled anger episodes. Being isolated and having few friends can also be an outcome of poorly handled anger over a

Anger consequences

	Positive consequences	Negative consequences
Short term	*I get respect* *No one messes with me at work* *I have a reputation for being tough*	*My wife is fed up* *My kids avoid me* *Stomachaches* *Too much drinking* *I'm always pissed off*
Long term	*My toughreputation at work*	*My wife might leave me* *I'll get an ulcer* *My drinking will kill me*

Figure 6.1 David's 2 × 2 anger consequences grid.

significant amount of time. An intervention to develop client insight is to bring the delayed or distal consequences into the present. The client visualizes the consequence (e.g., being fired, receiving a divorce decree, being friendless, having one's children fear and avoid them, being arrested for drinking and driving) and experiences it in the present. The therapist and client discuss how these potential longer term consequences might be avoided by actions taken earlier in the chain of events.

Anger Is Role or Identity Congruent

Some people identify as angry people, thinking of themselves as angry, hotheaded, and pissed off all the time. For others, anger is more role consonant. That is, in a role such as parent, supervisor, or coach, they believe they should be tough and angry. As such, anger and perhaps aggression are identity- or role-congruent. These emotions and behaviors are what they believe should be experienced and expressed, and, therefore, anger is not a problem, because it is what is expected and normalized.

Three interventions may help these individuals improve their therapeutic readiness. The first focuses on angry identity and role definition. Questions might include the following: *Is your anger getting what you want as a parent? You describe yourself as a hothead. How does that work for you? Are there other, less angry ways you would like to be?* Identify gaps in what anger is and is not getting them and inquire about how these gaps might be productively filled. The 2×2 consequence table described before can be adapted to anger as an identity or a role. The client can reflect on what anger is and is not doing and consider alternatives for reducing negative consequences and enhancing positive outcomes. Alternatively, the client can explore the perceptions of others especially in the given role. Open-ended questions exploring this might include things like: *How do others see you generally (in role as...)? How would you like them to see you? How are these different? What could you do to have a closer match?*

The second option is to create dissonance within current identity or role constructs. That is, identify valued elements of the role and discuss if these valued dimensions are violated by being angry or how anger is expressed. For example, if clients value not being quitters, exploration may show that an angry tirade can be a way of "giving up" or "giving in" to anger. If clients value not being taken advantage of, a discussion may reveal that the more they react to others in anger, the easier they are to manipulate. Clients may value being strong and in control; exploring examples may reveal that when they are angry, they are out of control and weak. Creating this dissonance provides the opportunity to discuss achieving positive characteristics and outcomes in alternative ways (e.g., being calm, clear headed, and problem-solving oriented).

A third option is to increase the range of possible, less angry role/identity options. For example, clients might be encouraged to describe other people who handle their anger in a very different way. Then, they could be encouraged to ask the other person how they handle their anger. An alternative is to help clients identify historical/movie/television/sports figures whom they like, but who handled their anger differently. For example, one angry college student identified a well-known basketball coach who was very calm and collected under pressure. Readiness was linked to discussions of how he could learn to be more like this coach.

Anger Is Justified by Prior Trauma

Some clients have been physically abused and traumatized by physical or sexual assault. For others, the trauma may not have a physical component, but be very negative nonetheless, such as a partner having an affair or going through a difficult divorce or relationship break up. They may be very angry about these events and recycling their anger, even years later. The anger feels justified because of the initial events (see discussion of "justified anger" in Chapter 3: Overview of Anger-Related Emotions).

In such cases, the therapist may need to consider PTSD as an important component of the case conceptualization. Some clients, however, can still be moved closer to anger- and alcohol-involved treatment. In doing so, it is important to openly explore and communicate back the clients' sense of anger, pain, and trauma. The therapist must legitimize the anger related to the trauma but also to empower clients to reclaim less angry options in the present. This is not necessarily an easy task, because clients may feel justified and may receive social support for thinking and feeling this way. Nonetheless, some of the following may be helpful.

One potentially helpful distinction is to describe the client's experience as primary and secondary trauma. Primary trauma is what the client experienced initially. Secondary trauma is what the client is experiencing currently which is related to the initial trauma. The therapist acknowledges and supports the client in both but identifies different degrees of choice related to each. The client had no choice about primary trauma. It happened. It cannot be undone. There is, however, some choice about secondary trauma and about what is done and felt now. Focusing on the secondary trauma, the client and therapist explore how and whether anger is productive in the present. That is, the goal is to evaluate the positive and negative consequences of focusing angrily in the present about a past event.

Some trauma has a specific perpetrator or group of perpetrators about whom the client continues to be very angry. In such cases, some clients find useful the notion of not giving additional power and control to the perpetrator(s). The therapist understands and acknowledges that the original events were painful and traumatic. However, if the client continues to be angrily preoccupied with the perpetrator, then power, influence, and control are still being given over to the perpetrator. Exploring how the client wants to reduce these secondary feelings may increase readiness for anger reduction and the connection to alcohol misuse.

A third strategy may be helpful when there is considerable separation in time from the initial trauma and the present. The cognitive therapy concept suggests that current feelings and reactions are not caused by initial trauma but are more the result of focusing upon, ruminating about, and thinking about the trauma in the present. If the client understands and accepts this conceptualization, then he/she may be in a position to identify how these thinking processes get triggered and how to think and react differently in the present.

A fourth option is to address the anger-related trauma within a mindfulness approach. Although beyond the scope of this book, trauma and related anger could be framed as entities that can be observed without having to be reexperienced.

Anger Is Externalized

Anger is often attributed to external events and conditions. Anger and perhaps aggression are seen as natural and reasonable extensions of and responses to these events. Moreover, clients with strong externalized anger may bring a narcissistic rule to bear: that they should not have to deal with negative events. Simply put, anger stems from external events which the clients believe they should not have to experience. Therefore, these clients are not ready for personal change–oriented interventions because they seek to make all of these external negative people and events go away.

If such clients are to change, they need to evaluate the belief that they should not suffer negative events, struggles, and difficulties in life. One strategy is to explore these beliefs via evoking and eliciting questions such as: *Why shouldn't difficult and challenging things happen to you too? Why does it have to go your way?* Throughout the discussion, it is important to gently reflect the clients' sense of hurt, indignity, and loss but respectfully challenge their assumption that they do not experience negative events.

For clients who strongly externalize their experience of anger, it may be helpful to introduce the notion of the "elegant solution" versus the "practical solution." The *elegant solution* represents the hope for a perfect and frustration-free life that is always the way clients believe it should be. As a result, these clients expect and demand that the world change to suit their needs. In contrast, the *practical solution* represents the 'real world,' with its typical frustrating, difficult, and negative events that all people encounter from time to time. In the real world, bad things happen to good people, and, naturally, some difficult events are going to happen to these clients. The practical solution is one in which clients make the best choices they can, constructively deal with negative events, and move on. The therapist can encourage clients to contrast the likelihood of the elegant solution (which is unlikely) with the likelihood of the practical solution (which is much more likely). Some anger and frustration are inevitable, but the clients come to accept this and cope appropriately even when life is not perfectly elegant.

Another strategy for encouraging insight with clients who externalize their anger is the therapeutic exploration of the paradox. These clients demand that the world always treat them in a perfectly fair way but often do not treat others by the same rules and demands. In other words, some clients "demand" that others behave in a certain way and then become angry and retaliatory when this does not occur. However, when these clients are asked if they, in contrast, always do what others want, the response is typically "of course not!" When asked why not, they typically respond that they do not want to, do not agree, or are free to choose not to. Having laid this dynamic bare, the therapist can inquire as to why they are free to choose, but others are not. A similar paradox is the demand that other people always be in emotional and behavioral control. That is, they always respond as the clients wish and never cause any problems. Again, the contradiction is explored; the clients are often not in emotional and behavioral control but believe others should always be that way. A third paradox explored in a similar manner is that of hurt. Specifically, others should not do things that are hurtful or painful. Yet, upon inquiry, clients often indicate that they have done hurtful things to others, yet are insisting others be perfectly pain-free toward them. These paradoxes have at their core an insistence that clients be treated perfectly even when not treating others perfectly. Gently exploring these contradictions may help clients release the insistence on perfect treatment and come to accept that we live in an imperfect world, one in which they can learn to be less angry and demanding.

SHIT HAPPENS

Sometimes axioms, bumper stickers, and metaphors may be a helpful code or shorthand to stay focused on the notion that bad things do happen and some of it will happen to them. As one angry client said, "Shit happens, but I have a choice about how I shovel."

THERAPIST TIP

A couple of suggestions are made for therapists working with externalizing clients. Avoid the trap of actively and directly talking them out of their maladaptive mindset. To the contrary, keep the focus on the clients verbalizing the premise of why their lives must be perfect. The focus is on the client "proving" the premise and not accepting the circular logic of "it's true because I think it." A second trap to avoid is having clients label the therapist as "lacking values" because of a refusal to clearly endorse their maladaptive mindset. The therapist can agree with the importance of having values, desires, and preferences, working toward them, and experiencing frustration when they are not achieved. However, the focus is gently returned to why the clients' values have the level of moral dictates for others.

Client Factors Summary

There are angry individuals who do not see their anger and the anger–alcohol linkages as personal problems and therefore do not seek help. Simply put, they are not at a point of readiness that is necessary for the interventions described in this book. They are more ambivalent and do not understand or accept anger–alcohol issues as problems. We are suggesting that therapists accept them where they are and gently intervene in a manner congruent with their motivation. It is possible to work with them to gain a better understanding of how anger and alcohol influence their lives. Some may come to accept that anger and alcohol link together in ways that have negative consequences. These clients are candidates for change. The focus must be on readiness enhancement with no rush to a change-oriented intervention. If not managed with patience and empathy, clients may feel misunderstood, the therapeutic alliance will be breeched, impasses will develop, and people will drop out of treatment.

Therapist Factors Influencing Readiness for Change

It may seem surprising to consider that therapist factors may influence clients' readiness for change. In our experience, however, there certainly are therapist characteristics that can use thought and attention.

Therapist Discomfort and Avoidance

Occasionally, behaviors of angry clients—talking in loud demonstrative ways, using emotionally charged language laced with obscenities, making denigrating comments, having negative nonverbal expressions—make therapists feel anxious and uncomfortable in session. This is not unusual and, even should be expected. However, this discomfort may lead therapists to pull back from exploring anger issues, possibly damaging the therapeutic relationship and slowing therapeutic progress. We offer the perhaps unusual advice that therapists list behaviors, phrases, ideas, and expressions that elicit anxiety and then desensitize themselves with repeated exposure. For example, therapists might make a list of words and phrases that make them uncomfortable and audio record them. The recording can then be used for desensitization via repeated listening. Alternatively, therapists might visualize a person saying, looking, or behaving in a certain way and repeatedly reexperience those images until they no longer elicit anxiety. If volume or intensity of the behavior is an element, then therapists can be exposed in more intense ways. For example, the audio might be turned up, so the words are being experienced at a high volume. This exposure can also be combined with the same relaxation skills therapists will teach clients. That is, therapists can be exposed visually or through sound and then relax in the presence of the anxiety laden cues. Over several exposures, the nature of the anxiety-producing dimensions can be increased in intensity. For example, in dealing with language, a therapist might move from "crap" and "damn" to "shit" to "stupid, lazy, f-ing asshole!"

In dealing with anxiety-producing issues, therapists need not like or agree with the language and concepts clients are putting forth. We are entitled to our preferences in dealing with others. We do not have to like sexist, racist, or, obscene language. What we are suggesting is that therapists learn to be therapeutically comfortable with this language so that they can calmly hear and explore the issues of anger and alcohol with clients. Just like depressed clients who may describe themselves in a very negative, hopeless way and want to express that loathing through self-destruction, therapists do not have to agree with and accept the clients' understandings. To the contrary, therapists explore those issues openly and compassionately. We are suggesting that therapists working with angry, alcohol-involved clients develop the same degree of comfort so that they can openly explore clients' angry lives.

The Therapist Is Judgmental

Sometimes therapists may label angry clients in judgmental, categorical ways. They may label the client as "rude," "being a jerk," "an asshole," "an insufferable narcissist," or so forth. Unfortunately, these labels distance therapists from clients. If therapists do not address these labels, distance will develop and clients will read and react negatively to it.

It is suggested that therapists monitor their thoughts and labeling and use, as necessary, the cognitive restructuring techniques outlined in this book. For example, clients might be reconsidered as "people who have learned dysfunctional ways of experiencing and expressing anger," "people struggling with developing different ways of dealing with their anger and alcohol," or "good people doing ineffective things." As noted previously, therapists do not have to like or agree with angry client behavior, but pejorative labeling will only increase distance and decrease chances of positive therapeutic gain.

Therapist Patience and Tenacity

Clients with anger issues may be frustrating and potentially intimidating to therapists. They often require considerable patience in listening to their concerns and intervening. Clients' cognitive, emotional, and expressive patterns are often highly engrained. It may take repetition of material and practicing the same skills multiple times before substantive change is made. Therapists need to expect this and check their impatience at the door. It often takes patient tenacity on the therapist's part to work through anger and alcohol issues. The good news is that some of the characteristics that may be initially off-putting such as being angrily stubborn and dogged may turn out to be therapeutic assets as the therapist and client turn these characteristics on the client's problems.

THERAPIST SKILL

Therapists need quality skills for conceptualizing and intervening in anger and alcohol problems. This book is focused on increasing therapist skill, self-efficacy, and confidence in addressing these client concerns. It is suggested that therapists actively increase their skills in a number of ways. For example, collect books and articles on relevant topics and become as informed as possible. Join up with at least one other therapist who is increasing expertise in the same area. Meet frequently and discuss case and intervention issues, supporting and helping each other improve skills. Finally, if a more seasoned professional with these skills can be identified, explore the possibility of in person or long distance supervision.

I THINK I FEEL. . .I FEEL I THINK. . .

One particular challenge for therapists who are new to anger management based alcohol treatment differentiating feelings from thoughts, or emotions from cognitions. Feelings can be defined as conscious mental reactions accompanied by physiological changes. We experience feelings in our bodies, and these feelings can usually be described in a few brief words such as, "I feel sad." Thoughts, on the other hand, are experienced in our minds and are typically expressed in several words, such as, "No one will ever love me." Thoughts can be defined as sentences in the mind, also called self-talk. Specifically, thoughts are beliefs, assumptions, organized views, principles, perspectives, opinions, ideas, attitudes, and judgments that have formed through a variety of life experiences. Some thoughts are obvious while others are more automatic and less evident. Thoughts and feelings are closely intertwined and the language used to express them also gets complex. For example, someone might say, "I feel disrespected." The goal for the therapist is to help separate the thoughts about disrespect from the feeling experienced when thinking about it. A more precise statement in this case might be, "I feel hurt (feeling); if he really cared, he'd call me back (thought)." Listening carefully in order to distinguish feelings from thoughts is a key therapy skill that develops with practice and experience.

Client–Therapist Readiness to Change

To achieve positive change, the client and therapist must readily agree on both the goals and means of therapy. Broadly speaking, for the kinds of interventions described in this book to be effective, the client and therapist need to agree that they are addressing the ways anger and alcohol link together in negative ways in the client's life. With that basic agreement established, they can begin to rehearse and learn skills with which to achieve anger reduction, abstinence, and to alter these connections. Therapists are likely to have this readiness, but clients might not. For example, the client may want therapy to be about getting others off his back, to stop harassing him, and to accept his alcohol use. Another client may be all about getting the therapist to write a letter to the court to lessen legal charges around alcohol misuse, rather than focusing on anger and alcohol changes. In these two examples, the client and therapist are clearly not ready to collaborate on the goals of therapy.

They also may not share the same view of the way therapy should be conducted. To be successful, both therapist and client must be ready for a skill base (cognitive, emotional, and behavioral coping therapy skills) to address anger and alcohol connections. Again, the client may have other ideas. For example, if the client thought therapy should explore medical interventions for anger and alcohol problems and the use of prayer and spiritual consultation to reduce problems, the therapist and client would have inconsistent expectations for therapeutic approaches and therapeutic readiness would be compromised.

Moving Forward

Agreement on the goals and means of therapy sets the stage for transitioning to the general Cognitive Behavior Therapy approach to anger and alcohol problems. Although the exact content will be shaped by the client's unique concerns, the general rationale is likely to include some of the following:

- First, problem behaviors are learned over time. The client has learned too much of some things (e.g., excessive emotional and physiological arousal, a tendency to yell and verbally attack others) and too little of some others (e.g., means of calming down when angry or how to resist peer pressure and refuse alcohol consumption).
- Second, new and adaptive approaches to problem situations can also be learned over time. Therapy will focus on identifying helpful ways of approaching and addressing problem situations. Once identified, these approaches or coping skills will be practiced so that they become learned and easy to use.
- Third, practice will take place both during and between sessions. In-session, various approaches (e.g., a roleplay of refusing alcohol, visualization of an angering situation and practicing relaxation to calm down, writing out new ways of thinking about angering situations) will be employed to practice helpful strategies. In-session practice will be extended to the external world via various targeted exercises and assignments. These exercises help make sure that the client can implement the new behaviors in the real world, and when they fail to do so, the exercises provide the feedback from which to make changes. New strategies can then be practiced.
- Fourth, practice will be graduated from easier to more difficult because people learn best when they can cope. For example, when learning to apply relaxation

coping skills, clients will practice first in non-angering situations and then move from mild angering to moderate angering and finally to extreme angering situations. At first, the therapist provides a great deal of assistance and support, with the client taking over as success in applying coping skills increases. Clients will not be left alone and floundering but will move in small steps with as much therapist assistance as needed.

Summary

In order for our skills-based anger management based alcohol treatment to be palatable and effective, the client must be prepared and ready for treatment, the therapist must be skilled, knowledgeable, and ready for treatment, and the client–therapist team must be ready to collaborate on a jointly developed treatment plan and method of treatment. We have identified client and therapist factors that may need preparatory attention to facilitate good outcomes.

The next section of the book focuses on the techniques and strategies for anger management based alcohol treatment. We will review alcohol-related sobriety skills, relaxation techniques, and cognitive therapy. After the client and therapist have developed rapport and a positive working alliance, these therapeutic techniques can be introduced.

Suggested Readings

Kassinove, H., & Tafrate, R. C. (2002). *Anger management: The complete treatment guidebook for practitioners*. Atascadero, CA: Impact.

This book provides many useful strategies for practitioners engaging in anger management. Of particular relevance for this book is their chapter on preparing the client for anger management therapy. The book also covers the topic of forgiveness, not covered in this book.

Kassinove, H., & Tafrate, R. C. (2006). *Anger management video program: An instructional guide for practitioners*. Atascadero, CA: Impact.

This video series provides a number of video segments that demonstrate portions of cognitive-behavioral therapy for anger reduction. Of particular relevance to this chapter is the segment of motivational interviewing.

Section III

ANGER MANAGEMENT BASED ALCOHOL TREATMENT TECHNIQUES

Chapter 7

Self-Monitoring and Self-Awareness

Chapter Points

- Self-monitoring is a useful behavioral strategy to increase self-knowledge, gain insight, and evaluate change over time.
- Regular self-monitoring of the various elements of anger emotions and alcohol use is a hallmark of this treatment approach.
- "Target exercises" are therapeutic tasks, including self-monitoring, that the client is encouraged to complete between sessions.

Questions for Self-Reflection

- What is your opinion on the effectiveness of self-monitoring?
- What experience, if any, do you have tracking your own behaviors?
- What do you do when a client does not complete home practice exercises or worksheets?

David: *Now that I'm listening and looking out for anger, I realize it's everywhere in my life! I can get pissed off at just about anything and I usually do! I wrote a lot down on the log this week and probably could've done*

Anger Management Based Alcohol Treatment. DOI: https://doi.org/10.1016/B978-0-12-812709-4.00007-X

more. I'm still pretty shocked by this. I think that fact that I'm not drinking is helping me tune in more too. I'll have to tell my wife at some point but I don't want to hear "I told you so." That would piss me off. Ironic, huh?

Rationale for Self-Monitoring

A highly effective way to increase knowledge about ourselves is to objectively, dispassionately, and routinely observe and record our behavior. The process of tracking, or self-monitoring one's own behavior, is an important strategy for gaining insight into our experiences, understanding how frequent and intense our emotions and responses are, and evaluating changes over time. In our case, the practice of observing behavior and monitoring it is a hallmark of anger management based alcohol treatment and the cornerstone on which insight and change is built. The self-monitoring process begins in the first treatment session and continues throughout the program.

Monitoring health-related behaviors in order to improve health is a common strategy. Foci of health-related behaviors amenable to self-monitoring include smoking (with a goal of smoking cessation), diet (with a goal of improved nutrition and/or weight change), exercise (with a goal of improved physical fitness), and excessive alcohol use (with a goal of drinking reduction or abstinence). Research has demonstrated that self-monitoring, as a component of behavior change therapy, helps improve these outcomes (van Achterberg et al., 2010; Michie et al., 2012). With regard to tracking for Alcohol Use Disorder behavior change, self-monitoring may include entries for amount of alcohol consumed, craving ratings, triggers, description of the setting, coping strategies used, effectiveness rating of the coping strategies, and mutual-help group involvement. As mentioned above, the goal of self-monitoring these thoughts, behaviors, and feelings is, in part, to increase knowledge into drinking quantities and frequencies. Clients often underestimate the quantity of alcohol consumed, especially when translated to standard drinks. Self-monitoring these domains may also produce important insights into high-risk situations and coping efforts.

HOW MANY DID I HAVE?

Knowing that a client has, for example, five "drinks" per day tells us little about the precise amount of alcohol consumed. Thus, we collaborate with the client in reporting alcohol quantities in terms of standard drinks. In the United States, a "standard drink" is any drink that contains approximately 14 g of ethanol (pure alcohol). This is about 0.6 fluid ounces or 1.2 tablespoons. Fig. 7.1 is the display that we use with the client to facilitate reporting of alcohol quantities in terms of standard drinks.

(*Continued*)

(CONTINUED)

What's a Standard Drink?

A standard drink in the United States is any drink that contains about 14 g of pure alcohol (about 0.6 fluid ounces or 1.2 tablespoons). Below are US standard drink equivalents. These are approximate, since different brands and types of beverages vary in their actual alcohol content.

12 oz. of beer or cooler	**8 oz. of craft beer**	**8–9 oz. of malt liquor**	**5 oz. of table wine**	**3–4 oz. of fortified wine** (such as sherry or port)	**2–3 oz. of cordial, liqueur, or aperitif**	**1.5 oz. of brandy** (a single jigger)	**1.5 oz of spirits** (a single jigger of 80-proof gin, vodka, whiskey, etc.)

Many people don't know what counts as a standard drink and so they don't realize how many standard drinks are in the containers in which these drinks are sold. Some examples:

- For **beer**, the approximate number of standard drinks in
  - 12 oz. = 1
  - 16 oz. = 1.3
  - 22 oz. = 2
  - 40 oz. = 3.3
- For **craft beer**, the approximate number of standard drinks in
  - 8 oz. = 1
  - 12 oz. = 1.5
  - 16 oz. = 2
- For **malt liquor**, the approximate number of standard drinks in
  - 12 oz. = 1.5
  - 16 oz. = 2
  - 22 oz. = 2.5
  - 40 oz. = 4.5
- For **table wine**, the approximate number of standard drinks in
  - standard 750 mL (25 oz.) bottle = 5
  - 1.5 L (50.8 oz.) "magnum" = 10
  - 1.5 L box = 10
  - 3 L box = 20
  - 5 L box = 33
- For **80-proof spirits**, or "hard liquor," the approximate number of standard drinks in
  - a mixed drink = 1 or more*
  - 200 mL "half pint" (6.8 oz.) = 4.5
  - 375 mL "pint" (12.7 oz.) = 8.5
  - 750 mL "a fifth" (25 oz.) = 17
  - 1 L "quart bottle" (33.8 oz.) = 22.5
  - 1.75 L "half gallon" (59 oz.) = 39

Figure 7.1 A standard drink explanation chart.

The premise for anger management based alcohol treatment is that anger-related emotions are intertwined with drinking and related problems. Therefore, self-monitoring also includes reporting on dimensions and aspects of anger. Specifically, the self-monitoring target exercises for anger-related emotions include report on their intensity, situational, inter- and intrapersonal triggers, anger-increasing cognitions, and coping strategies. Perhaps most importantly, clients are asked to reflect on the linkages between anger-related emotions and craving for alcohol or drinking. Examples of questions used to explore these connections include the following: *On any given day, are cravings for alcohol triggered by any anger-related emotions? Is drinking a method to cope with anger-related emotions? Does alcohol consumption influence the experience of anger-related emotions? If so, does drinking calm these emotions or intensify them? Do the linkages between anger-related emotions, drinking, and craving change from day to day? If so, what are the inter- and intrapersonal factors and situational characteristics that are associated with this variability? And, finally, do these linkages change over the course of anger management based alcohol treatment?* Clearly, the therapeutic insights gleaned from the client's ongoing daily self-monitoring of these circumstances will inform and guide therapy and will allow the client and therapist to track changes (and hopefully improvements!) over the course of therapy.

In the initial treatment session, we introduce the practice of daily self-monitoring as the first in a series of "target exercises." In the first session, the client is provided with a daily self-monitoring log to notate experiences of anger-related emotions, physical reactions, any alcohol consumption, cravings, and whether the experience of anger-related emotions was in any way linked to the experience of craving or drinking. One side of the form provides spaces for recording details. The other side of the log contains specific monitoring instructions and examples of a completed log.

TARGET PRACTICE

Instead of the negatively-laden word "homework," we use the concept of "target exercises" to describe between-session therapeutic assignments. A target exercise is a therapeutic task that connects the in-session counseling material with the client's between-session activity and practice. Our approach to introducing any target exercise is to (1) discuss the rationale and usefulness of the target exercise, (2) provide a concrete example of the task, (3) facilitate the client's completion of an initial entry during the therapy session, and (4) negotiate and obtain the client's good faith agreement to try to complete the task during the week.

As mentioned above, self-monitoring of drinking, craving, and the experience of anger-related emotions is a hallmark of anger management based alcohol treatment. Thoughtful recording of these experiences and ongoing review of entries during therapy sessions will facilitate insights into a client's behaviors and the treatment's impact. These insights may include deeper understandings of (1) frequency and quantity of alcohol consumption; (2) frequency and intensity of anger-related emotions; (3) how anger-consistent cognitions intensify the experience of anger; (4) how alcohol craving and consumption is both caused by, and results from, the experience of anger-related emotions; and (5) how moderating and managing anger-related emotions may have a beneficial effect on alcohol involvement. Monitoring these concepts over the course of therapy will allow the therapist/client team to track changes in drinking, craving, anger-related emotions, and their linkages.

In developing and sharing the rationale for the target exercise with the client, the therapist should minimize the degree to which this material becomes a "lecture" or monologue. An important stylistic characteristic of anger management based alcohol treatment is borrowed from Motivational Interviewing (Miller & Rollnick, 2013). Instead of the therapist "teaching" this material, it is critical that the therapist evokes the client's insights into the rationale for self-monitoring and facilitates a discussion regarding its potential benefits for the client.

THERAPIST TIP

Self-monitoring is an unusual behavior; most people do not systematically self-observe. Start the task as simple as possible. Then provide demonstrations, examples, concrete in-session practice, and encouragement. Do everything you can to support acquisition of this new and often unfamiliar behavior.

THERAPIST TIP

The therapist and client should discuss the previous week's self-monitoring at the beginning of the next session. If the therapist does not openly review the material, the client may understandably assume that it is unimportant and may discontinue self-monitoring. If it is important enough to assign, it is important enough to review. Clients should be encouraged to bring self-monitoring forms with them each session.

David's *Intro to Self-Monitoring (Self-Monitoring Log 1)*

Therapist: *Before we end today's session, I'd like to take some time to introduce you to the process of self-monitoring. One of the best ways to increase knowledge about behavior is by observing it. Noticing and then writing down what happens with both your drinking and your anger emotions can help give both of us a clearer picture of what's going on for you and where to focus on changing. This tracking process will begin today and continue each week throughout the program. How does that sound to you?*

David: *You mean like keeping a journal or something?*

Therapist: *Kind of, but what I have in mind is a bit more structured, something we call a target exercise because it focuses in on a target behavior. For this week I'd like you to begin to keep track of your experiences with anger emotions and whether or not they are alcohol-related in any way. You can do this using a daily log that covers both your anger emotions, cravings, and any drinking. Here, take a look. (Self-Monitoring Log 1)*

David: *I like this. I like things organized and structured.*

Therapist: *Great! If you turn it over, you'll notice there are specific instructions as well as example situations to give you a better idea on what to include.*

David: *These examples are helpful and it seems pretty self-explanatory.*

Therapist: *If it's ok with you, I'd like to spend a few minutes going over how to fill it out and even get it started with you. The first column is the date and time. Most people find that filling it out as close to the frustrating event as possible is the best way to make sure you get all the details, but obviously that's not always realistic. Let's fill in the first line with something that happened recently, something frustrating and possibly linked to drinking.*

David: *Sure. I've got a good one. Tuesday when we got all that snow. It happened after work around 6:30.*

Therapist: *Ok. Tuesday the 21st around 6:30. The next column asks for the frustrating situation, a brief description of what happened that made you feel angry or frustrated. It's up to you how much detail you include. Either a couple short sentences or even a few words or phrases can help you describe what happened. So what happened Tuesday that was frustrating for you?*

David: *I called my son and asked him to shovel the driveway before I came home. I know he's just sitting around playing his stupid game and he'd never even think to just go out and shovel on his own. I swear kids these days don't want to lift a finger if they don't have to. And of course, I come down the street and my driveway is completely buried in snow and I can't even pull in. I was furious and called him again from the car and he said he was just about to start shoveling. Seriously?*

Therapist: *Sounds like you were pretty angry when you got home. The next column asks you to put a number to how intense those angry feelings were for you. Again, it might help to picture a thermometer where 0 is cool or cold and 100 is your boiling-over point. Another way to think about it is the speedometer on a car. At what speed do you feel like you might start losing control? How intense was your anger reaction on that 0–100 scale Tuesday?*

David: *I'd put it at 85 or 90—I was really pissed off. He is so freaking lazy and disrespectful. Plus it was a long day and I couldn't even pull in my own driveway. And my wife didn't back me up! She says I'm too hard on him. Please! She's the reason he's so spoiled and soft.*

Therapist: *You were really angry, almost at 90. As we talked about last week, anger emotions can affect the body in different ways. The next column has space for you to include what you noticed in your body when you felt that angry. Include things like an upset stomach, any muscle tension, headaches, etc. What did you notice in your body on Tuesday?*

David: *Well, I was already tense from the drive home—stupid drivers that can't handle the weather—it's ridiculous! I was gripping the wheel pretty tight and my stomach was hurting.*

Therapist: *You noticed a lot of tension in your body, your hands, and your stomach was hurting. In the next column, you're asked to decide if your frustration was related to alcohol at all for you. What do you think about that?*

David: *It was definitely alcohol related. I was so mad I drove straight to the liquor store while he was shoveling. I drank a lot of that bottle when I finally got home.*

Therapist: *You clearly saw a connection between your anger and drinking on Tuesday. The next column has a 0–10 scale for you to rate the level of the alcohol craving you noticed with 0 being no craving and 10 being the most intense craving possible. How would you rate your craving level on Tuesday?*

David: *My craving was probably 9. I needed a drink.*

Therapist: *Your craving level was also high that day. The final column asks you to write down the number of standard drinks you had. About how many do you think you drank that night?*

David: *I'm guessing about 10 or 11 drinks the way you guys measure them.*

Therapist: *Thanks for sharing all that. Hopefully as we go along, that last column will include some "0's" for you but again, the main goal of keeping a log like this is to help gather information about both your anger emotions, craving, and any drinking. I'd also like to clarify that while the goal of this program is abstinence, it's important for you to be honest, especially with yourself, but also with me about what's going on. What questions do you have at this point?*

David: *What happens if I don't have a real angry situation one day?*

Therapist: *Good question! If you have a day with absolutely no frustration situations you can always write "none" in that row. There may also be a day when you have more than one frustrating situation so you can use 2 rows on that day. It's basically up to you how to use the spaces. I do want to stress that I'm hoping we can use this information to get a clearer picture of the range of your anger reactions so even if you're intensity level is on the lower end, like 40 or less, I'd like you to include it. The highs and the lows can both offer useful information. How does that sound to you?*

David: *That sounds reasonable.*

Therapist: *Great. I'm wondering how willing you are to fill out this log over the next week. What are the odds?*

David: *I'm willing to do it and 95% sure I'll get it done.*

Therapist: *I'm glad to hear that. What could get in the way of you filling it out?*

David: *Not much. I'm good at paperwork. The only thing is I don't want anyone to see it at work or at home so I'll have to find a good place to hide it. Maybe in the trunk of my car.*

Therapist: *It makes sense that you want to keep this private so that might work. I'm just thinking that for some people, out of sight means out of mind. Would it be helpful for you to have a way to remind yourself to fill it out each day?*

David: *Probably. I can set a reminder on my phone.*

Therapist: *Great. Do you have any other questions about self-monitoring before we move on?*

David: *Nope. I've got it.*

Therapist: *Ok. Next time we meet, this log will help us review your week and focus in more on your anger emotions and any drinking or cravings to drink so please remember to bring it with you.*

Progression of Self-Monitoring

As treatment sessions continue, therapeutic content progresses to the management of anger-related emotions and their associations with craving and any drinking. In tandem with this progression is the evolution of the nature and content of the daily self-monitoring target exercises. Our treatment protocol utilizes three self-monitoring logs. As therapy moves toward a focus on coping skills for anger management, the logs reflect this change as clients are asked to identify and record their anger-increasing thoughts and their various coping efforts. At each transition to the next self-monitoring log, the therapist is encouraged to again discuss and evoke the rationale for the log in its new form, review the examples, facilitate completion of an entry during the session, and renegotiate commitment to the target exercise.

Self-Monitoring Log 1

During the initial session, the therapist and client focus on identifying anger-related emotions, recording the situation and triggers for the affect, intensity, physical symptoms, any relation to craving, and, if relevant, the number of

Self-Monitoring Log 1

Date/ time	Frustration situation	Emotion intensity 0–100	Physical symptoms	Alcohol related? If yes, how?	Craving 0–10	No. of drinks?
8/20 7:00 p.m.	*Stupid drivers on the way home from work slowed me down and I missed my daughter's big game. My wife was really upset*	85	*Gripped wheel*	*I had to get away from my wife*	9	10
8/21 7:00 p.m.	*Home late from work, my son never mowed the lawn, someone left a sink full of dishes, and all the lights were on in the house*	90	*Stomach*	*Drank as soon as I walked in the door*	10	9
8/22 6:00 p.m.	*Crappy day. Late for work, missed a meeting, boss was pissed, wife was nagging, and spilled coffee on my new shirt*	75	*Stomach*	*Started a bottle on the way home*	10	9

Figure 7.2 Self-monitoring log 1 example.

standard drinks consumed (see Fig. 7.2). It is imperative that throughout treatment the therapist and client review and discuss the previous week's log at the outset of each treatment session. The drinking pattern during the week is reviewed, focusing on successful abstinent days as well as any craving and drinking that may have occurred including details on the triggers. Attention is then turned to the anger-related emotions that were experienced during the week, focusing on the words the client used to describe the affect (e.g., angry, annoyed, pissed off), its frequency and intensity, and situations and triggers that were associated with the affect. As the therapist and client review this material, the therapist uses the client's own language and words to discuss the entries, allowing and accepting whatever intensity of emotion the client displays and describes. It is important that the therapist not judge, shut down, or minimize the client's affect but instead accepts the client's report, thus allowing the client to present and discuss anger openly with the therapist.

In these early sessions, the therapist and client begin the practice of exploring the links between the client's anger-related emotions, reports of craving, and any drinking. Using open-ended questions and reflections, the therapist guides and evokes the client's understandings of how anger is associated with the client's cognitive and affective experiences of craving and any drinking that is occurring. It is not unusual that linkages between anger and craving and drinking are quickly apparent and the client has insight (or already had insight) into these associations. Other times, especially when the linkages are more sporadic or not proximal, it may not be clear how (and whether) anger and alcohol are associated. Review and discussion of the self-monitoring logs will help identify the anger—alcohol triggers and insights for the upcoming foci of treatment content.

THE "DRINKING POLICE"

Over time, a client who is self-monitoring cravings and drinking may begin to feel as though the therapist is the "drinking police." The client, beginning to feel emotions such as annoyance, self-consciousness, embarrassment, and guilt becomes reluctant or embarrassed to report alcohol consumption. The therapist can help to address these feelings with empathy, unconditional positive regard, and a matter-of-fact approach to problem solving as necessary. Also, the therapist might bring up the notion of "drinking police" directly and, with some humor, reassure the client that they are working together to support the client's sobriety.

Self-Monitoring Log 2

As the treatment content turns to cognitive therapy, self-monitoring logs change to include both the description of the anger-related situation and the thoughts that are associated with the situation (see Fig. 7.3). We encourage clients to be as brief or as detailed as they choose when completing the logs.; the purpose of monitoring these cognitions is to aid recall in-session so that they may be discussed and reviewed. The rationale for recording thoughts associated with anger-producing situations is that they are central for identifying and eventually modifying anger-inducing thoughts and unhelpful generalizations. Simply put, anger-management cognitive therapy focuses on anger-increasing thoughts; once identified, these cognitions can be evaluated, tested, and modified as appropriate.

Self-Monitoring Log 2

Date/ time	Frustration situation	Thoughts	Emotion intensity 0–100	Alcohol related? If yes, how?	Craving 0–10	No. of drinks?
10.23 11:00 a.m.	*Running errands. Every stupid driver was on the road and I hit all the red lights too*	*Some of these moronic asses shouldn't even have licenses*	55	*The wine store was on the list of errands*	7	10
10.24 all day	*Woke up feeling awful. Decorated the house for Halloween with no help from Michael*	*Why am I the only one who cares about taking care of this house?*	75	*Drank all day because I was alone and pissed*	9	10
10.25 11:00 p.m.	*Hungover, slept all day, went to work. The chef was in a nasty mood*	*I can't stand this job anymore! He's an asshole*	80	*Drank at work and at home*	9	6

Figure 7.3 Self-monitoring log 2 example.

Stephan's *Self-Monitoring* (*Self-Monitoring Log 2*)

Therapist: *I really appreciate the effort you put into filling out your self-monitoring log last week. If it's ok with you, I'd like to take a few minutes to explain the second version of the log that you'll be using this week.*

Stephan: *I didn't mind doing it and I think when Michael saw me doing homework he realized how serious I am about this. He's knows I used to blow off work when I was actually in school! Not because I was dumb, I just didn't care about most of that crap.*

Therapist: *This is something you really care about.*

Stephan: *Absolutely!*

Therapist: *Here's Log 2. Like the first one, there are instructions and examples on the back. The main difference with this one is that instead of writing down your physical reactions to the anger emotions, you're going to focus on the thoughts that come to mind when you're feeling angry, frustrated, annoyed etc. Let's take a look at some of the examples on the back.*

Stephan: *It seems pretty simple to me.*

Therapist: *It can be simple. Some thoughts are obvious and for most people, there are a few thoughts that are "regulars" and pop in pretty frequently. It can almost be like pushing a "play" button and the thoughts just start running. But sometimes, thoughts happen so fast we don't necessarily recognize them. Another benefit of keeping a log like this is that you can take some time after the situation to consider these less obvious, automatic thoughts. Does that make sense? Can we practice by filling out the first line using one of your situations, maybe the one that happened yesterday since it's still fresh in your mind?*

Stephan: *Sure. Like I said, it was the usual bullcrap at work and I was just pissed at everyone.*

Therapist: *What were some of the thoughts that may have been running through your mind? Again, it can be helpful to imagine a small microphone in your head. What were you saying to yourself yesterday?*

Stephan: *Ha-ha! That microphone again! I'm sure it was things like, "This job sucks. I'm not getting anywhere in life. A monkey could do my job. Why do I work with such losers?" I may have used some bad words but I don't want to offend you.*

Therapist: *Don't worry—I've heard a lot and I'm not easily offended. It's more important for you to listen for your thoughts and use the words that feel natural for you.*

Stephan: *In that case, I know I thought about what a total bitch my boss is. She's the queen of the bitches and was on my case all day yesterday. No wonder her husband left; no one can stand her. It's like it's her job is to make us all f-ing miserable while she sits on her throne. She's the worst and has no clue how much we all hate her.*

Therapist: *Those are some great examples of thoughts that happen when you're angry. Are you willing to listen for that kind of stuff this week and include it on your log?*

Stephan: *Absolutely! I just hope I have enough room on the sheet!*

Self-Monitoring Log 3

The third iteration of the self-monitoring logs has an added column for the client to describe coping efforts ("What did you do?" "How did it turn out?") (see Fig. 7.4). Clients come into therapy with their own ideas on coping with strong emotions including both effective and less effective methods (like drinking). In addition, some clients may already be skilled at coping with anger in one area of their life (e.g., work) while less skilled in other areas (e.g., personal relationships). At this point in treatment, the client has also started practicing multiple skills to moderate anger-related emotions such as relaxation skills (see Chapter 9: Relaxation Coping Skills), use of cognitive coping thoughts (see Chapter 10: Cognitive Coping Skills) and coping skills rehearsals (see Chapter 11: Coping

Self-Monitoring Log 3

Date/time	Frustration situation	Thoughts	Coping efforts	Emotion intensity 0–100	Alcohol related?	Craving 0–10	No. of drinks?
11/07 6:00 p.m.	*Every day I come home to an empty apartment*	*I can't stand being alone. Why me? My life is a hot mess*	*Tried to do some deep breathing but I was too wound up*	80	*Yes I drank*	10	5
11/08 3:00 p.m.	*My mom wonders if I'll ever give her grandbabies*	*She says shit like that just to piss me off*	*I left her and went to the gym*	65	*Drank the rest*	7	3.5
11/09 7:00 p.m.	*Sore from the gym and disgusted with my body*	*No one will ever want to be with me* *I'm gross*	*Called my friend but he wasn't home*	95	*Drank a whole bottle*	10	8.5
11/10 6:00 p.m.	*Some days I absolutely hate my job*	*I wish I could just quit. Why didn't I stay in college?*	*Did some relaxation and actually calmed down*	70	*Didn't drink*	4	0

Figure 7.4 Self-monitoring log 3 example.

Skills Rehearsal). The rationale for monitoring coping efforts and their effectiveness is to increase the client's awareness of primary "go-to" coping strategies that can be rapidly and positively implemented in difficult situations. This third version of the log will be used most frequently throughout the program.

Tiffany's *Self-Monitoring (Self-Monitoring Log 3)*

Therapist: *I really appreciate the effort you put into filling out your frustration logs the last couple weeks. If it's ok with you, I'd like to take a few minutes to explain the third and final version of the log that you'll be using this week and actually it's the one you'll be using until the end of the program.*

Tiffany: *That's fine.*

Therapist: *This is Self-Monitoring Log 3. Like the first one, there are instructions and examples on the back. The main difference with this one is that in addition to writing down the thoughts that come to mind when you're feeling angry, there's now a column for what we call 'coping efforts.' Basically, it's where you can write what you did to try and handle the situation. It can be the things we're practicing in here and other things that work for you. I want to be clear that both successful and not-so successful ideas are important to include. Let's take a look at some of the examples on the back.*

Tiffany: *I get it. I just got to write down what I did when I was mad.*

Therapist: *That's right. Can we practice by filling out the first line using one of your situations, maybe the one that happened yesterday since it's still fresh in your mind?*

Tiffany: *All right. Like I said, I was mad at my friends. I saw that post on Instagram of them all out together and I was pissed. They didn't even ask me to go. What the hell?*

Therapist: *You felt pretty angry—an 85 on the intensity scale. What were some of the thoughts running through your mind?*

Tiffany: *Bitches! Who needs friends like that? I deserve to be alone. This blows. No one wants to be with me. I hope they all get sick.*

Therapist: *That's a lot of thoughts. What did you do then?*

Tiffany: *I paced around my apartment. I kept checking my phone. I ordered a pizza. I had a few drinks. I tried to sit and relax with my cat but he was ignoring me too.*

Therapist: *So you tried a few different things. How did it work out overall?*

Tiffany: *I didn't drink too much if that's what you mean. I ended up watching a sad movie and falling asleep. I wanted to text them and give them a piece of my mind but I didn't.*

Therapist: *That sounds new for you.*

Tiffany: *Yeah—it sucked and I'm still pissed as hell but at least I didn't make it worse by cursing them out.*

Therapist: *So for next week, are you willing to fill out this new log with thoughts and coping efforts?*

Tiffany: *Sure.*

Enhancing Adherence and Compliance

In our experience, perfect adherence and compliance to daily self-monitoring is infrequent (although we have also worked with "super" self-monitors who describe their days in full detail!). Our strategy is not to label irregular self-monitors as "noncompliant," "unmotivated," or "uncooperative." Instead of creating a negative experience for clients who are less-than-perfect at self-monitoring, we remain positive and appreciative of the monitoring that has been completed and focus on it as fodder for review. During this discussion and review of the week, if other anger-related instances are mentioned, the therapist uses discretion as to whether to encourage the client to complete additional monitoring in session. Clients who have not completed any of the self-monitoring task or who have forgotten their log at home are provided with a fresh log, and the therapist guides the client to completing several entries. These in-session generated entries are then the basis of discussion.

At times, brief therapist-guided problem solving is helpful for assisting clients who mention barriers to self-monitoring. Such barriers may include lack of time or opportunity to monitor, not being able to remember the task, and lack of understanding for the increasing complex components of self-monitoring. These barriers may have reasonable strategies to address them, so identifying them and obtaining commitment to try is facilitative. Again, the therapist's nonjudgmental and objective demeanor will increase the likelihood of increasing compliance.

IT'S ALL UP TO YOU...

Choice and autonomy are important factors to respect when describing and reviewing self-monitoring logs. Encouraging clients to "make the task their own" and adapt it to their needs and situation will improve the ease of the task and motivation to complete it. Olson, Schmidt, Winkler, and Wipfli (2011) randomly assigned people to choose (or not) a health-related target behavior to monitor. Findings revealed that those individuals instructed to choose their own target behavior and aspect to monitor were more successful at daily self-monitoring than those who were assigned a specific target behavior to monitor.

THERAPIST TIP

As mentioned before, the therapist's adherence to the general principles of Motivational Interviewing (Miller & Rollnick, 2013) is important as a positive approach to enhancing compliance. Genuine empathy and understanding, reflective listening, evoking self-monitoring rationale, and compliance strategies from the client will aid in the client's interest and willingness to self-monitor.

Summary

Self-monitoring alcohol use, cravings, anger-related emotions, and relevant situations is the initial critical component of anger management based alcohol treatment. This task will guide and focus the implementation of discussion, practice, and application of the coping skills. Providing and discussing a rationale, clearly explaining and practicing the task, and remaining positive and appreciative of the work completed is critical to good treatment outcomes. Our next topic is a review of skills to help the client to achieve abstinence and support sobriety.

Suggested Readings

Michie, S., Whittington, C., Hamoudi, Z., Zarnani, F., Tober, G., & West, R. (2012). Identification of behaviour change techniques to reduce excessive alcohol consumption. *Addiction*, *107*, 1431–1440.

Focusing on 42 studies of behavior change techniques to reduce excessive alcohol consumption, this review concludes that prompting self-monitoring of alcohol use was associated with greater reductions in drinking. Although this review focused on reduction of excessive drinking, rather than alcohol use disorder per se, this article provides support for this behavior change strategy.

Olson, R., Schmidt, S., Winkler, C., & Wipfli, B. (2011). The effects of target behavior choice and self-management skills training on compliance with behavioral self-monitoring. *American Journal of Health Promotion*, *25*, 319–324.

Sixty individuals were randomly assigned to choose their own, or be assigned, one of seven health-related behaviors to self-monitor. In addition, subjects were randomly assigned to receive (or not receive) computer-based self-management skills training. Subjects were then asked to complete daily monitoring for 2 weeks. Although the online self-management skills training had no effect on compliance with the self-monitoring tasks, subject choice did. Those subjects who chose a behavior to monitor were significantly more compliant with the self-monitoring tasks when compared to those subjects who were assigned their target behavior by study personnel.

van Achterberg, T., Huisman-de Waal, G. G., Ketelaar, N. A., Oostendorp, R. A., Jacobs, J. E., & Wollersheim, H. C. (2010). How to promote healthy behaviours in patients? An overview of evidence for behaviour change techniques. *Health Promotion International*, *26*, 148–162.

This review collected and summarized research studies on smoking cessation, physical exercise, and nutrition in order to describe the effectiveness of behavior change strategies including increasing knowledge, behavior facilitation, self-monitoring, and social support. Among the conclusions supplied by this review, the practice of self-monitoring was one of the most effective behavior change strategies across these domains. Two other effective strategies were communication of risks and use of social supports.

Chapter 8

Sobriety Skills

Chapter Points

- Sobriety skills are an essential component of anger management based alcohol treatment.
- The SOBER problem-solving model is a structured format for working through both general and alcohol-related life problems.
- Drink refusal is a key skill in the treatment for alcohol use disorder. Repeated therapist modeling and client role plays are essential to learning and rehearsing this important skill.
- Multiple additional sobriety skills are available to achieve and support abstinence.

Questions for Self-Reflection

- Are you more likely to tell people what to do or evoke their own ideas?
- What are your thoughts on mutual-help groups like alcoholics anonymous (AA)?
- How do you feel about doing role plays in session with your clients?

David: *I'm nervous about a weekend we have coming up. We only see these folks once a year and it's always a huge booze fest, especially for me. I'm not sure if they know I'm not drinking and I have to find a way to*

Anger Management Based Alcohol Treatment. DOI: https://doi.org/10.1016/B978-0-12-812709-4.00008-1

tell them. I'm fine with not drinking but I mostly don't want to be a party pooper and ruin all their fun. I'm always the weekend bartender and I'm worried that me not drinking will make them uncomfortable. I'm not sure what to do.

Overview of Sobriety Skills

As can be inferred from the name of this treatment approach, a core component of anger management based alcohol treatment is a package of sobriety skills to achieve and maintain abstinence from alcohol. Research suggests that clients in treatment benefit from regular use of a broad and varied range of coping skills. For example, Roos and Witkiewitz (2016) report that the better posttreatment alcohol outcomes were found for clients who reported consistent use of numerous alcohol-specific coping skills, relative to outcomes of clients who reported a narrower range of coping skills use. Specifically, those individuals reporting the consistent use of a broad range of both behavioral and cognitive alcohol-specific coping skills also reported drinking less and having fewer alcohol-related problems. Skills included strategies such as talking to others, avoiding drinking-related triggers, self-calming when craving, thinking about how drinking hurts self and others, feeling good about not drinking, and positive self-talk and commitment.

Another study, Dolan, Rohsenow, Martin, and Monti (2013), identified specific coping skills that predicted good alcohol outcomes. Researchers asked 131 alcoholic clients about their use of urge-specific coping skills as well as general life change strategies. Uses of 31 of the 42 total strategies were predictive of positive drinking outcomes. Effective behavioral strategies included engaging in an alternative activity, problem-solving, drink refusal, and social support; effective cognitive strategies included thinking about drinking consequences, positive self-talk, thinking distracting thoughts, challenging negative thoughts, and telling self to "wait it out." A third category—spiritual coping—was also associated with positive outcomes. Use of these strategies was reported as helpful even 1 year following treatment. A powerful implication of these research studies is the importance of teaching, role playing, and encouraging the use of a wide variety of behavioral skills (e.g., self-reward of positive changes, self-calming, and avoiding triggers) and cognitive coping skills (e.g., thinking about problems from drinking, making a commitment to sobriety, and positive self-talk) during treatment. These coping skills should be alcohol-specific (e.g., coping with urges and lapses) as well as general lifestyle skills (e.g., problem-solving).

A variety of sobriety skills can be weaved throughout anger management based alcohol treatment. These skills should be taught, practiced, and reinforced in session and through home practice. Although not comprehensive by any means, a set of skills regularly used in our treatment protocols is reviewed here.

Our focus has been on skills including general and alcohol-specific problem-solving, drink refusal, sober social support (e.g., mutual-help groups), and life skill training (communication and assertiveness skills, listening skills, challenging negative thinking, and increasing pleasant activities). Although many of these skills are utilized with most, if not all, clients (e.g., problem-solving, drinking refusal), others are included based on individual client needs (individual life skills training).

Ongoing Progress Updates

Although not a sobriety skill *per se*, each therapy session begins with a review of the client's report since the last session with a particular interest in substance use that may have occurred, cravings experienced, sobriety skills used, and high-risk situations identified. This review is important for multiple reasons including tracking the client's progress toward sobriety and identifying and problem-solving upcoming high-risk challenges. This review often takes 10 minutes or so, and more time is allotted as warranted by the client's report and current challenges.

In addition, we have the client provide an exhaled-air breath sample for a BAC (blood alcohol concentration) reading to detect recent alcohol use and intoxication at each therapy session (see Chapter 5: Assessment Instruments and Considerations). The therapist and client make an agreement at the outset that therapy sessions will be conducted only in a sober environment. Occasionally, a client will arrive to therapy with a positive BAC. Most therapists and clinics will have guidelines and procedures in place and, in large part, are based on the client's BAC reading. Depending on the circumstances and the client's history, procedures, compassion, and support can make the experience therapeutic for the client.

CLIENT CRISES

When a client presents an urgent and timely issue, such as a serious relapse to drinking, a personal crisis, or suicidal ideation, the session content originally planned for that session should be delayed in order to focus on problem-solving and caring for the crisis. The client-centered approach we encourage necessitates the individualization of treatment to meet each client's needs. If ongoing crises and emergencies regularly take precedence over the planned anger management based alcohol treatment material, the therapist and client should review the treatment contract to determine whether additional or different treatment content or intensity may be required.

SOBER Problem-Solving

A structured format for focusing on life's problems and challenges is another core component of this treatment. Alcohol Use Disorder (AUD), for most individuals, is concomitant with numerous life problems in realms such as family, work, health, legal, financial, and emotional states. These problems and challenges, often alcohol-related, are usually quite serious and overwhelming. Further, addressing these issues may sometimes detract from alcohol treatment and anger management, making the delivery of treatment content difficult. The problems may also negatively impact drinking outcomes and stand in the way of sobriety. Teaching, practicing, and successful implementation of a standardized strategy for problem-solving is important for positive treatment outcomes. Research backs this up; Demirbas, Ilhan, and Dogan (2012) found that, among alcohol-dependent inpatients, clients who reported more active engagement in problem-solving were more likely to be abstinent 6 months later relative to those who reported less problem-solving efforts.

Our "SOBER" model of problem-solving is introduced to the client early in treatment (often in Session 2; see Fig. 8.1). The therapist and client team take time to review the paradigm, practice it in session, and then use it as a target exercise in the upcoming week. As treatment continues, SOBER problem-solving is used for problematic issues during the ongoing progress updates as warranted.

> Therapist: *One important skill I'd like us to talk about today is problem solving. We all face problems in life, both big and small. For some people, drinking becomes a way to handle problems and to avoid thinking about them. Learning and practicing a constructive strategy for solving problems is essential in maintaining sobriety. What do you think about that?*

SOBER Problem Solving

S: Stop and See the problem – describe it as clearly and accurately as you can

O: Organize your Options (brainstorm) – come up with a list possible solutions

B: Be aware of consequences – consider positives/negatives and short term/long term

E: Evaluate and select the best options – choose the best idea(s) and try it out

R: Review the Results – Did you make progress? Great! If not, go back and start again

Figure 8.1 SOBER problem-solving paradigm.

Stephan: *It makes sense. I think I'm pretty good at solving problems but I also know I drink more when I'm dealing with a lot of problems.*

Therapist: *So you notice both in yourself—you have some good problem solving skills and you notice more drinking when you face problems. If it's ok with you, I'd like to take a few minutes to review the model we use called SOBER Problem Solving. Then we can spend some time practicing it with a problem you're dealing with.*

Stephan: *Sure, go ahead.*

THERAPIST TIP

Asking permission. Notice that the therapist here asks for permission to discuss and educate Stephan on the SOBER problem-solving strategy, "If it is OK with you, I'd like to take a few minutes. . ." Asking for permission to present therapeutic educational material is both respectful and consistent with a client-centered approach. Watch for the therapist's use of permission throughout these case study materials.

Therapist: *The S stands for "**Stop and See the Problem.**" Sometimes problems are easy to recognize. At other times you have to look for clues that there is a problem like physical symptoms, emotions, thoughts, behaviors, and other people. Once a problem is identified, it's important to try and define the problem as clearly as possible using as much information as you can. Occasionally, you need to think carefully about the true nature of the problem. An example of this is "Ron" who says the problem is that his landlord is a jerk. However, the missing information is that Ron has not paid his rent on time for the past 6 months.*

Stephan: *Haha! I'm guilty of that kind of thing. I blame other people and forget that I sometimes have a big part in creating the problem in the first place!*

Therapist: *Recognizing your role in the problem can really help in this model, especially because it's a lot easier to change yourself than it is to change other people. Sometimes, what you actually need to change is how you react to a person or situation.*

Stephan: *That's true. Other people can be so stubborn!*

THERAPIST TIP

S: The therapist mentions here, and will implement shortly, the strategy of "Stop and See the Problem" in full detail. Instead of simply stating the problem, the therapist will guide Stephan in describing the small details and underlying issues and thoughts related to the problem. Also, several different problems may be tangled together. It is important to identify them separately because they may have very different solutions.

Therapist: *So once you have a clear picture of the problem, it's time to move to the O which stands for "**Organize your Options**," otherwise known as brainstorming. This is where you consider all the things you can do to solve the problem. It's important in this step to come up with as many ideas as possible, without judging them as right or wrong or helpful or not, but just writing them all down. Some people find it useful to consider other viewpoints, for example, if your friend had this problem, what would you suggest? You can also think about past solutions that have worked for you or for other people you know and include those.*

Stephan: *We do something like this at work when we have a big event. We come up with different scenarios and brainstorm how we'll handle them. We don't call it SOBER though.*

Therapist: *So you're familiar with this at work. That's true for many people. They have and use these skills effectively in one area of their life but may need to practice more for other areas.*

Stephan: *That's me—I'm one of the best at work but at home, I usually just give up and drink.*

Therapist: *You can understand the benefits of finding other ways to solve problems in all areas of your life.*

Stephan: *For sure.*

THERAPIST TIP

O: At this point during brainstorming, the therapist emphasizes that possible "Options" and strategies are suggested broadly, without consideration of their usefulness and effectiveness. Good or bad, Stephan will be encouraged to list (and write) a broad range of problem responses. This list may include drinking; often this can be a therapeutic moment for the client.

Therapist: *So the next step in SOBER problem solving is to "**Be Aware**" where you start to consider the possible consequences of each idea on* *your list. You basically ask "What will happen if I do this?" for each idea. It's important to think about both positive and negative as well as the long term and short term consequences. Drinking can be a great example of this. It'll most likely be on your list of options and might take you mind off you problems in the short term...*

Stephan: *But the next day my problem is still there, I'm hungover, and probably in trouble with my husband!*

Therapist: *You got it. Ideally you want a solution that maximizes positives in the long run and minimizes the negatives.*

THERAPIST TIP

B: The therapist emphasizes "Being Aware" of both *positive and negative consequences of each problem-solving strategy as well as the short- and long-term consequences* associated with each strategy. Again, when considering drinking as a problem-solving strategy, Stephan may again recognize that although drinking may have a short-term positive effect, the longer term consequences are negative.

Therapist: *E is the step where you "**Evaluate**" and select one or more options that have the best chance of working for you and decide how to put them into action.*

Stephan: *Like I said, I'm a man of action...*

THERAPIST TIP

E: Stephan will "Evaluate" and select option or options that are most likely to be effective in both the short and long term. As necessary, the therapist will guide Stephan's considerations and, likely, put forth drinking as a viable option. Allowing Stephan the moments to reject drinking because of its many negative consequences may encourage therapeutic insights.

Therapist: *Right. And the final step is to "**Review the Results**" after you've implemented your idea and given it some time. It's important to check in and see if it's working as well as you hoped it would. If it is, great! If not, you need to decide to whether to give it more time or to go back to an earlier step in the process. Maybe redefine the problem, maybe choose a different option. It's important not to stick with a solution when it's no longer effective.*

Stephan: *That reminds me of the definition of insanity—trying the same thing over and over and expecting different results!*

THERAPIST TIP

R: It will be important for the therapist and Stephan to "Review the Results" of his efforts to implement the options he has chosen. The therapist should take responsibility for returning to the problematic situation during the next session (or two) and help Stephan to consider any impact he has had on the problem issue and whether his options can be tweaked. This "R" step is sometimes forgotten as it happens later on.

Therapist: *These skills really seems to make sense for you. Can we take a few minutes to practice this with a problem in your life right now?*

Stephan: *Sure, how about my job?*

Therapist: *Great. Can you put the problem into your own words? What is the problem with your job?*

Stephan: *I hate my job. My boss is a bitch, my co-workers are slackers, everyone gossips, the customers complain constantly, I know I could be doing more with my life, the money is inconsistent, and I feel like I'm wasting my time and not living up to my potential.*

Therapist: *So there are a lot of reasons you are unhappy at your job, both external and internal. Let's sum up the problem as "I hate my job" and write down these details. Now let's go to the next step, considering options.*

Stephan: *The way I see it, I have a few options. I can suck it up and be glad I have a job. I can quit and look for something else. I can look for something else and then quit. I can quit and go back to school full time. I can keep working and take some classes part time. I can keep doing what I'm doing and be miserable and drunk. Or I can quit and let Michael support me after we sell our house and move into a tent.*

Therapist: *That's a great list of options. Let's talk about the consequences of some of these ideas.*

Stephan: *I'm tired of being drunk and miserable and the last one is kind of a joke, we really need both of us working, so let's get rid of those and start at the top.*

Therapist: *Ok, get rid of the last two and start at the top.*

Stephan: *If I just focus on being grateful to have this job, I may be less miserable but I'm still stuck spinning my wheels. If I quit first it might cause some financial stress if I don't find something right away. If I look around for another job while I'm still there, they could find out and make my life miserable. I would like to quit and go back to school full time but I don't know if I can afford that. It's probably more realistic to take some classes part time while I'm still working but I'm worried I'll have trouble with my homework.*

Therapist: *You can see benefits and drawbacks to each of your ideas. As with most life problems, there isn't usually one perfect solution. If we move to step E, which option seems to offer you the most positives over the long term?*

Stephan: *I'd have to say it's to take some classes while I keep working. I'll still have an income and I'll be doing something to give me more opportunities in the future. I'll have to stop drinking and probably cut down on weed to get homework done but I can do that if it means I won't be stuck in this job forever.*

Therapist: *You're really thinking about what you can do to make this plan work for you.*

Stephan: *Yeah. I think about this stuff a lot. This has actually been helpful, seeing it in writing and talking it out. I think I'll go home and talk to Michael.*

Therapist: *I'm glad you found this helpful and you realize you're already pretty good at this. Sometimes just taking some time to think things through carefully can make a difference. I'll be interested to hear what you decide to do after you talk to Michael.*

Stephan: *I'll be sure to let you know.*

Therapist: *I'd also like to offer you this worksheet on Problem Solving. It has reminders of what we discussed today with room to use this with another problem, or even to review this one. Are you willing to fill this out and bring it back next week?*

Stephan: *Sure, maybe Michael and I can do it together.*

Drink Refusal Skills With Role Play

A research study by Witkiewitz, Donovan, and Hartzler (2012) sums it up well: "This [drink refusal skill training] approach rested on the notion that training individuals with alcohol dependence to invoke an alternative social response to alcohol-involved situations should deter temptations to drink and enable clients to develop more adaptive social responses." (p. 441). Their research demonstrated that the 302 clients who received the drink refusal treatment module (35% received the training once and 65% received the training multiple times) reported significantly fewer drinking days during treatment and 1-year after treatment compared to those who did not receive training. The training module included the rationale for training, understanding the social pressure to drink experienced by the client, and reviewing the client's common strategies to cope with this pressure. The behavioral skills training for drink refusal was next in the treatment module. As demonstrated below, the therapist and client role play drinking situations relevant to the client's experiences. First, the client plays the role of "pusher," and the therapist demonstrates a clear, positive, and assertive style of drink refusal. Then the roles are reversed; the therapist plays the "pusher" and the client practices refusal techniques. The therapist provides feedback to the client and the role plays continue until the client and therapist are comfortable with the client's skills and confidence.

DRINK REFUSAL GUIDELINES

(1) "No" should be the first word spoken to yourself and then to others; don't hesitate. Be clear right from the start!
(2) Use effective non-verbal behavior including a firm, clear voice and maintain comfortable eye contact.
(3) Suggest something else to do; "Let's go for coffee instead."
(4) Say "No" and then change the subject; "No thanks. How's your new job?"
(5) Assertively ask the person to stop offering; "Please stop offering, I really don't want a drink."
(6) Try to avoid vague excuses or time-limited answers; "I'm on medication right now." These can imply that you might have a drink later.
(7) Have a nonalcoholic drink in your hand already; "No thanks, I'm all set."
(8) Don't feel guilty—you have a right not to drink!
(9) Practice, and practice again, using multiple relevant situations.

Therapist: *Another important sobriety skill that I'd like us to talk about today is Drink Refusal Skills. Unless you never leave your house again, it's almost impossible to avoid all events and situations that have alcohol.*

Tiffany: *That's the truth. Pretty much everyone I know drinks and that's what my friends and family do when we get together.*

Therapist: *So these skills will be especially important for you. If it's ok with you, I'll spend some time explaining the skills and then we can practice using an example from your life.*

Tiffany: *Sure but this isn't going to be easy!*

Therapist: *You're right. Learning skills to help you refuse drinks isn't easy and takes a lot of practice before it feels natural. And it all starts with the first skill, saying no to yourself. It's essential that you're clear with yourself, before you even leave the house, that you won't be drinking. If you leave it up in the air, chances are...*

Tiffany: *I'll drink. I hear you and I've been there, telling myself I'll see what happens when I get to the party—ha! I know damn well what's going to happen when I get there, I'm going to drink.*

Therapist: *What happens when you decide not to drink?*

Tiffany: *Then I don't drink.*

Therapist: *So if "no" is clear in your own mind, there's also a better chance that "no" will be the first thing you say when someone offers you a drink. It's even more effective if that clear "no" comes with some non-verbal messages that back it up.*

Tiffany: *What do you mean?*

Therapist: *Well, if you say "no" clearly, with a strong voice, and make direct eye contact with the person, it sends an even clearer message that you mean it. If you say "no" and your voice is hesitant or weak and you're avoiding eye contact, the person might not believe the "no" and think you actually want to be convinced. Let me show you...*

THERAPIST TIP

The Therapist can demonstrate saying "no" using the two different styles of communication – stronger versus weaker – to give the client a better idea of the power of non-verbals which are usually more convincing than verbal messages.

Tiffany: *I see what you mean, when you were saying it all unsure like that, someone definitely would have wanted to give you a drink.*

Therapist: *You got it. When we say things more assertively, our message is usually heard loud and clear. In some situations, another idea is to ask the person if you could do something else together, maybe something not drinking related like going for coffee.*

Tiffany: *I've tried that a few times with my one friend Denise. We went for coffee one day and went to the movies another time. She knows what I'm going through and she doesn't drink as much as some of my other friends. I just feel bad asking other people to not drink just because I have a problem.*

Therapist: *It sound like Denise likes to spend time with you even if you're not drinking.*

Tiffany: *Yeah, she's cool like that. Some of my other friends won't be though. They'll just keep offering me drinks.*

Therapist: *That's tough but pretty common, especially if most of your social life involves drinking. Sometimes, you have to be clear and just ask the person to stop offering you drinks. Again, this skill takes some strength and certainty on your part.*

Tiffany: *I guess I can find out who my real friends are. If they know how bad my drinking is, why would they be pushing drinks on me?*

Therapist: *So you think the people who truly care about you will listen and respect you. Keep in mind that for many people, pushing drinks on you may say more about them than about you. The people in your life might need some time to get used to the idea that you don't drink anymore. It's a big change.*

Tiffany: *Most of them won't believe me... I'll have to prove it to them and to me.*

Therapist: *And someday it will seem normal for you to say no to a drink. Another skill people find useful is to say "no" and then immediately change the subject. Ideally you can take the focus off your drinking and avoid any awkward conversation. Most people would probably rather talk about themselves than about your drinking anyway.*

Tiffany: *Haha—that's the truth!*

Therapist: *Another option is to have your own non-alcoholic drink already in your hand so you can just say "I'm good." You can bring your own or order for yourself and no one needs to know.*

Tiffany: *I could try that. I like sweet tea and could bring it with me.*

Therapist: *That's a good idea. Sometimes people use excuses like "I'm on medication, or on a diet right now so I'm not drinking." If that's what you need to say to get you out of a tough situation, it could work. The only worry is that it may leave the door open for next time, especially if it's someone you see often. Does that make sense?*

Tiffany: *Yeah, but I'm not telling everyone the truth, they don't need to know everything.*

Therapist: *Absolutely. It's up to you how much to share. I also want to remind you that you don't need to use excuses because you have the right to not drink. What do you think about that idea?*

Tiffany: *I have the right not to drink? I never thought of it that way but I guess it's true. Nobody can make me do anything I don't want to do.*

Therapist: *That's right. And this also goes back to something you said earlier about feeling guilty about your friend Denise. If she's choosing to be with you and not drink, that's her choice. Maybe she cares more about you than about alcohol.*

Tiffany: *I feel like I'm depriving her of fun by not drinking with her but maybe that's not what she thinks.*

Therapist: *So of all these skills I've mentioned, which do you think will be most useful for you?*

Tiffany: *I think saying no to myself, being clear, and trying to not feel guilty.*

Therapist: *Great. Can we take a few minutes and practice using a situation from your life where you might need drink refusal skills?*

Tiffany: *I guess so. One of my friends from high school is in town and a bunch of us are planning to hang out with her Saturday night. There'll be lots of alcohol.*

Therapist: *Ok, so who'll be offering the drinks?*

Tiffany: *We're going to Alicia's house and she's got a bar in her family room.*

Therapist: *Ok. To start out, how about you be Alicia offering a drink and I'll be you saying no.*

Tiffany: *This feels weird but here goes: 'Hey girl, I got your vodka and sweet tea here. You want a big glass with ice?*

Therapist (as Tiffany): *Thanks. Just sweet tea with ice for me.*

Tiffany (as friend): *I got this lemon vodka just for you. Come on, we're partying tonight.*

Therapist (as Tiffany): *Nah, just the sweet tea.*

Tiffany (as friend): *What's up with you? You never turn down a drink at my house.*

Therapist (as Tiffany): *First time for everything. Hey, how's your boyfriend doing...*

Tiffany: *Ha—that would get her talking! I don't know about this.*

Therapist: *It does feel strange at first. How about we switch; I'll be Alicia and you can practice saying no to her.*

Tiffany: *Ok.*

Therapist (as friend): *Hey girl, I've got your vodka and tea. You want ice?*

Tiffany: *I'll just have the tea and no ice.*

Therapist (as friend): *Just tea? Oh come on. We're partying tonight!*

Tiffany: *Just tea for me. Hey, how's Duane doing?*

Therapist (as friend): *He's good. You sure you don't want some vodka in here? It's the good stuff I got just for you.*

Tiffany: *Nah—I'm good with the tea right now. Tell me about the wedding plans.*

Therapist: *You did it. How did that feel?*

Tiffany: *Awkward. Maybe I can just bring my own drink and not even tell her.*

Therapist: *That's an option. Remember, refusing drinks is a skill that needs practice and time to feel natural.*

Tiffany: *I can see that.*

Therapist: *I have a worksheet for you that has a different situations where you might need to refuse drinks. For most people, if you practice what you would say in advance, the words come out easier. Are you willing to fill this out before our next session?*

Tiffany: *These don't all apply to me but I'll do it.*

Mutual-Help Group Support

The oft-interchangeable terms of mutual-help group, self-help group, 12-step organization and AA refer to groups of members who both give and receive support, encouragement, and advice regarding recovery from addictions and, in our case, alcoholism. Humphreys et al. (2004) defines self-help groups and organizations as "non-professional, peer-operated organizations devoted to helping individuals who have addiction-related problems" (p. 151). They provide a positive and useful review of the variety of mutual-help groups available in the United States including AA, Secular Organization for Sobriety, SMART Recovery, and Women for Sobriety. These organizations are readily available, do not charge fees, appeal to a broad spectrum of people, and vary in their philosophies and beliefs. Especially useful for a long-term support approach, mutual-help groups are often recommended and used both as an adjunct to formal addictions treatment as well as for continuing care and post-treatment support.

Briefly put, qualitative, quantitative, and longitudinal research on mutual-help groups (predominantly focusing on AA) has concluded that these groups improve abstinence outcomes, social functioning, self-efficacy, and reduce health care costs. Humphreys et al. suggest a variety of strategies for encouraging and fostering involvement in mutual-help groups among individuals in treatment for addictions, including using empirically validated counseling methods (e.g., 12-step facilitation therapy, motivational enhancement strategies), offering a menu of mutual-help options, and respecting cultural and belief diversity. The interested clinician is referred to the substantial literature in existence for further discussion of mutual-help groups, their philosophies, and their effectiveness.

Summary

Our goal in this chapter has been to describe several sobriety skills that we routinely use in our treatment and to illustrate their use in our case studies. It is important to recognize, however, that the AUD treatment field encompasses a broad and varied menu of efficacious research-based options. A complete review of these additional skills is beyond the scope of this text, although we have mentioned a few of them here. Comprehensive resources exist on reviews of efficacious individual psychosocial AUD treatments and also on the individual treatment approaches. These approaches include motivational enhancement treatment, brief interventions, cue exposure treatment, coping skills training, negative affect management, behavioral couples therapy, community reinforcement approach, and behavioral self-control training. Several of these approaches can be integrated into anger management based alcohol treatment (e.g., coping skills training and negative affect management) while other strategies would pose a challenge (e.g., behavioral couples therapy and community reinforcement approach).

Suggested Readings

Demirbas, H., Ilhan, I. O., & Dogan, Y. B. (2012). Ways of problem solving as predictors of relapse in alcohol dependent male inpatients. *Addictive Behaviors, 37*, 131–134.

At the initiation of inpatient treatment, 128 alcohol-dependent men answered questions regarding their problem-solving skills and confidence and, 6 months later, their drinking [abstinent (43% of the sample) versus relapsed (57%)]. Those who were abstinent were more likely to have reported using more reflective and more avoidant problem-solving styles relative to those who relapsed. Specifically, a problem-solving style that was more thoughtful and cognitive (i.e., reflective) was at less risk of relapse. Interestingly, those who reported a more avoidant problem-solving style were also at less risk for relapse. Confidence in problem-solving was unrelated to drinking status.

Dolan, S. L., Rohsenow, D. J., Martin, R. A., & Monti, P. M. (2013). Urge-specific and lifestyle coping strategies of alcoholics: Relationships of specific strategies to treatment outcome. *Drug and Alcohol Dependence, 128*, 8–14.

This study sought to identify lifestyle and situation-specific coping skills which were particularly predictive of positive treatment outcomes among alcohol clients. Findings included that many behavioral and cognitive coping strategies, some alcohol-specific and others general lifestyle, were positively related to outcome; several were not. The effective strategies included problem-solving, drink refusal, social support, positive and encouraging self-talk, and distracting thoughts. Ineffective strategies included willpower alone, self-punishment, exercise, and beverage substitution. An important implication of this research is to teach and encourage use of a variety of cognitive, behavioral, alcohol-specific, and general lifestyle coping strategies during treatment.

Humphreys, K., et al. (2004). Self-help organizations for alcohol and drug problems: Toward evidence-based practice and policy. *Journal of Substance Abuse Treatment, 26*, 151–158.

This expert consensus statement was developed by a national workgroup on substance abuse self-help organizations. This review article presents the group's conclusions regarding the effectiveness of self-help organizations and suggested policies for clinicians, addictions programs, and policymakers.

Roos, C. R., & Witkiewitz, K. (2016). Adding tools to the toolbox: The role of coping repertoire in alcohol treatment. *Journal of Consulting and Clinical Psychology, 84*, 599–611.

Over 2600 AUD clients reported the degree to which they used 40 alcohol-specific coping skills and strategies after alcohol treatment. Coping skills included both behavioral skills such as talking to others, avoiding drinking-related triggers, and self-calming when craving and cognitive skills such as thinking about how drinking hurts self and others, feeling good about not drinking, and positive self-talk. Clients who reported consistent use of many of these skills drank less and reported fewer problems as compared to clients who had a narrower range of skills consistently used. The implication of this research is to teach and practice a broad range of alcohol-related skills—both behavioral and cognitive—during AUD treatment.

Witkiewitz, K., Donovan, D. M., & Hartzler, B. (2012). Drink refusal training as part of a combined behavioral intervention: Effectiveness and mechanisms of change. *Journal of Consulting and Clinical Psychology, 80*, 440–449.

This study demonstrated that drink refusal skill training and the subsequent improvement in self-confidence are important and effective components of alcohol dependence treatment. Over 300 alcohol-dependent clients who received drink refusal skill training reported significantly fewer drinking days during and after treatment. Also, drink refusal training improved clients' self-confidence to not drink and this important change also contributed to positive drinking outcomes.

Chapter 9

Relaxation Coping Skills

Chapter Points

- Achieving a rapid and effective state of relaxation is the critical first step for anger management based alcohol treatment.
- Relaxation targets the physiological arousal component of anger-related emotions.
- A variety of relaxation exercises and techniques are presented and regular skills practice is strongly encouraged.
- Several barriers to relaxation exercises and practice are described as well as potential solutions.

Questions for Self-Reflection

- What is your attitude toward relaxation skills in your own life?
- How comfortable are you with silence?

Stephan: *When I hear relaxation, I picture some spaced out hippie sitting cross-legged and chanting nonsense. He's probably high on something too. Smoking weed relaxes me. The first few drinks relax me. My garden is relaxing. I tried yoga once and threw out my back. I'm just not into this new age crap. If I'm too relaxed I'll lose my edge. I need to be tough to*

Anger Management Based Alcohol Treatment. DOI: https://doi.org/10.1016/B978-0-12-812709-4.00009-3

put up with all the assholes in my life. My dad used to ask us, "You wanna be the hammer, or you wanna be the nail?" I choose the hammer—I've had enough of being the fucking nail.

The Rationale for Relaxation

Multiple research studies support the effectiveness of relaxation coping skills for anger reduction. Relaxation coping skills are effective with general anger and angry drivers (e.g., Deffenbacher, 2009; Deffenbacher, Demm, & Brandon, 1986; Deffenbacher, Filetti, Lynch, Dahlen, & Oetting, 2002; Deffenbacher, Huff, Lynch, Oetting, & Salvatore, 2000; Deffenbacher & Stark, 1992; Deffenbacher, Story, Brandon, Hogg, & Hazaleus, 1988; Hazaleus & Deffenbacher, 1986; Novaco, 1975). One study (Novaco, 1975) suggested that relaxation was somewhat less effective than cognitive and cognitive-relaxation interventions. However, when the relaxation intervention was lengthened and included active coping skills training, relaxation was as effective as cognitive, behavioral, and cognitive-relaxation interventions.

Initiation of Relaxation Interventions

During anger management based alcohol treatment, the introduction of relaxation strategies is initiated early in therapy. Typically, clients intuitively understand the contradictory relationship between anger and relaxation and readily accept the rationale for learning and practicing relaxation techniques. Relaxation interventions are, therefore, uniquely linked and adapted to the client's own experience of anger including thoughts and behaviors when calm.

RELAX, THEN THINK

Early research (e.g., Hazaleus & Deffenbacher, 1986) found that relaxation interventions facilitated the therapeutic relationship and reduced initial resistance to cognitive interventions. That is, clients liked relaxation but fought cognitive interventions when presented before relaxation. In contrast, when relaxation preceded cognitive interventions in a combined cognitive-relaxation therapy, clients received the cognitive intervention more willingly (e.g., Deffenbacher, Story, Stark, Hogg, & Brandon, 1987; Deffenbacher & Stark, 1992).

Therapist: *In tracking your experiences with frustration and anger over past couple weeks, you've noticed some of the effects on your body.*

David: *Yeah, I never realized how tense I get when I'm mad, and the stomachaches have to be connected somehow.*

Therapist: *All this tension has been happening without you realizing it. So what does that tell you about the relationship between anger and physical tension?*

David: *It tells me that when I'm pissed off, I tense up. I feel it in my jaw, my shoulders, my neck, my hands when I'm driving. I guess if I didn't get so mad, maybe I wouldn't get so tense.*

Therapist: *That's certainly true. I also wonder about thinking of it the other way around.*

David: *You mean if I can avoid getting so tense, I would get less mad?*

Therapist: *It's possible. What do you do in your daily life to relax?*

David: *Honestly, I drink.*

Therapist: *What else do you do to relax other than drinking?*

David: *I tinker in my garage. And when the weather's nice, I like to walk in the woods.*

Therapist: *How do you feel when you're doing those things?*

David: *I feel good. I can get lost in a project in the garage and I feel energized in the woods and calm when I get back home.*

Therapist: *Let's focus for a minute on your walks in the woods. You're up, energized, moving your muscles and then when you're done, you feel calm.*

David: *Yeah, it's a great feeling.*

Therapist: *And what about your anger emotions at those times?*

David: *I'm usually not angry as long as no one bugs me too bad. After I've been in the woods, I don't seem to let stuff get to me as much.*

Therapist: *And it sounds like part of what helps you feel calm and relaxed is moving around, using your muscles.*

David: *Yeah—I used to be a daily runner and I loved the feeling after a good run.*

Therapist: *What else do you notice when you feel like that?*

David: *It seems like I can handle anything; I feel confident and optimistic.*

Therapist: *What if you could learn to find that feeling of calm confidence at any time during the day?*

David: *I don't think that's possible with my life but if it was, I'd probably feel more in control.*

Therapist: *If you could be more relaxed, you would feel more in control of how you react to situations and people.*

David: *You could say that.*

Therapist: *If you were more in control of your reactions, what would be different in your life?*

David: *I probably wouldn't fly off the handle so easily and may be I wouldn't need to drink so much.*

Therapist: *What else?*

David: *Maybe my family wouldn't avoid me.*

Therapist: *Being more in control, not drinking as much, and having your family choose to be around you would be important benefits for you.*

David: *Sure but I can't just go off walking in the woods every time I'm mad.*

Therapist: *You're right. I'm wondering if you'd be interested in practicing some skills that may help you get that "walking in the woods" relaxed feeling anytime you need it?*

David: *I'm not sure what you mean but tell me more.*

As demonstrated by David's therapist, likening relaxation procedures to a positive, relaxed, and calm experience in the client's past is an effective introduction to this phase of anger management based alcohol treatment. Relaxation strategies and exercises are described as a means of learning how to physically relax and, with repeated practice, achieve relaxation, any time, any place, in a minute or so. The ultimate goal of this practice is the ability to initiate relaxation and calm down anytime when angry or upset. Clients are often interested but skeptical that this can be achieved. It is suggested that the therapist offers reassurance that it can be done but that it will take 2–4 weeks to develop reliable, quick relaxation and a few more to employ it for anger reduction. It is emphasized that it will take repeated practice both in-session and between sessions to develop these relaxation skills. The therapist can also indicate that initial procedures are a bit cumbersome (anticipating the tension-release exercises of progressive relaxation training) but that with repeated practice, the client will become much quicker and effective in initiating relaxation.

The therapist might take a few moments and make an introduction something like the following:

> *I'd like to describe what relaxation therapy looks like. Today, we'll start with a couple of basic relaxation methods. Specifically, I'll ask you to develop a personal relaxation scene and then we'll systematically tense and release the muscles in your body. This'll help you get the kind of feeling you get when you're walking in the woods* (making reference to the client's earlier conversation), *because muscles go into a deeper state of relaxation after they've been tensed. As you practice this at home during the next week or two, you'll learn to relax without the tension-release exercises, and you'll be able to achieve relaxation in a few seconds to a minute or so. Then, you'll have relaxation tools to address anger and other feelings of stress. But, this isn't enough. Together, we'll practice applying relaxation to reduce feelings of anger. I'll help you to think about, remember and visualize situations that've made you angry, feel these feelings of anger, and then relax away those feelings. At first, we'll start with mild to moderate anger situations, and I'll guide you through relaxation. As you get better and faster at relaxing in the face of anger, we'll kick up the level of anger you're dealing with and I'll reduce my help, so at the end you can visualize what angers you the most and cope with those feelings on your own. How does that sound? How do you feel about working together on this plan?*

Relaxation Scene Development

Visualization of a personal moment of calmness, relaxation, and peace is both an effective relaxation strategy, as well as a positive strategy for initiating relaxation therapy. To facilitate the client being able to rapidly enter into the scene and maximize the retrieval of relaxation, the scene should be of a clear, specific moment in a client's life. The therapist should pay attention to specific cues that can help the client experience the scene in as much sensory detail as possible. These include environmental, auditory, tactile, visual, olfactory, temperature, and emotional cues. If the scene involves a situation experienced several times (e.g., being at the same spot on a lake on multiple occasions), then the therapist should attempt to get the most relaxing time or at least a very specific single occasion. Otherwise, clients often report switching back and forth between memories and images and not fully experiencing any single one. Thus, the scene should be a specific memory, a moment in time, like an emotional snapshot from the person's file of life experiences.

These guidelines suggest that the therapist exclude some types of scenes even though they may be relaxing. First, the scene should be a real experience, not a fantasy. When the material is fantasy in nature, clients report a greater likelihood of embellishing or changing the image in ways that are not relaxing and perhaps even angering or distressing. Second, the scene generally should not include a great deal of physical exertion (e.g., engaging in a vigorous bike ride or a hard work out). Although these may have been relaxing, the exertion may become the focus, rather than the relaxing quality. Competitive situations should also be avoided. For example, a person may feel very relaxed after a highly competitive game of tennis with a friend. In a scene like this, however, the focus may be on the competitiveness rather than the feelings of relaxation. Sexually involved scenes may also be relaxing for some people, but they have mixed qualities of relaxation and sexual arousal, so these scenes generally should be avoided. A final issue is substance-involved relaxation scenes (see Tiffany's example below). Visualizing having drinks with good friends is not a useful scene, even though it may be relaxing. If the scene involves alcohol or other substances, there is a risk of encouraging and rehearsing relaxation through behaviors that are dysfunctional in other ways.

Relaxation Scene (David)

Therapist: *One way some people lower frustration is by imagining a scene or image that's relaxing. Last week you spent some time thinking about what scene or image might work for you. Can you please describe that scene to me now? I'm going to take notes to make sure I get it right.*

David: *I chose walking in the woods.*

Therapist: *Can you describe the scene in more detail for me? Sights, sounds, smells, temperature, emotions etc. It's usually helpful to try and focus in on a specific day if it's something you do frequently.*

David: *I see myself hiking along the path and there's the creek on one side and trees everywhere. It's a sunny day but the woods are shady. The temperature is perfect, not hot or cold, and I can hear the wind in the treetops. I hear birds too. I feel relaxed and glad to be away from work.*

Therapist: *I'm not sure if it's true for you, but for some people, an active scene, like hiking or walking, even though it's relaxing, can be challenging to use. I'm wondering if there's also a moment of stillness on your hike, maybe sitting or lying down.*

David: *Again, I'm not one for just sitting around doing nothing but once in a while I like to stop and sit on a big tree stump.*

Therapist: *Are there any other details you want to add when you're sitting on the stump? The purpose of these details is to help you to put yourself right back in that moment, so the clearer they are, the better it should work.*

David: *When I'm sitting on the stump, I usually hear the creek running and I love the smell of the woods but I'm not sure how to describe it. It feels like everything is right with the world for a few minutes.*

Therapist: *So let me just review what you've told me so far. You're in the woods, sitting on a large tree stump* (environmental cues). *It's a sunny day but shady in the woods* (lighting and visual cues). *The temperature is perfect* (temperature cues). *You can hear the wind in the treetops, the running creek, and the chirping birds* (auditory cues). *You're also aware of the smell of the woods, that "woodsy" smell* (olfactory cues). *You feel calm and centered and peaceful. It feels like everything is right in the world* (psychological/emotional cues). *Anything else?*

David: *Nope. That's about it.*

Relaxation Scene (Tiffany)

Below is Tiffany's relaxation scene. It is important to note that this scene was selected specifically as to not involve alcohol consumption. She had previously consumed alcohol when petting and cuddling the cat, and it was important to select a specific, special time not involving alcohol:

Therapist: *It's about three weeks ago. You're sitting on your couch with Tiger (her cat) on your lap. You're petting Tiger* (environmental and scene setting details)*, his fur is really soft (*tactile cues*), and he's purring loudly* (auditory cues). *On this particular day, you're not drinking any alcohol but you have a glass of sweet tea on a coaster on your table* (more external details). *It's the middle of summer and the windows are open. You're feeling comfortably warm* (temperature cues). *You can hear traffic outside and the sound of some birds nearby* (auditory cues). *The air smells tropical because of your air freshener* (olfactory cues). *You're feeling calm and relaxed and grateful to have Tiger who loves you unconditionally and is always there for you* (emotional/psychological cues).

IT'S ALL ABOUT YOU!

During the presentation of relaxation training skills and in-session practice, the therapist weaves in gentle and positive comments to encourage the client's self-attribution of these skills. It is important that the client views him or herself as successfully retrieving relaxation as opposed to believing that this is "done" to the client by the therapist. These gentle comments might include "good, I can see that you are feeling your relaxation," "enjoying the sensations of relaxation that you have created for yourself," and "choosing whichever of the relaxation skills that you do best." Self-attribution is important for all skills acquisition so that the client will begin to feel confident in trusting him or herself to use these skills in the real world.

Progressive Relaxation Training

Progressive relaxation training is introduced as a basic technique for relaxation. The clinician describes it as a way of learning how to relax the body by systematically tensing and then releasing muscle groups. Clients learn how to relax by paying attention to the feelings of tension in the muscles and then the sense of relaxation when they are released. The therapist may want to use the analogy of the feeling relaxed after exercise when the muscles have been tensed and released.

There are many variants of the exact order and means of tensing and releasing muscles during progressive relaxation. One is probably not superior to any other, except that the number of tension-release exercises should be sufficient to address all major muscle areas. The procedure below is the variant used in our work, but other similar approaches could be employed if the clinician is more familiar with those.

BEFORE WE BEGIN...

Here are a number of issues the therapist should consider before starting the first relaxation session:

Glasses that slide down the client's nose. If the therapist notices this happening, the client may be encouraged to remove glasses during relaxation to prevent them from sliding and being distracting.

Jewelry. If the client has jewelry that flops around or makes noise when moved (e.g., bracelet) and proves distracting, the therapist may suggest removing it.

Gum or candy. If the client is chewing gum or sucking on candy, it should be removed. Otherwise, as the client relaxes, it may pose a choking hazard.

Areas of injury, pain, or recent surgery. If the client has areas that are painful or difficult to tense without pain or discomfort, then tension-release exercise sequence should be adapted to prevent the pain or discomfort, which is counterproductive to relaxing.

(*Continued*)

(CONTINUED)

Patients with a history of angina. If the client has a history of angina, clenching the fists tightly may bring on pain. If this is the case, check with the client and modify tension-release sequence accordingly.
A visible signal system. When the client is asked to visualize the personal relaxation scene, the therapist will want to ask if the client is visualizing the scene clearly. This requires a visible signal from the client. Common signals are raising an index finger or a hand a little bit. The therapist should notice positioning of the client and select a signal system that is easily visible.
Questions about hypnosis. Occasionally, clients will ask if the relaxation process is hypnosis; indeed, it is not. The relaxation training is a learning procedure that, with practice, clients can use to rapidly bring feelings of relaxation under their own personal control.

The therapist begins by modeling and demonstrating how the muscles will be tensed and released. This demonstration both provides an example of the technique and also decreases the chances that clients will need to open their eyes and watch the therapist for instruction during the tension-release process. The therapist might introduce this by saying something like:

> *In a few moments, I'm going to have you systematically tense and release the muscles in your body. Before I do that, I want to show you what it'll look like so that you'll know what I'll be asking you to do. We'll start by tensing your hands. I'll ask you to clench both of your hands into tight fists* (Therapist demonstrates). *I'll have you keep them tense for about 10 seconds and ask you to pay attention to the tension in your fists. Then, I'll ask you to release and relax that area. Let the muscles relax quickly and go limp* (as opposed to slowly opening the hands which keeps tension in some of the muscles—Therapist demonstrates). *I'll ask you to pay attention to the difference between tension and relaxation and let the muscles of the hands relax even more and to notice the feelings in that area. After 20–30 seconds, we'll move to the next muscle area which will be the forearms. You'll tense this area by extending your arms in front of you and bending your hands back at the wrist tightening those muscles like you're pushing a heavy object in front of you* (Therapist demonstrates). *Same process, about 10 seconds tension and then 20–30 seconds of releasing tension and increasing relaxation. We'll repeat this through the following muscles* (therapist demonstrates each).

- *Upper arms* by clenching fists and bending the arms about 45 degrees flexing the upper arms and forearms.
- *Shoulders* by shrugging and pulling the shoulder blades back and together.

- *Forehead* by frowning deeply or by lifting the eyebrows upward (client chooses which will tense the area best).
- *Eyes and bridge of the nose* by squinting very tightly.
- *Cheeks, jaw, and lips* by grinning widely from ear to ear with lips pressed together.
- *Chin and neck* by pressing chin downward and forward trying to bury the chin on the chest and tightening neck and throat at same time.
- *Chest and back* by taking a very deep breath and holding it while arching the back from the shoulders and hips.
- *Stomach* by hardening the stomach and abdominal muscles while continuing to breathe normally.
- *Thighs* by lifting the feet off the floor slightly and clenching the thighs and upper legs.
- *Lower legs* by lifting the feet off the floor slightly and bending the toes back toward the knees.
- *Lower legs and feet* by lifting the feet off the floor and point the feet and toes down and away.

Describing the last tension-release exercise is a good place to reiterate the purpose and process of progressive relaxation.

> *That covers the tension-release process we'll be going through, but be careful with this last exercise. If tensed too hard the toes or the arch of the foot can cramp up. With all the exercises, tense the muscles firmly but not to the point of pain or cramping. Remember also to tense and then let go quickly and focus on the difference between tension and relaxation in that area. Do you have any questions about what we're going to do with tensing and releasing the muscles?*
>
> *I'll start by having you close your eyes and take a few deep breaths. Then, I'll have you tense and release the muscles like I just showed you. When we've completed the tension and release process, I'll have you visualize your relaxation scene a couple of times before we're through. How does that sound? Do you have any questions?*

SUPPLEMENTAL TENSION-RELEASE EXERCISES

There are additional tension-release exercises that may be useful for some clients, especially if they tend to be tense in these areas.

- *Lips and mouth* by pressing the lips together very firmly.
- *Back of the neck from the base of the skull to shoulders* by pressing head backward and downward firmly.

(*Continued*)

(CONTINUED)

- *Middle and lower back* by arching the back from the hips and shoulders (i.e., splitting the single tension-release exercise described above into two parts by taking a deep breath expanding the chest an upper back as one exercise and tensing the middle and lower back as another).
- *Stomach and abdominal area* by sucking the stomach in as far as possible as if trying to have the navel reach the backbone.
- *Waist, hips, and buttocks* by clenching the buttocks together very firmly.

Ok, we're now ready to begin the relaxation process. Let's begin by having you settle in the chair comfortably with your arms and legs uncrossed (this is done to reduce the chances of some muscles falling asleep as the client relaxes). *Now, just close your eyes and settle back...*(5–10 seconds)... *Now let's have you take 3–4 big deep breaths to start clearing out tension* (This is partly done to anticipate deep breathing cued relaxation in the next session)...*That's it. Take a big deep breath* (therapist taking an audible, deep breath and breathing out to cue the client) *and let the tension out as you exhale...That's it. Now another nice big deep breath, holding it for a moment and then exhaling, letting tension flow out as you breathe out...* (therapist repeats another 2–4 times).

Now let's start tensing and releasing the various muscle groups we went through earlier. Let's start first with the hands. So, clench both hands into tight fists...That's it. Feel the tension around the fingers, knuckles and hands as you tense those muscles...Hold it and now relax and let those muscles go quickly (tensing lasting approximately 10 seconds)...*Now notice the feelings in the fingers, knuckles and hands...Notice how they feel different than a few moments ago when they were all tight and tense...You may notice that your hands are warmer or that the muscles or fingers twitch a little bit as they relax...Letting the feelings of tension flow out and relaxation flow in around the fingers and hands...*(focus on the hands for about 20–30 seconds)...*Ok, now let's move to the muscles of the forearms...*(in a similar manner, the therapist moves through the remainder of the muscles tensing and releasing them in a similar manner).

Insert *muscle reviews without tension* in four places: (1) after the shoulders, to review the arms and hands; (2) after tensing the neck, to review the head and neck; (3) after the stomach, to review the chest, back, and stomach/abdominal area; and (4) after the feet, to review the legs. We do this to increase a sense of relaxation and to anticipate relaxation without tension in the next session or two. Instructions for shoulder/arms/hands review might be like the following with other reviews without tension being similar, but focusing on the other three areas:

> (after completing the shoulder tension-release exercise)...*Let's take a moment or two to review the muscles we've just been through. I'm going to mention each muscle group, and when I do, I want you to focus on it and increase the relaxation a bit more but without tensing the muscles. So, focus on the shoulders and let a little more tension out of there without tensing that area...It may be like a wave or flow of relaxation increasing in that area...Just let that wave of relaxation now move down through the muscles of the upper arms...just loosening and relaxing the upper arms more...and now letting it flow down through the forearms...allowing the forearms to become more relaxed...and now moving it through the wrists, hands and fingers...just draining remaining tension out the tips of your fingers...taking a moment to enjoy the feelings of relaxation that you've been creating and will be able to use to reduce your anger* (Therapist is giving a suggestion of future self-control and self-efficacy)...*So, now let's shift our attention to the head and neck region, starting with tensing the forehead*...(continuing with tension-release exercises).

When the lower legs, feet, and the muscle review without tension have been completed, then the therapist is ready to transition to presentation to the client's relaxation scene. It is suggested that the relaxation scene be presented twice. Sometimes, the first visualization is harder to do than the second, so repeating it provides a greater opportunity for success. Instructions might be something like:

> *Now I'd like to help you relax by visualizing your relaxation scene. In a moment, I'm going to ask you to visualize your scene involving* (provide brief description to remind the person of their scene). *When I ask you to switch that scene on, I want you to put yourself right back into that situation. Be there like it's happening to you right now. When you're visualizing it clearly and are relaxed, please signal me by raising your right index finger* (or whatever signal system is easy and visible to the therapist). *So, right now, put yourself back into this situation*...(Therapist describes scene along with the emotional/psychological detail) (the therapist acknowledges the signal of scene visualization)...*Good, I see your signal...Just continue visualizing that scene and really being there* (Therapist description along with suggestions to be there and experience the relaxation, calmness, peaceful feelings, etc. involved in the scene)...(after a minute or so of visualizing the scene, it is terminated)...*Ok, now switch that scene off now, and shift your attention back to the sense of relaxation in your body....Just relaxing more and more...perhaps relaxing more with each*

normal breath out. . .(20 seconds or so later, the relaxation scene is presented again). . .*In a moment, I'd like you to visualize your relaxation scene again. Like we did before, I want you to put yourself right back in that situation, really be there and experience it and the relaxation, signaling me when you are visualizing the scene clearly. So right now, put yourself right back into*. . .(therapist describes and then terminates the scene as before).

At this point, the client is at least moderately relaxed and so a procedure is needed to gently terminate the exercise and help the client become more alert and focused in order to debrief the relaxation training experience. A simple procedure is to slowly count backward from 5 to 1 as in the following:

(after the relaxation scene has been cleared for the second time). . .*Just focusing on the feelings of relaxation you have been creating for yourself*. . .*You're probably feeling more relaxed than you were before we started. I'd like to alert you gently from this state of relaxation by counting backwards from 5 to 1. On the count of 4, move your arms and legs gently to help them become more alert. On the count of 2, open your eyes and look around. On the count of 1, you will be alert, but still relaxed and refreshed*. . .*So, I will now begin counting*. . .*5*. . .*4*. . .*beginning to move your arms and legs a bit*. . .*3*. . .*feeling no aches or pains*. . .*2*. . .*opening your eyes*. . .*1*. . .*alert and refreshed.*

The client is given a few moments to become more alert and refreshed, and then the experience is debriefed. Typically, the therapist would inquire in an open-ended manner about (1) the general nature of the experience, (2) areas that were easy to relax, (3) areas that were difficult to relax, (4) any uncomfortable experiences or difficulties, and (5) the clarity and feelings of calm from the personal scene visualization. Generally, experiences tend to be positive, which is reinforced and linked to the notion that clients will become better and faster at relaxing as they practice these procedures. Regarding areas that were difficult to relax, two suggestions are made. First, that the client pay attention to see if anger is experienced more intensely in these areas. Often, this is the case. Clients can be encouraged to track these and use increased tension in these areas as a cue to initiate relaxation coping. Second, the client might be encouraged to repeat the tension-release exercise for a difficult area twice before moving to the next tension-release exercise. Minor difficulties (e.g., feeling itchy, jumpy, having one's mind wander) may be noted by the client. It is suggested that the therapist acknowledge the issue but not focus on it too much. The client can be reassured that these issues tend to generally decrease as the client practices the procedures. This reassurance is not hollow. In fact, most of these problems tend to fade with time. If the scene was not clear or easily visualized on the second presentation, clients may be asked what additional detail would make it more realistic. If scene clarity and involvement do not improve in home practice, a new relaxation scene may need to be generated.

Target exercises for relaxation for the coming week involve practicing relaxation procedures daily, or at least 5 of the next 7 days, and recording experiences on the relaxation log (see Appendix II). Home practice of relaxation is facilitated by a written set of instructions for setting up home practice and a list of the muscles and how they can be tensed (also available in Appendix II).

CAN I BRING YOU HOME WITH ME?

Sometimes, clients will ask for a recording of the therapist giving the relaxation instructions so that they can use this recording for home practice. We have come to discourage this. For many clients, it may initially be easier to have the therapist's voice and instructions. However, there is a tendency for them to become reliant to the recorded instructions rather than internalizing the processes and being able to do it on their own. Use of written instructions reduces the reliance on an external source (the therapist's voice and instructions) while providing information and memory prompts sufficient to support home practice.

ZZZZZZZZZZ. . .

Infrequently, clients will become so relaxed that they fall asleep during the in-session relaxation practice. Therapists may suspect this if a client does not follow instructions to do a tension-release exercise or if the client appears inattentive. The following simple procedures are effective in addressing this problem. The therapist might say, "Give me a signal if you can hear my voice." If no signal is apparent, then the same question can be asked in a negative way. Specifically, "If you cannot hear my voice, please signal me." Absence of a signal to both questions suggests that the person is asleep. If that is the case, then the therapist can tell the client that the therapist will get up and gently shake his or her wrist. Then, the therapist can put the thumb on one side of the wrist, the fingers on the other side, and gently rotate the wrist back and forth until the client wakes up (e.g., opens eyes, gives some verbal acknowledgment). The relaxation procedures are continued with an instruction something in the order of "Ok now we return to relaxation. So, now staying at a higher level of alertness."

The Next Session's Review

At this point in anger management based alcohol treatment (about the beginning of the fourth session), the client will have completed two target exercises relevant to anger reduction. These are the initial relaxation skills (relaxation scene and progressive relaxation training) and identifying angry thoughts and anger-provoking situations on the self-monitoring log. These should be reviewed at the beginning of the subsequent session.

Clients' between-session use of the relaxation exercises is tracked on the relaxation log which is reviewed for amount of and experience with practice. Clients typically practice sufficiently at five or more times in the past week or insufficiently with none, one, or two times.

- If practice is sufficient and experiences have been good, then the client is ready to move to a modification of relaxation training (see later descriptions). If the client practiced, but experienced difficulties, then the nature of these difficulties is explored. Modifications in procedures are made as needed, and the client continues the initial relaxation practice for another week, including any modifications made.
- If practice is insufficient, reasons should be explored:
  - A fairly common problem is that the client keeps falling asleep when starting to practice. Often, this can be addressed by finding another time to practice, for example, at 5:00 p.m. when just home from work, rather than at 7:00 p.m. when more tired and sluggish from dinner. Alternatively, it may be important to find a less comfortable place to practice, for example, sitting up in a chair rather than lying on a bed.
  - Other explanations for noncompliance involve not having time or other things interfering with practice. Reasons should be explored nonjudgmentally and pragmatically while also reviewing client reasons for engaging in anger reduction therapy and encouraging therapeutic tasks like relaxation practice. Following discussion of these issues, recommitment to completing relaxation is garnered and the relaxation target exercises are reviewed.
- Sometimes, either of two misunderstandings regarding relaxation practice is involved in the client not practicing.
  - First, the client may have thought he/she was only to practice when angry. He/she did not practice relaxation because he/she was not frequently angry the past week. The importance of practice for skill development is reiterated and rationale for home practice of relaxation activities is given again.
  - Second, the client may have misunderstood, thinking that the initial form of relaxation will be the way they cope with anger and, therefore, did not see the utility practicing. Here is an example of such a misunderstanding:

Therapist: *How did the relaxation practice go this past week?*

Stephan: *I practiced once, but quit about half way through. I was thinking that this didn't make any sense. I can't stop in the middle of a big hassle at work and do all of this muscle tension stuff. I would look stupid and it would take too much time. I don't see the point.*

Therapist: *You were thinking that you'll have use the full process we went through last week to cope with anger.*

Stephan: *Yeah. Isn't that what you said?*

Therapist: *Not exactly, but you're absolutely right on one thing: what we practiced last week would not be very useful, especially in your line of work! The goal was for you practice those skills so you can start to develop a relaxation response. With time and practice, you'll be able to find a way to relax in a minute or less. I want you to find effective, quick tools that you could use anytime, anywhere. So, basically, what we went through last week is not the final product. Practicing the skills for a couple of weeks will give us the basis for shortening them. Does that make sense?*

Stephan: *Ok. That makes a lot more sense. I just kept picturing myself lying down in the busy kitchen at work and tensing up my muscles while everyone threw food at me and laughed hysterically!*

Therapist: *That's quite an image! So to make sure we're on the same page, can you tell me in your own words what you now think the practice is good for?*

Stephan: *Yeah—I practice all this stuff now and eventually find quick and easy ways to relax anytime without everyone knowing and harassing me!*

Therapist: *You've got it.*

Relaxation Coping Skills and Their Development

Five relaxation coping skills or combinations thereof have shown both effectiveness and acceptability among clients. Each skill is described below along with ways to train and practice them.

Breathing-Cued Relaxation

Breathing-cued relaxation is an extension of the deep breathing from progressive relaxation training. It involves the client taking a very deep breath, pulling the diaphragm down so that the stomach rises or pushes out. That breath is held a few moments and then is released slowly, releasing tension and increasing relaxation as the air is slowly exhaled. This is repeated 6–8 times with the client relaxing more on each out breath. The number of breaths taken and released is up to the client. One client may find 3–4 breaths sufficient, whereas another may prefer 8–12. The number is not as important as the effect that it has on the client. Instructions for breathing-cued relaxation might be introduced as follows:

> *Ok, now let's increase relaxation by focusing on our breathing. Take a big deep breath and hold it...That's it...Now exhale and relax. Let the tension flow out with the air and be replaced by relaxation...Ok, now another big deep breath...Hold it and now breathe out and relax...Focusing on increasing that relaxed feeling as you breathe out...One more time now. A big deep breath and hold it...Exhale and relax...Ok, now you repeat it a few more times on your own. Big breath in and relax as you exhale...*(watching the client and maybe 20 seconds later another prompt)*...That's it. Big deep breath really filling up the stomach area and relaxing as you exhale.*

Breathing-cued relaxation is a very flexible coping skill. It can be employed in most situations that do not require continuous talking. Even in situations involving talking, clients can usually take 2–4 slow deep breaths and relax during the natural breaks in conversation. Additionally, breathing-cued relaxation is easily combined with many other relaxation coping skills.

Cue-Controlled Relaxation

Based on learning and conditioning principles, if a word or short phrase is repeatedly paired with a deep state of relaxation, the word itself will become conditioned to the relaxed state and help to trigger relaxation. A single word or a short phrase is developed by or tailored to the client. Common cues include "relax," "calm," "calm control," "peaceful," or "chill." It might even be a color like "green" or "yellow" that has a calm association or meaning to the client. Whatever the word or phrase, it is paired and associated with a state of relaxation through instructions such as:

> *Let's now relax in a little bit different way. I'm going to slowly repeat the word "relax." Each time you hear it the word "relax," focus on your feelings of relaxation and let yourself relax just a little more. So, just let yourself "relax"...*(The space between repetitions is about 10 seconds. The therapist may want to take slow breaths as a cue for saying the word relax.)*...That's it just "relax."...."Relax"...Just "relax"...* (This is repeated 8–10 times total.)*...Now you do that on your own. Say the word "relax" slowly to yourself and let yourself relax more each time you say it. Perhaps, saying it each time you breathe out slowly....*(after 20–30 seconds the therapist may want to add a prompt)*...Good. Just relaxing more*

each time you say the word "relax" to yourself....(This is discontinued when the therapist has estimated that the client has repeated the word or phrase 8–10 times.)

Cue-controlled relaxation is also a very flexible skill and can be applied almost any place and time. It is easily combined with other relaxation coping skills, especially by being said on each exhale during breathing-cued relaxation.

Relaxation Without Tension

By this time in treatment, relaxation without tension has been previewed in the muscle group reviews built into basic progressive relaxation training. Initially, relaxation *without* tension involves focusing on each muscle group and letting the tension out while relaxation increases, all without tensing the muscles first. If the clients have time, they can do a full body scan in this manner. However, many clients find that there are certain areas (e.g., jaw, shoulders, neck, or fists) where the experience of tension is particularly noticeable. Attention is therefore focused on those muscles, letting tension flow out and relaxation flow in. Initial instructions follow the sequence as in initial relaxation training, focusing on each muscle group for about 10–15 seconds much like:

This week we're going to relax the muscles, but without tensing them. When I mention a muscle group, I want you to focus your attention there and relax it without tensing the muscles. Just focus there and relax, retrieving that comfortable feeling. So, let's start with the hands. Focus your attention there and relax your hands... increasing the relaxed, perhaps warm feeling around the fingers and hand...feeling more relaxation there...Now shift your attention to the forearms...Just let relaxation replace the tension in your forearms...you may feel that comfortable wave of relaxation moving through your forearms...And now let that relaxation flow into the upper arms...(and so forth through the remainder of the body).

As noted previously, clients will often focus on a specific set or group of muscles that are most problematic for them. Many find that letting a flow or wave of relaxation move through that area 3–4 times consecutively helps bring about the relaxation. This is often combined with deep breathing. The client takes a deep breath and lets the wave of relaxation flow through an area such as the neck and shoulders. A variation of this is that some clients will use the four muscle review areas, take a deep breath, and let the relaxation wash through the full area, repeating this 3–4 times. Once developed, relaxation without tension is very flexible, can be adapted to the client's personal experience of tension, and is easily combined with other relaxation coping skills.

Adaptation of Tension-Release Exercises

If a client finds specific tension-release exercises useful to release tension from one problem muscle area, then it is possible to tailor tension-release exercises as an active coping skill. For example, the client might shrug the shoulders for 10–15 seconds and then relax them for 20–30 seconds. This could be repeated 2–4 times. A client with stomach tension might tighten the abdomen in a similar way 2–4 times. The use of specific tension-release exercises can be adapted to the type of provocation and frustration encountered. The skills can be deployed in almost any situation where the client is alone (e.g., a time before or after a provocation, when alone ruminating). Use of the skills in more active, ongoing anger is dependent on the exercise and the situation. For example, squinting the eyes is inappropriate for driving but might be adapted to angry phone calls. However, the shoulder shrugging and stomach clenching might be easily adapted to driving. In summary, specific tension-release exercises may be adapted for clients who found them useful for a specific area of problem anger tension.

Personal Relaxation Scene

The personal relaxation scene described earlier can be deployed as a relaxation coping skill itself. Obviously, use of the personal relaxation scene as a coping skill is limited in situations where the person must keep the eyes open (e.g., driving or interacting with other people). However, it can still have many applications. For example, the relaxation image can be used while planning for or just before dealing with an angering event. It can also be used to cope with the aftermath of an angering situation, either just after the event or later when reviewing what happened. When experiencing the latter, the personal relaxation scene can be employed to help calm the mind in the face of angry ruminations. And finally, the relaxation scene (and other relaxation coping skills) can be used to combat a number of distressing states associated with alcohol and other substances (e.g., irritation, agitation, cravings, and lowered frustration threshold).

I JUST CAN'T SEE IT...

Occasionally, clients find that relaxation scenes are ineffective. Two reasons typically account for this. First, some clients find visualization a difficult task. We suggest that clients not worry because visualization often improves with practice. The relaxation scene can be sharpened with details that may help when it is rehearsed again. If problems continue, we suggest the relaxation scene be de-emphasized because the client will likely find other relaxation coping skills effective. Second, some clients are

(*Continued*)

(CONTINUED)

unable to identify an image that is relaxing. They should be encouraged to continue to think back over time to see if they can identify such an experience. If one is located, then develop the scene as outlined and add it to the relaxation activities. Some clients, however, continue to report that they cannot locate a relaxation image, often reporting life is just too stressful to have relaxation in it or that alcohol and drugs were always present. We suggest two things. First, as with those who cannot visualize easily, they will likely find other relaxation methods that work. Second, consider the issue of depression. Sometimes, clients who report a lack of relaxation and calmness can be depressed.

READY TO TRY IT...

An issue that commonly comes up is whether clients should at this point start to employ relaxation coping skills for the reduction of anger or other negative emotions (e.g., anxiety, fear, embarrassment). This is a clinical dilemma. On the one hand, the client may try the skills on their own and gain benefit. On the other hand, active in-session coping skills rehearsals (Chapter 11: Coping Skills Rehearsal), which maximize the probability of success, have not yet taken place. Our suggested approach is to support client application but caution that efforts may not work yet and that future sessions will provide practice controlling anger and increase chances of success.

Summary

A variety of relaxation exercises and techniques have been reviewed. Although we encourage substantial practice of these exercises to develop the client's ability to relax rapidly, it is not uncommon for the client to eventually focus on three or four skills on a regular basis. This ability to relax rapidly is the key first skill step in anger management based alcohol treatment. In the next chapter, we will prepare the therapist to take the second step for this treatment: development of cognitive coping skills.

Suggested Readings

Deffenbacher, J. L., Demm, P. M., & Brandon, A. D. (1986). High general anger: Correlates and treatment. *Behaviour Research and Therapy*, *24*, 481–489.

Authors suggested that lesser effects for relaxation in Novaco's (1975) study may have been due to the compressed time frame and lack of active coping skills training. Intervention time was lengthened from 2.5 to 8 weeks and coping skills training to reduce anger elicited by anger imagery was included. Relaxation was significantly more effective than the control, and effects appeared more robust than those found by Novaco. Subsequent research has supported the effectiveness of relaxation coping skills and its equivalency to other interventions.

Deffenbacher, J. L., & Stark, R. S. (1992). Relaxation and cognitive-relaxation treatments of general anger. *Journal of Counseling Psychology*, *39*, 158–167.

This study compared relaxation and cognitive-relaxation interventions for general anger reduction. Both interventions were equally effective and significantly better than the control. Effects were maintained through short- and long-term follow-ups.

Novaco, R. W. (1975). *Anger control: The development and evaluation of an experimental treatment.* Lexington, MA: Heath.

This landmark research was the first well-controlled anger intervention study. Cognitive, relaxation, and combined cognitive-relaxation interventions were compared to a control for general anger reduction. The relaxation intervention was somewhat effective, but the cognitive and cognitive-relaxation interventions were superior to relaxation. The author concluded that the cognitive element was the critical component in the combined condition.

Chapter 10

Cognitive Coping Skills

Chapter Points

- Cognitive therapy focuses on identifying, challenging, and modifying thoughts about alcohol, anger-increasing thoughts, and other cognitive distortions.
- Cognitive restructuring has several overlapping steps, and completing each step is important to achieve good outcomes.
- We present eight categories of anger-increasing cognitive distortions, common examples of each, and potentially relevant coping thoughts.

Questions for Self-Reflection

- How do you separate thoughts from feelings in your own life?
- How do you react to clients whose thoughts or ideas you find unlikeable?

Tiffany: *It's funny. At work I'm actually good at dealing with customers on the phone and some of them get real angry; it's part of our training and they use my recordings a lot to show new workers how it's done. I know the people calling aren't mad at me so I'm good at staying calm*

Anger Management Based Alcohol Treatment. DOI: https://doi.org/10.1016/B978-0-12-812709-4.00010-X

and talking them back down so I can help them. But I can't find a way to do that in my real life. I fly off the handle at the smallest thing and can't walk by a mirror without getting pissed off and almost wanting to cry. It's like there's two of me.

Introduction to Cognition

Relaxation interventions target the increased physiological arousal components of anger and cravings for alcohol. Cognitive processes are also heavily involved in the development and experience of anger and alcohol problems. It is important to assist clients in understanding that anger and anger-alcohol connections are strongly influenced by the way that they think about, make meaning out of, and mentally process events. That is, anger and alcohol use are strongly influenced by certain beliefs, ways people think about themselves and others, primary and secondary appraisals, attributions, internalized cultural and family norms, important personal rules for living, and tasks to be achieved. We respond to our internal cognitively-constructed world in addition to our immediate physical and social environment. Some cognitive processes leave us grounded and may lead to mild to moderate anger or other negative states such as disappointment, sadness, and concern. Other cognitive processes, however, distort and exaggerate, leading to strong anger (e.g., fury, rage, "mad as hell") and potentially to aggression or other dysfunctional ways of expressing anger including problematic drinking.

As described in Chapter 2, cognitive interventions, as part of Cognitive Behavior Therapy (CBT), are effective in the treatment of alcohol use disorders. Cognitive interventions are also empirically supported for anger reduction (Dahlen & Deffenbacher, 2000; Deffenbacher, 2009; Deffenbacher, Dahlen, Lynch, Morris, & Gowensmith, 2000; Hazaleus & Deffenbacher, 1986; Novaco, 1975). Cognitive coping skills are effective for both general anger and angry drivers. Cognitive interventions for anger are as effective as relaxation, behavioral, and cognitive-relaxation approaches.

Cognitive restructuring targets dysfunctional cognitive processes, lowering both anger and cravings while freeing up capacities to plan, solve problems, and cope in more constructive ways. That is, cognitive interventions help clients identify their personal cognitive processes, develop calmer, less distorted coping thoughts, and rehearse them so they can employ cognitive coping skills for anger reduction and sobriety in everyday life.

Cognitive restructuring involves five overlapping steps. The first three are described in this chapter and the latter two in the next chapter where we discuss how cognitive coping skill training is integrated with relaxation coping skills. These five steps are:

- Becoming aware of and identifying anger and anger/alcohol cognitive processes.
- Understanding and accepting the influence of cognitions on anger and alcohol use.
- Recognizing cognitive distortions and developing reality-based alternatives and coping thoughts to challenge these distortions.
- Rehearsing these cognitive coping thoughts with guidance in a controlled environment.
- Transferring cognitive coping to the everyday environment so that clients have reliable application of cognitive coping skills to manage anger and support sobriety.

Enhancing Awareness of Cognitive Processes

Cognitive processes are highly automatic and may operate quickly and outside of consciousness. People are often unaware of what they are thinking, and they do not naturally "think" about their thinking. An important first step then is to assist clients to become aware of cognitive processes.

A simple, but effective way to assist clients in understanding the importance of cognitions is the ABC (**A**ctivating Events → **B**eliefs → **C**onsequences) model. "A" stands for activating event (triggers). The "B" or beliefs (thoughts, images, attributions, appraisals, and interpretations) filter and shape the "C" or the consequences (emotional and behavioral outcomes). Often, clients think A (the event) automatically causes C (their anger and/or drinking). Cognitive interventions are about understanding how the Bs (the beliefs) lead to elevated anger, cravings, and dysfunctional behavior.

For example, in introducing the ABC model (see Fig. 10.1) the therapist might say to Stephan:

> *When you're angry and pissed off, it often seems like someone or something (activating event or "A") causes all the anger ("C" or emotional consequence). But that's not the whole story. What's really happening is the event leads us to start thinking about how bad, and unfair things are, about how someone is threating, harming, taking advantage of or disrespecting us. It's these thoughts or beliefs that trigger the anger, not the event alone.*
>
> *Remember when you got so pissed at Michael for expecting you to do most of the household chores and ended up drinking too much? You were really angry, and you were thinking a whole bunch of things like: "Damn it. He*

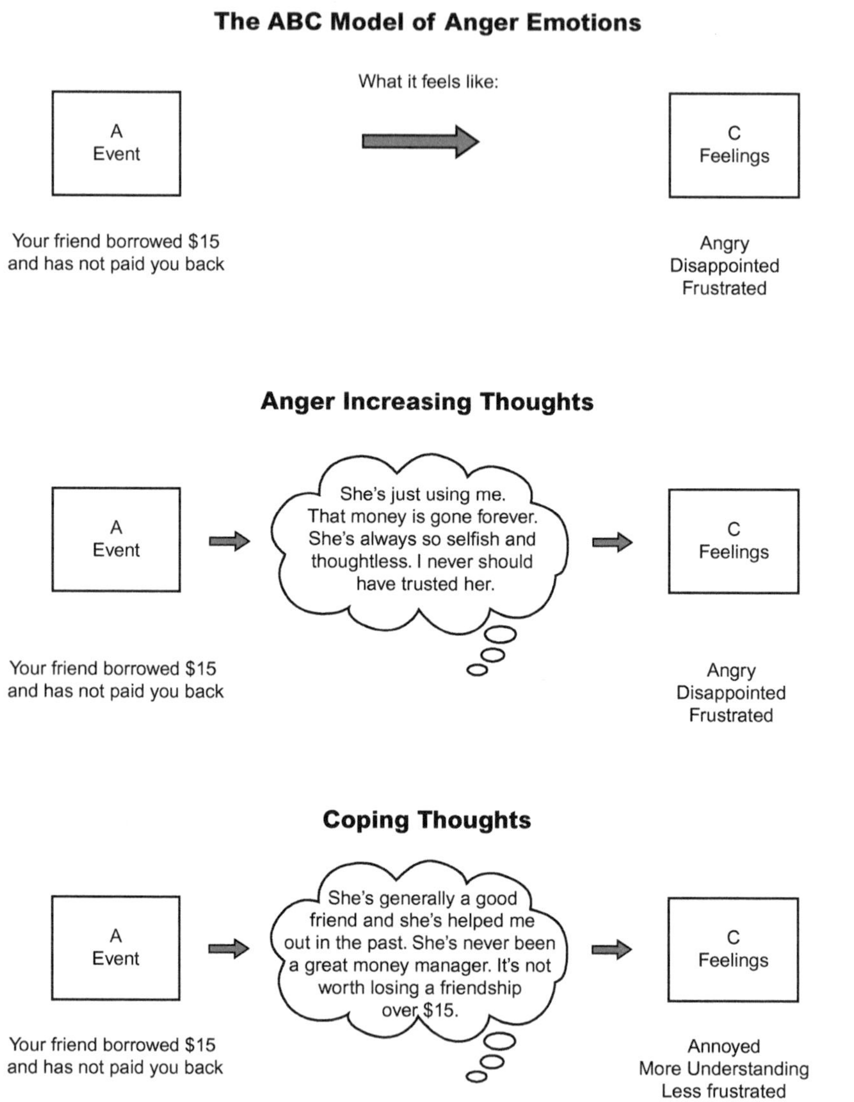

Figure 10.1 The ABC model of cognitive processes.

doesn't give a shit about how I feel." "He's taking me for granted." "He's so selfish." "He doesn't respect me or how hard I work." "He looks down on me because I earn less money than he does." "He does this just to piss me off and get back at me." His snobby attitude makes me drink! What I'm suggesting is that it was those thoughts, in addition to his behavior, that made you so angry, and led you to yell at him, start another fight, and get drunk.

We're going to work together to understand how those thoughts influence your anger and your drinking. Thoughts are kind of like marriages; some are for better and some are for worse. We'll want to help you strengthen the better ones and change the worse ones.

The ABC model of cognitive restructuring provides a general way of understanding the influence of cognitive processes (B) on emotions and behaviors (C). However, clients are often unaware of these mediating thoughts. The first step is thus to enhance awareness. In the initial alcohol and anger assessments and discussion of angering events, the therapist can help clients identify cognitive processes by using open-ended questions that focus on cognitions. For example, *What was going through your mind as you experienced that? Tell me what you think about that? If I could have a recorder in your head when that was going on, what would I hear you thinking about it? When you're really craving a drink, what thoughts run through your mind?* Answers to such questions help clients begin to identify their thought processes.

A good way to help clients identify cognitive processes is by having them self-monitor angering events and cravings for alcohol between sessions and identify their thoughts in real time on the self-monitoring logs. Exploring logs in an open-ended manner helps clients begin to become aware of their cognitive processes.

One of the early steps in CBT for alcohol use disorder is to help clients recognize and change drinking-related cognitions. With help from the therapist, clients learn to identify thoughts that reinforce drinking, challenge those thoughts, and replace them with alternatives.

Examples of drinking-related thoughts:

- *A drink will help me calm down.*
- *Drinking gives me a break from my problems.*
- *I deserve a drink.*
- *Alcohol relaxes me.*
- *I drink a lot but I still function.*

Examples of challenging/alternative thoughts:

- *Drinking doesn't always calm me down; sometimes it gets me in more trouble.*
- *Drinking is just a temporary break; it doesn't solve the problem, and it usually makes things worse.*
- *There must be a healthier way to reward myself.*
- *I want to be able to relax without all the other problems drinking causes.*
- *Maybe I'd be doing more with my life if I wasn't drinking.*

Some clients, even those who are easily able to recognize their thoughts about alcohol, have considerable difficulty identifying the cognitive processes around anger. Hyperbole, perhaps to the point of silliness, may help. Here's an example of Stephan who was significantly angry (60–70 ratings) with his husband but resisted identifying his thoughts.

Therapist: *You're good at telling me how you FEEL about your husband, but not how you THINK about his treatment of you. I'm wondering how you'd feel if you were thinking the following: "Michael is the worst husband ever. A total jerk! I'm completely fed up with his game playing. He deserves the worst, maybe three life sentences without the possibility of parole. And I'd like to turn the key on his jail cell!"*

Stephan: *Well, I'd feel really pissed off if all that was true but I don't think he's that bad. He's just insensitive at times and can't express his feelings very well. He has a tough time listening and being really present when we have something important to talk about.*

Therapist: *You think Michael has difficulty listening and being comfortable with emotional communication.*

Stephan: *Exactly. And given his parents' crappy relationship, it's no wonder he can't deal with emotional things. All they ever did was fight or give each other the "silent treatment."*

Therapist: *Sounds like you have a pretty good understanding of why Michael may have these problems and that's helpful. On the other hand, you don't like how Michael's issues cause problems in your relationship. It's frustrating for you.*

A hyperbole in the opposite direction could have also been taken.

Therapist: *You're good at telling me how you FEEL regarding your husband, but not how THINK about his treatment of you. I'm wondering how you would feel if you were thinking the following: "Michael is the most wonderful husband ever. I love it when he doesn't listen to me, closes me out, and doesn't tell me how he feels. I'm really looking forward to another 30–40 years of this."*

Stephan: *You've got to be kidding me! I told you I'm really angry and frustrated about communicating with him.*

Therapist: *I understand, but what I'm curious about is how you would be feeling if you had the kinds of thoughts I just mentioned.*

Stephan: *Well, I guess I'd feel happy with Michael and thrilled with the way he communicates.*

Therapist: *Exactly. You'd feel very different from how you do feel, which is angry and frustrated with your emotional communications. As silly and wrong as the thoughts I suggested were, you acknowledge that different* ***thoughts*** *would lead you to* ***feel*** *differently. That's why it's important for us to continue to work on identifying thoughts and how they influence your feelings. How does that sound to you?*

Accepting the Importance of Cognitive Processes

Relaxation interventions make intuitive sense to most clients. Being able to relax allows them to calm down and achieve better control. However, with cognitive interventions the link is not so obvious. Even as clients become more aware of their cognitions, they often still accept them as "truths" or "face valid" without questioning. Therapists, therefore, will need to help clients accept that their thoughts influence their feelings and that they can question and change their thoughts.

In reviewing self-monitoring, the therapist might notice that the intensity of anger and cravings to drink differs in similar situations. Clients often use phrases like "I thought about it differently," or "I had a different perspective," or "I was having a good day." The contrast in reactions to similar circumstances provides the bridge for accepting that cognitions make a difference.

Therapist: *In reviewing your anger log, I noticed something. On Monday when Michael made a comment about the dishes not being done, you didn't seem too angry, you gave it a 40, but on Friday when you made a similar entry, you were really pissed at 75. Why are they so different?*

Stephan: *Well, on Monday, I'd been working in the garden and it was a beautiful day so I was in a good mood when he got home. He commented on the dirty dishes but it didn't bother me so much.*

Therapist: *What do you mean it didn't bother you so much?*

Stephan: *I was in a good mood and decided it wasn't worth ruining the day with a fight.*

Therapist: *You were feeling good and decided it wasn't worth getting mad. So what happened on Friday that made it so much worse when you encountered the same thing?*

Stephan: *I was exhausted and crabby from work and I just wasn't in the mood for his sanctimonious critical asshole routine.*

Therapist: *So, you were thinking he was being an asshole and being critical. What else were you thinking at the time?*

Stephan: *This isn't fair; I work hard too. Why should I have to do all the housework? He always pulls crap like this. He's so f-ing judgmental. I was really pissed.*

Therapist: *So, on Friday, when you were thinking this isn't fair, he always does this to me, he's so judgmental, you were really mad. But on Monday, when you were thinking it's just not worth ruining a beautiful day, it wasn't so bad.*

Stephan: *That's right.*

Therapist: *The situation was similar both days so what made the difference in how mad you were and whether you yelled at him?*

Stephan: *Well, I was looking at things differently.*

Therapist: *You hit on an important point. How you look at it makes a big difference. We're going to spend some time figuring out ways for you to have more reactions like the one on Monday. That make sense?*

Stephan: *Sure does. Monday we ended up doing the dishes together and I didn't even think about a drink. I'd rather have that than the horrible fight we had on Friday and the hangover I had on Saturday!*

To further examine the connection between thoughts and anger emotions, the therapist can use a description of a recent anger event in different way to get an emotional contrast. Before exploring the event, the client would be asked to rate his/her current anger level for the event on the 0–100 intensity scale. Next, the client and therapist explore the event. The therapist makes every effort to engage the client cognitively in discussing the event by focusing on the anger increasing thoughts. At the end of the discussion, the therapist again asks the client to rate his/her current anger level. The rating is likely to be higher. The therapist points out the contrast by noting that nothing in the situation had changed. The therapist helps the client to realize that it was *thinking about and recalling* the anger event that made the difference. Again, the point is made that what one is *thinking about* makes a critical difference.

In summary, an important task of cognitively oriented therapy is not only an awareness of cognitive processes but also an understanding and acceptance of their impact. Activities like the one above have the client experience and explore how reactions change as a function of different thought patterns, while situational parameters are the same. That is, thoughts matter.

An example of introducing the cognitive concept of anger with Tiffany is presented below.

Tiffany's Cognitive Anger Concept Introduction

Therapist: *The main goal of our session today is to recognize how thoughts impact anger emotions. Once you understand how your thoughts influence emotion, you can choose to distance yourself from thoughts that increase anger emotions and open the door to more calming thoughts.*

Tiffany: *I don't know what you mean.*

Therapist: *Ok, let me back up a bit first and talk about having anger emotions. Having anger emotions is something we all experience—it's a normal process. So how do we move from experiencing an event to feeling these angry emotions? When we get frustrated, we usually blame a situation or event for causing our frustration.*

Tiffany: *I get that. Someone disrespects me and I get pissed off.*

Therapist: *That's usually how it feels when it's happening. But I'd like you to consider this: what if the event, someone disrespecting you, starts you thinking about how bad or unfair the situation is and it's these thoughts that set off your anger? In your mind, you're labeling the behavior as "wrong," "bad," or "unfair." It's these judgments of the event that actually trigger your angry feelings. In a way this is good news because by changing how you think, you can change your experience of emotions. What do you think of that idea, that it's your own thoughts that determine the level of anger you experience?*

Tiffany: *I don't really know. This is confusing.*

Therapist: *Let's use an example... Say there's a driver on the highway. She's stuck in traffic and is late to work. A car suddenly cuts her off. She's having thoughts like: "What a jerk!" "I hate this damn road," "I'm going to be late again," "That asshole almost hit me," "I can't stand this drive," and so on. What might that driver's anger emotion level be on the 0 to 100 point scale?*

Tiffany: *Pretty high.*

Therapist: *You're probably right. Now, what if our driver was having these types of thoughts: "I'm glad I didn't get hit; that would really make me late," "This is annoying, but I can deal with it," "I'll use this time to listen to music," "I'll take a couple of deep breaths." What might that driver's anger emotion level be on the 0 to 100 point scale?*

Tiffany: *It'd be lower.*

Therapist: *Exactly. Can you relate to these 'two' drivers; how their feelings are influenced by their thoughts?*

Tiffany: *I do get mad when I drive, especially if I'm late. I get all pissed off, I curse people out, and sometimes I'm the one cutting people off if I'm really late.*

Therapist: *What are some of the thoughts that go through your mind when you're late because of traffic?*

Tiffany: *If I'm late for work I know my boss is going to be mad, I know I won't get a good parking spot, I'll be running in there looking foolish, and my co-workers will be judging me.*

Therapist: *So when you're stuck in traffic and late for work, all kinds of thoughts pop up. You're not just worried about being late, you're worried about what other people will think about you being late and where you'll have to park. What happens if you're stuck in traffic and don't have to be anywhere at a certain time?*

Tiffany: *I'd still be mad but maybe not as bad if I'm not late.*

Therapist: *So without all the extra thoughts about being late, you wouldn't get as angry.*

Tiffany: *Yeah, that's probably true.*

Therapist: *So by having different thoughts about being stuck in traffic you can change how angry you feel.*

Tiffany: *I never thought about it that way.*

Therapist: *If it's ok with you, I'd like to talk about ways to manage thoughts that work for many people. I'll be interested to find out if these ideas would seem helpful for you.*

Tiffany: *Ok.*

Therapist: *Thanks. There are two basic steps for managing your thoughts. The first step is learning to recognize anger increasing thoughts when you have them. The second step is to reduce the anger increasing thoughts and then replace them with calming, coping thoughts. When you're feeling angry, what thoughts run through your head?*

Tiffany: *I don't know. It depends on what's pissing me off.*

Therapist: *That's certainly true. Here are examples of some common anger increasing thoughts:* ***Anger Increasing Thoughts Handout****; see Appendix II Keep in mind, nobody's perfect. At one time or another, everyone has these anger increasing thoughts. The key is to look at how these thoughts might influence your emotion level. Can you look back to your self-monitoring log and find a time you think you had one or more of these anger increasing thoughts?*

Tiffany: *Oh yeah—I hear me saying a bunch of these. Just the other day with my asshole brother who never showed up to help me.*

Therapist: *What are some of the thoughts you were having about your brother?*

Tiffany: *He's a lazy, selfish, no-good, bastard. He doesn't care about anyone but himself. He never does what he says he's going to do. He could've at least called. I'm always stuck doing everything on my own.*

Therapist: *So it's possible that some of these thoughts might have made your anger even more intense, turned it up to a boil instead of a simmer.*

Tiffany: *Maybe. But what am I supposed to do, just sit there and take other people's abuse? That's pathetic.*

Therapist: *You're right. Sometimes anger emotions are helpful, they let you know something isn't right and motivate you to fix it. But other times, angry reactions are out of proportion and end up hurting more than they solve anything. What do you make of that idea?*

Tiffany: *I see your point. I probably get more angry than I need to but I just have so many things in my life that piss me off!*

Therapist: *You're starting to think you get angrier than you need to and that may be affecting you in some negative ways. It's possible that learning how to turn your anger down from a boil to a simmer would be helpful.*

Tiffany: *It's possible.*

Therapist: *This* ***Anger Increasing Thoughts Handout*** *also has lists of calming, coping thoughts that are related to these different themes. Are any of these coping thoughts especially relevant to you and your situations?*

Tiffany: *I like this one: "I'm not going to let him/her get to me." I use that at work a lot.*

Therapist: *You're good at that one in your work and I wonder if it could be helpful in your personal life.*

Tiffany: *I'm sure it would. I'm sick and tired of letting people get to me. Especially my brother.*

Therapist: *You're starting to recognize that you have the power to choose how much you let people get to you. I'd also like to offer you a handout of* ***General Coping Thoughts*** (see Appendix II). *This list includes the Serenity Prayer, which some people find calming. Which of these coping thoughts are likely to be helpful to you?*

Tiffany: *Sometimes I pray but not I don't know this one. I'll have to look at these other ones.*

Therapist: *What we've been talking about is both listening for thoughts that increase your anger and then replacing them with calming, coping thoughts. This is something you're good at when you're at work and you'd like to be better at it in your personal life.*

Tiffany: *I am good at doing that at work. I'll have to pay more attention to this stuff in the rest of my life.*

Therapist: *Ok—so you'll spend time this week listening for anger increasing thoughts and trying to replace them with calming, coping thoughts. This'll be something we'll add to your relaxation skills and practice them together in here starting next week.*

Tiffany: *Fine.*

Anger-Increasing Thoughts and Their Alternatives

As clients become more aware of their cognitive processes and accept their impact, they are in a position to begin separating the thoughts that may lead to mild or moderate anger from the thoughts that incite high anger and potentially aggressive or dysfunctional behavior, like heavy drinking. In the earlier angry driving scenario, thinking about what could have happened and not wanting any part of it would likely result in frustration and annoyance. These are reasonable thoughts that lead to mild or moderate anger emotions and most likely little or no craving to drink. On the other hand, thinking the other person is "a complete idiot" who cut you off on purpose to make you mad and who ought to be punished, elevates anger emotions to fury and rage and potential aggressive behavior (e.g., screaming at the other person, flipping the finger, and dangerous tailgating). This level of anger can also trigger strong alcohol cravings for many people.

The following section describes eight common cognitive distortions that engender anger, along with examples of each and their antidotes. For each distortion, change strategies are outlined.

Catastrophizing/Magnifying

This cognitive distortion involves labeling situations in extreme, negative terms. Situations are "awful," "terrible," "the worst," "reprehensible," "sickening," "intolerable," "horrendous," or "devastating." The person reacts to these extreme characterizations which go far beyond the reality of the situation. Catastrophic labels exaggerate the painful, threatening, and negative factors and minimize possible positive, tolerable, and mitigating factors. As such, they play to anger-enhancing primary appraisals and to overwhelming, aggression-supportive, and alcohol-involved secondary appraisals.

Examples of magnifying/catastrophizing:

- *I can't stand how she's treating me.*
- *This is horrible.*
- *This is the worst thing that's ever happened.*
- *My job is the pits.*
- *What he did was devastating.*

Examples of coping thoughts:

- *It's frustrating how she's treating me, but it's not the end of the world.*
- *This is frustrating and I don't like it.*
- *This is not the worst, it's just a big hassle.*
- *My job has a number of issues and I'm going to have figure out how to deal with them or whether I want to find a new job.*
- *What nonsense. He just did it, and you're surviving. Stop exaggerating his influence.*

Change strategies: When we engage in catastrophizing, we expect the worst of all outcomes. A simple, but effective way to generate coping thoughts is to ask the client to concretely answer the question, "How bad is it really?" Often the answer is negative but not nearly as bad the catastrophic label implies. Clients are encouraged to ask themselves this question when catastrophic thinking is identified and to stay with the realistically negative answers.

Another helpful approach is to have the client describe events with more realistic negative emotional descriptors. Things are "frustrating," "disappointing," "annoying," "hassling," or "sad." Life often serves up negative events, and everyone, including the client, will experience them. Staying emotionally accurate keeps the client at these mild to moderate states and does not escalate them to high anger.

A third antidote is for the client to describe situations in specific, concrete, positive and negative ways. For example, a car that does not start is not a worthless, horrible piece of junk. Rather, it is a car that may have served you well, but now has a dead battery which needs to be replaced at some financial cost. Moreover, the car's failure to start is frustrating because you will be late for work and have to make arrangements to have it repaired. This description is concrete and accurately describes the external situation, reasonable emotions, and other consequences. It is consistent with feeling frustration and mild anger, rather than fury.

Another alternative method is to widen the perspective and look at the whole picture. Catastrophizing focuses on the extreme negative. Looking at the entire situation considers the downsides as well as the upsides, positive aspects, possible help, coping resources, and support. For example, a person that has been labeled "horrible" in one context may also be a person who has been a good listener and supportive in another. When solely focused on catastrophizing, these positive features are lost, and anger ensues from the unbalanced view.

Overgeneralizing

In overgeneralizing, people take the details of one event and make broad sweeping conclusions across events, characteristics, and time. Person and situation overgeneralizations are identified by things like "all," "total," "everybody," and their negatives like "not at all," "none," and "nobody." Time-related overgeneralizations are marked by labels of "always," "all the time," "never," and "none of the time." Such cognitive coding makes things bigger, more negative, and more inclusive. They also obscure positive aspects and coping resources.

Stereotypes and group labels are also examples of overgeneralizations. They apply broad negative characteristics to all members of a group and therefore, dehumanize individual members of that group. Phrases like "Women do...", "African Americans are...", and "All Democrats think..." capture these aspects. If the stereotype is negative and something devalued by the individual, he or she is more likely to feel threatened and to respond with more intense and broader anger than if responding to a specific individual from that group.

Examples of overgeneralizing:

- *He never gets anything right.*
- *She's always late.*
- *Nobody cares.*
- *The kids are always lazy and irresponsible.*
- *They're all freeloaders.*

Examples of coping thoughts:

- *He made a mistake. That's all.*
- *She's late today but she's on time on other occasions.*
- *I have friends. I just don't have a friend nearby me right now.*
- *The kids didn't do what they were supposed to do today.*
- *Some of those people got better treatment than we did. Maybe we can look into it and see how we can balance things out.*

Change strategies: One strategy for reversing overgeneralization is to describe things in concrete, accurate, situation-specific terms and to react to those, rather than the overgeneralization. A second strategy is to look for the exceptions. When the person has identified exceptions, it is harder to respond to the over-inclusive emotional meaning of a broad conclusion. The person may still be dealing with a specific negative situation but will react with an appropriate level of anger.

Polarized Thinking

This distortion is also called either/or, black/white, all/nothing, or dichotomous thinking. In making this error, people conceptualize things into one of two categories. One has a very positive emotional valence and the other very negative. Things and people are good or bad, smart or dumb, right or wrong, strong or weak, in or out of control, winners or losers, perfect or worthless. Any single experience or evidence that disproves the positive polarity automatically triggers the negative polarity and, along with it, strong anger because of the extreme state of affairs. The person is not responding with lesser anger that might come from seeing the shades of gray between the extremes of white and black.

Examples of polarized thinking:

- *I'm dumb, a failure.*
- *He's such a loser.*
- *She hates me.*
- *This is worthless.*
- *This is wrong, just plain wrong.*

Examples of coping thoughts:

- *I'm not dumb. I got a B on the test. Wanted an A but didn't get it. Frustrating, but I'll study more for the next one.*
- *He's not a loser. Sure, he's making mistakes now, but he does well at some other things.*
- *She's probably upset with me because I missed her birthday. I'll apologize, but if she truly hates me and doesn't get over it, I'll have to think about what kind of friends we are.*
- *Worthless? Imperfect for sure, but that's hardly a crime. Mistakes happen to all of us.*
- *Wrong? It's frustrating to get late notice on this project, but that's all it is.*

Change strategies: One strategy for dealing with polarized thinking is for the - person to use qualifying adjectives, adverbs, and phrases. For example, the individual might start quantifying amount (e.g., a little, somewhat, a lot, instead of "always"), degree of performance (e.g., poor, average, good, instead of "terrible" or "failure"), and time (e.g., occasionally, sometimes, often, instead of "never" or "always"). These qualifiers introduce complexity into the person's perception and help modulate anger.

Another approach is for the person to ask and answer the following question, "Where is the evidence that if something isn't *all* good, then it must be *all* bad?" Answering this question honestly forces the person the break down the polarity into a continuum, which in turn helps modulate anger more appropriately.

Another alternative is to assist the individual in considering multiple dimensions of the polarity. Take, for example, the notion that a person either loves or hates you. In reality, there are multiple aspects to consider. The person might strongly like one characteristic (e.g., your patience), strongly dislike another (e.g., your bluntness), and not care much at all about another (e.g., your vocational choice). Love or hate simply misses the mark. The person likes, dislikes, and is indifferent, depending on what element is being considered. Most dichotomies miss the multiple aspects or dimensions involved. So, the goal is to begin considering the variety of parameters or elements of the person or situation and to accurately label the degree of positive or negative reaction.

Global and Inflammatory Labeling

A major trigger for anger arousal is the highly negative, often obscene, labels applied to people or situations. Examples of labels that are generally not obscene include things such as "idiot," "slob," "worthless," "wimp," "jerk," "slime," "loser," "a joke," "ugly," "lazy," "selfish," and "evil.". A few examples of obscene labels include "bitch," "sonofabitch," "ass," "asshole," "shithead," "shit," "dick," or "f-up." Such labels are highly negative and inaccurate because they are applied to the whole person, situation, or behavior of the person without exception. Such labels add highly angering interpretations to events and are like pouring a cup of cognitive gasoline on the situation, only inflaming things further.

Examples of global/inflammatory labeling:

- *Asshole! (referring to another driver)*
- *He's a lazy bum.*
- *The kids are being stupid little shits. (two labels for the price of one)*
- *They're complete jerks.*

Examples of coping thoughts:

- *Asshole? Nope. Just another poor driver. I've made mistakes behind the wheel too. So, I'll cut him some slack.*
- *Nope. That goes way beyond the facts. He doesn't appear to be working hard today, but I've seen him work hard before.*
- *The kids are neither stupid nor shitty. They're just not following through as agreed.*
- *Jerks? I'm not even sure what that means. What's true is that they're doing things I really don't like. They have a right to be wrong, and are they ever exercising their rights!*

Change strategies: Inflammatory/global labeling can be addressed by having people describe things in very specific, concrete ways. What specifically happened? When did it happen? How many times? Individuals are to ask and answer these types of questions. An element of this is encouraging people to describe another person's behavior and react to that, leaving out labels of the person. People are not what they do. People are too complex to have a single, broad emotive label apply to all of their characteristics.

Another approach to dealing with global/inflammatory labeling is for the person to concretely define the terms that they are using (e.g., jerk = a sudden pull, stupid = a person with lesser intelligence, bitch = female dog, sonofabitch = male dog, etc.). Once defined, the person is to be asked how these specific definitions apply in the specific context. Many simply do not fit. The person is then asked to use concrete descriptions and experience emotions that fit (e.g., "He's not a stupid sonofabitch, just a person who's doing things that are frustrating me.").

Looking for and defining exceptions to the label often applies as well. Exceptions break down the label and humanize the person. This lowers anger as the person considers exceptions to the broad label (e.g., "He's not an egotistical prick. Yes, he's behaving in ways that seem pretty self-serving to me today but I've seen him be caring and sensitive at other times.").

Finally, many examples are nonsensical and absurd and therefore open to silly humorous reframes. For example, calling another driver an "ass" can be funny. Looking up the definition of "ass" provides two general definitions—a burro and the buttocks. The client is asked to think about this and perhaps visualize or draw a picture of each definition driving a car. Such thoughts and images often significantly shift the frame of reference and provide an anger-lowering chuckle. Another example is the rage at someone else giving them the "finger." This action is often interpreted in highly angering ways. However, there are alternative interpretations that are silly. For example, the person might think that the person was signaling them that they were Number 1. Alternatively, in our society a "thumbs up" is a very positive communication. Therefore, the finger giving person just got the wrong digit and has a bad case of digital confusion. Another interpretation is that the person was very poorly communicating an invitation for a sexual encounter. Maybe the person was sadly communicating the number of friends he has. All of these alternative interpretations have in common a sense of the absurd and silly humor is antithetical to being highly angry. A chuckle often is an antidote for anger. So, with inflammatory/global labeling consider having clients concretize their concepts and where relevant drawing pictures of or visualize these potentially absurd and humorous ideas.

WHAT ARE YOU LAUGHING AT?

Silly humor is not typically recommended in psychotherapy. However, consider it in the specific case of global/inflammatory labeling. Be alert, and avoid the possibility that the client may feel laughed at. If this happens, quickly indicate that the two of you are exploring the humor in some of the descriptions used. Some *thoughts* are funny but *not* the client. A chuckle can often provide some relief and reduction of anger. As a group, individuals with anger issues tend to be durable. They are not likely to fall apart at attempts to see the humor in some of their thinking. It is, however, suggested that attempts at humorous reframes be delayed a few sessions into therapy until rapport is well established and enough trust and goodwill is present to offset any problems stemming from introducing humor.

Single Assumptions and Attributions

People with problematic anger often jump to highly egocentric assumptions and attributions about the thoughts, feelings, and motives of others. They tend to mind read and are convinced they know what others are thinking and why they are behaving in certain ways. They tend toward a hostile attributional bias. That is, they assume that others want to hurt, harm, take advantage of, exploit, manipulate, deceive, lie to, and compete with them. Moreover, they are convinced that others do these things consciously and intentionally. They are highly certain about their assumptions; they know they are right. The result is a single, powerful understanding of others which is biased toward harm and threat and the need to defend and/or attack back in response. A high level of anger is evoked because of the perceived threat from others. A key problem is that the attributions and assumptions are often not true and therefore the anger is misplaced.

Examples of single explanations/attributions:

- *He said that to embarrass me and make me look stupid.*
- *They did that just to piss me off.*
- *I know she's spreading rumors about me.*
- *She's trying to steal my boyfriend.*
- *They're jealous.*

Examples of coping thoughts:

- *Where's my evidence that that's the reason they did it?*
- *Don't jump to conclusions. This probably didn't have anything to do with me personally.*
- *Don't try to read their minds. Ask them why before you go off on a rant.*
- *There are often many possible reasons why people do things. Let me think through this before I reach a conclusion.*
- *They probably aren't trying to take advantage of me. Most people are just trying to get by the best they can.*

Change strategies: It is often useful to ask clients about occasions when they made assumptions about a person's intentions or motives only to find out later that they were wrong. Further exploration can inquire about the consequences of acting on those conclusions. Probably the most important question is what they could have done differently to check out their assumptions. Often responses include that they should have slowed down, thought things through, considered alternatives, and asked other people about what was going on.

One of the best approaches for dealing with misattributions is helping clients to literally test their assumptions, to help them learn how to tactfully but directly see if their understanding is correct. Clearly, others will not always be able or willing to answer questions, but the client is likely to have a better idea of what is going on and to feel positive that they asked and tried to clarify things.

Another approach is to encourage clients to develop and write out lists of possible reasons why people behave in a certain way. Encourage clients to develop as many alternatives as possible and to continue to add to the list over time. Encourage brainstorming rules where clients are to consider all possible explanations including the unlikely and farfetched (e.g., they were brainwashed by a cult, they really are shapeshifting aliens). Silly humorous possibilities may be appropriate for some clients. For example, consider the possibility that the reason a person is being very controlling and grouchy is because he is totally constipated or experiencing bad gas. Whatever the method, the goal is to increase the range of alternative explanations and to slow reacting emotionally while these alternatives are considered.

Another intervention is to return to the notion of the paradox. A good place to start is to ask people if they always try to harm, take advantage of, or manipulate others. The answer is often a firm "no" with a fairly benign explanation of their own motives. This can be gently contrasted with the assumptions they make about other people's motives. In this context, the therapist can introduce the general notions that others are doing the best they can, most people are not consciously and intentionally trying to take advantage of others, and many people are just struggling to get by. These are more benign and less hostile biased interpretations of human nature. It also provides a frame of reference for when people explore the evidence to support more hostile attributions.

THE SAD TRUTH

Therapists need to be prepared for the possibility that the client's negative attributions are true. There are spouses who do not care and continue to have affairs. There are employers who do take advantage of and cheat employees. There are parents and partners who are abusive. When situations such as these are discovered, the focus of therapy shifts to helping clients clarify their choices, some of which may painful (e.g., terminating a flawed but important relationship or quitting a well-paying, but abusive job). Other interventions might focus on empowering clients to remove themselves, set limits, or to mobilize intra- and interpersonal resources. If the situation poses imminent danger, then shifting to crisis management and harm prevention is warranted.

Over- and Underestimating

Angry individuals tend to overestimate the probability of negative, threatening events and to underestimate personal and other coping resources. That is, primary appraisal processes are skewed toward identifying wrongs and frustrating events, while secondary appraisals underestimate capacities to solve problems and cope. The antidote is to help people become more accurate in assessing the probabilities of negative events and the probabilities of personal and environmental coping resources. A corollary cognitive change is that individuals may encounter and need to tolerate situations where probabilities are unknowable and/or subject to change without notice.

Examples of over-/underestimating:

- *I just know I'm not going to get the job.*
- *I don't have a clue about how I'm going to cope with this.*

- *I'm so pissed at her. I know I'm going to get drunk after we talk.*
- *I'm certain the kids will have trashed the house while I was out.*
- *I bet I screw it up.*

Examples of coping thoughts:

- *How can I be so certain that I won't get the job? Hell, I haven't even interviewed yet. The odds may be low because of all the applicants. At least they offered me an interview. I'll do my best and see what happens.*
- *So, how will I cope with this? Well, first I'll try to break it down and deal with one piece at a time. I'll try to stay calm and think things through with SOBER problem solving* (see Chapter 8: Sobriety Skills).
- *I'm going to try to manage my anger and talk about things calmly. Maybe we'll work out our problem and maybe we won't. However, getting drunk is NOT a choice. I'm not going to drink, even if things go poorly.*
- *I don't know what the kids have been doing. I doubt they've been angels, but I have no way of knowing if they left a mess. I'll wait until I'm home and deal with whatever did happen.*
- *I don't feel very skilled at this. I think the odds are about 1 in 4 that I can solve the problem. If I get it, great. If not, I'll get some help.*

Change strategies. Over- and underestimates are often implicitly accepted as truths or givens. Encouraging individuals to ask questions like, "What are the chances this will happen?" or "What evidence do I have that things will happen as I am predicting?" helps them become more realistic in their predictions.

People can also be given the task of making bets on predictions about how things will happen (e.g., what topics will come up in an interaction, how another person will treat them, whether someone will be late or not), and then collect the data and see how close their predictions were. A typical finding is that their predictions are not nearly as accurate as they think. They can also begin to identify factors that influence or change the odds. Some observations provide opportunities for people to do things differently and see if they can change the odds of things happening a certain way. For example, one client tended to interrupt conversations to offer his opinion and this often lead to arguments. In contrast, his friend almost always listened and made sure he understood the other person's point of view before sharing his own opinions. The client adopted this strategy and found that the amount of arguments dropped dramatically.

Some people become angry when they cannot know or predict events. An exploration of the idea of the uncertainty and sometimes fickle nature of life may help. Once they accept the general idea, it is important to concretize them in coping thoughts like "*Sure, I like to know what's going to happen, but it looks like it's one of those times that I can't. I'm just going to relax and wait to see what happens,*" or "*Sometimes things are clear and sometimes they're not. No need to get angry because I don't have a crystal ball.*"

Another common issue comes up relative to over-/underestimation. Individuals will often overestimate how bad things will be while underestimating their ability to cope if the event happens in the future. However, when asked to consider what they would do if it actually happened, they often report lower anger and frustration and identify several ideas about how they would handle the situation. In a case like this, the contrast between the high anger and poor coping versus more moderate anger and positive coping is pointed out. People are encouraged to do two things: (1) not borrow distress about whether or not an event could happen and (2) bring future coping and problem-solving into the present and think concretely about how they plan to cope should the event happen. This tends to lower anger and increase a sense of empowerment and control.

Demanding and Commanding

Having personal preferences and desires is healthy and adaptive. It is good for people to want things, to actively pursue them, to be pleased when they are achieved, and to feel frustrated and disappointed when they are not.

However, that is not what happens with this cognitive distortion. In demanding/commanding, people raise their personal desires, wants, and preferences up to the level of moral dictates and commandments which become rigid, inviolate rules. They no longer simply want and prefer; instead, things, other people, even one's self *must* be a certain way. Now things "should," "ought to," "have to," "must," "need to," "got to," and "are expected to" (or their negatives such as "should not") be a certain way. Life is judged against these rigid standards. When the "should" is met, then all is well, but when it is not met, things are very, very wrong. Offenders, which can be people, events, and oneself, are the focus of high anger and perhaps blame and punishment. Anger is externalized to the offending source, people feel righteous in their anger, and may use mild aggression or verbal rebuke to force compliance. These "shoulds" and dictates are often deeply held beliefs. The person is not aware that the intense anger does not stem directly from the offending person or event but from the violation of this rigid, personal rule. In addition, the individual often believes that others share the same set of "shoulds." This is often not the case. Others have their own desires and preferences which do not necessarily overlap with those of the angered person. When this is encountered, the person is more confused and angry, a sort of "*How dare they not agree*" which is only one further demand (i.e., "*I'm right and they should agree.*").

People have their own idiosyncratic demands. Clinicians can identify these when they hear the keywords or phrases listed in the prior paragraph (i.e., "should," "need to," and "have to"). However, there are also a number of themes clinicians commonly encounter; these demanding themes are described in the extreme but can be identified by keywords (especially "should") used by the client.

- Perfection—*I/others/events should be done right, correctly, perfectly.*
- Agreement—*Others should agree with me and with what I want and think.*
- Control—*Things/people should be controlled, in control, and orderly, not chaotic or disorganized.*
- Liking/love/appreciation—*Key people should like me, care about me, appreciate me, and love me.*
- Disliking/being critical—*Others should not dislike, judge, be critical of, or be negative toward me.*
- Respect—*Others should show me respect.*
- Punishment/retribution—*Offenders deserve to be and should be punished.*
- Justice/fairness—*People and events should be fair, right, and just.*
- Kindness—*People should be treated with caring, kindness, warmth, and courtesy.*
- Bad things should not happen to me—*I should not have to experience, put up with, deal with, or cope with difficulties, impediments, frustration, pain, delays, or difficult people.*
- Alcohol/other drugs—*I need to have, or must have, a drink.*

These themes are described individually, but two or more may be entwined into the thinking about a single angering event. For example, the person may be demanding perfection and then be angered further because the offender does not agree and show respect. This example involves demands for perfection, agreement, and respect. All three likely need attention with regard to a specific angering event and across events. That is, people often have one or more demanding/commanding themes that are triggered across time, people, and events. For example, a person may demand respect from a spouse, children, coworkers, and friends. The therapist will want to lift out the general theme so that the client can more readily identify and change how the general theme(s) will play out.

Examples of demanding/commanding thoughts:

- *He should pay attention.*
- *This has to be done right.*
- *They should know better.*
- *I shouldn't have to put up with this shit! Nobody should.*
- *I have to have a drink.*

Examples of coping thoughts:

- *I wish he would pay better attention. It's frustrating to have to help him focus. Oh well, maybe he's just a little scattered.*
- *I sure hope we can do this well. I don't want to come back to it again. But it's not the end of the world if we have to struggle with it.*
- *They should know better? Obviously not. I wish they had it together, but they're probably doing the best they can.*
- *I sure don't like this and wish I didn't have to deal with it. But who (other than me) says that some bad things shouldn't happen on my watch? Chill and deal with it.*
- *I do NOT have to have a drink. I've coped with stress and anger for years by drinking. I definitely am not going to drink. I am going to...* (person makes plans to do something else).

WHY ME?

Often, clients will frame cognitions in the form of rhetorical questions, such as "Why can't they get things done on time?" or "Why me?" or "Can't she see that she's being so rude and mean?" It is suggested that therapist turns these questions into statements. When this is done, the question usually morphs into a demand that things should be the way the client wants them to be. For example, the above questions might change into "They should get things done on time." "This shouldn't be happening to me." and "She shouldn't be so rude and mean." When the rhetorical questions are reframed as statements, they can be treated as demands which then can be changed using the suggested strategies.

Change strategies: The general antidote for demanding is to think in preferential terms. The person has important wants, desires, and values; works hard to pursue them; while also accepting the inevitable disappointments that go with not always achieving them. A commonly employed strategy is the repeated explorations and gentle challenges to the person's "shoulds." Open-ended inquiries such as the following might be employed:

- *Having things be perfect would be great. Help me understand why it has to be perfect according to your standards.*
- *You get to have your own values and preferences, but do you have the right to impose them on others?*
- *You seem to be saying that you shouldn't have to deal with difficulties. It certainly would be preferable for you not to have to deal with them. But, why shouldn't you have to deal with some tough stuff like other people?*
- *Where's the evidence showing that others have to think like you do?*

- *How angry do you get when you want something and aren't able to get it?* (This is explored.) *Ok, how angry are you when you demand and insist that the world has to give you what you want and you still don't get it?* (This is explored with usually greater anger and consternation in response to the second question. Then, the contrast is posed and the relative consequences are compared). *In both cases you don't get what you want. When you are pursuing your wants and don't get them, the anger is about 30–50. When you are demanding them, anger is in the 60–90 range. Which one would you rather experience, given that either way you don't get what you wanted?*

As clients answer such inquiries, they begin to understand the differences between wanting and demanding. Reframing these demands as wants/preference/likes can be written down in the client's own language and related metaphors can be used as coping thoughts. Sometimes, especially after the person has begun to identify "shoulds" and created alternatives to them, short statements may prove helpful to get the person to switch from demanding to preferential thinking. Examples include:

- *Shouldhood is shithood.* (meaning that when people think in terms of shoulds they are going to feel very bad, which in our case is high anger)
- *Bad things happen to good people.* (This is especially useful for those demanding that bad things should not befall them.) *Some people find it useful to add on with something like I am a good person, and some bad things are likely to happen to me. It looks like one of those has happened. So, how do I want to deal with it?*
- *My oughts condemn me to a personal hell.* (The idea that the person does not want to go or to experience hell. Frustration, annoyance, and irritation are bad enough.)
- *There I go 'shoulding' again. Let me focus on wanting.*
- *My needing pushes me over the edge, and I don't like the fall.*

Blaming

Blaming involves identifying an external event or person(s) as responsible for their anger. If blaming did nothing more than this, it might not be so bad. Identifying sources of anger, frustration, and provocation is an important step in adaptive coping and problem-solving. However, blaming does much more than identify an external source of anger. In blaming, the individual attributes total source and responsibility to the person or situation and attaches the notion that the source should be made to pay. When people are involved, the notion of intentionality is often embedded as well. That is, the person did it on purpose. The person was trying to hurt, harm, make life difficult, etc. (depending on the context). This increases and justifies anger and behavior directed toward the other person(s).

Blaming leads to two very negative consequences. First, as total responsibility is attributed externally, the individual him or herself has no responsibility. The individual is helpless to do anything about the situation. Anger may spike more as the person feels out of control. Second, notions of punishment and retribution justify the client's intense anger and aggressive or other means of extracting payment for offense.

Examples of blaming thoughts:

- *You taking so long to get ready always makes us late.*
- *We could be having a good time if she wasn't in such a bad mood.*
- *Damn you!*
- *Her leaving me makes me so damned angry and depressed.*
- *I wouldn't be drinking so much if you weren't hassling me.*

Examples of coping thoughts:

- *Taking a long time to get ready contributes to us being late. But, me being so pissed just means that I'm late and pissed. So, I'm going to talk to him and see if we can't figure out a better solution.*
- *Sure, I wish she was in a better mood. Maybe I should check and see what's going on. Maybe I can do something to help.*
- *Where do I get off damning anybody? Nobody appointed me supreme ruler. Let me express my concerns respectfully and see if we can't find something that works for all of us.*
- *I couldn't prevent her leaving, but I can do something about the anger and depression. Sitting around all angry and upset is NOT helping me.*
- *I don't like you being on my case as much as you are, but drinking is on me. I'm the one who pours the drink down. Now, what am I going to do about my relationship and, more immediately, about my drinking?*

Notice that nearly all of the coping thoughts do two things to blaming. First, they at least partially shift the focus away from the perceived source and include the angry person. Second, the angry person is taking some responsibility for what is happening and looking to what can be done about it. The individual is no longer helpless.

Change strategies: Interventions for blaming typically need to separate two components—laying total responsibility on an external source and thinking in terms of punishment and retribution. Occasionally, an event or outcome is 100% determined by a single source. More often, however, there are multiple contributing factors. A series of open-ended inquiries like the following may help clarify what led to the blameful event:

- *What things do you think contributed to the situation*? (Usually, the client will repeat the single source interpretation. This can be followed up with a summary and a question.) *And what others things contributed*?
- *What's the evidence that this was the only cause*?
- *Are there other things that could have fed into the situation*?
- *Do you think you had any part in what happened*? *If so, what part*?

A SLICE OF PIE...

Adding a pie chart of responsibility can be helpful to concretize this. The client is handed a piece of paper and a pencil, asked to draw a circle, and asked to think of it as a pie that represents factors responsible for outcomes. As each factor is identified, it is written on the pie. When the list of factors appears to be exhausted, the client is asked to draw a piece of pie that represents the percentage of contribution and to write that % on the piece. Reviewing the final pie often identifies several things. First, there were multiple contributors, rather than a single one. Second, no single slice took up the whole pie (i.e., no factor was totally responsible). Third, some of the pieces may directly or indirectly involve the angry blaming person. In turn, this helps point to the person's own contribution. Fourth, the sum total may be greater than or less than 100%. Over 100% disproves the single source theory. Less than 100% also weakens the single source notion and introduces the idea that there may other, as yet unidentified, factors that created the experienced outcomes.

Punishment, and more specifically the blaming individual meting out punishment, needs to be addressed. The difference between accountability and punishment can be discussed. People can be held accountable and some natural negative consequences may follow. Punishment in this context means that the blaming person is going above and beyond accountability and adding pain and other negative consequences. Punishment may not be the person's prerogative. If need be, it is the role of other institutions such as the police and the courts.

The therapist will want to listen for another possibility to be explored. It may be that in blaming others, the client is actually distracting from and avoiding issues such as drinking. For example, a client may blame a spouse (e.g., "I wouldn't be drinking if you weren't so damn frigid.") or an employment situation (e.g., "I have to stop off for a few drinks after work, because work is so crazy and stressful."). This kind of blame can shift the focus away from the alcohol use while creating relationship conflicts. In addition to alcohol use, therapists should watch for other avoidance and deflection that serve to keep another problem from being identified and addressed.

Some coping thoughts may not address a specific cognitive distortions but help clients endure frustration and provocation. Examples include thoughts like *"And this too shall pass," "Hang in there. You'll get through this," and "Anger is like fire. It can heat the house or burn it down. Let's just heat the house.*" These general coping thoughts are pulled together in a **General Coping Thoughts** list (Appendix II). Clients are encouraged to add to their list and use their additions when developing cognitive coping thoughts.

Some people like to conceptualize themselves in nature with certain characteristics. For example, they see themselves as turtles who can pull in their appendages so as not to get hurt and simply let insults and disrespect ping off their shell. In a somewhat similar manner, they might see themselves as a duck in the rain and let negative things, like rain, not ruffle or penetrate their feathers, but drip onto the ground. They might see themselves as cool as a penguin in a windstorm. Other images can take on a metaphorical anti-anger quality. For example, one client developed a relaxation scene involving lying in the sun on a big rock in a local river. Over time, she began to see herself like the rock. She could be solidly anchored and let the dark and turbulent waters of the spring runoff (things that angered her) just flow on by, knowing that the clear, tranquil waters of early fall would return. When clients find images like these, they are added to their general coping list. Clients are encouraged to visualize such images to lower anger.

Putting It Together: The Early Stages of Cognitive Coping

The general rationale, introduction to the ABC model, and exploration of cognitive aspects of anger and alcohol use are typically introduced in the first or second session after relaxation training has begun. Self-monitoring log 2, which includes a place to record cognitive aspects of anger, is introduced in the second session. In the next few sessions, contrasts in degree of anger and craving in similar situations are introduced to increase the understanding and importance of cognitive processes. Cognitive distortions and how they increase anger are discussed. This is facilitated by giving the client the **Anger Increasing Thoughts** handout (see Appendix II) which includes short descriptions of the distortions and how they influence anger, followed by examples of less angering coping alternatives on the **General Coping Thoughts** handout (see Appendix II). The first portion of the next sessions is devoted to reviewing self-montoring logs, discussing drinking/cravings, identifying examples of cognitive distortions, and developing coping alternatives. An example of these kinds of steps is presented below.

After two to four sessions of these activities, the final two components of cognitive restructuring are added. These are in-session rehearsal of cognitions for anger reduction and the transfer of cognitive coping skills to real life anger- and anger-alcohol involved situations. Since these latter steps are integrated with the application and transfer of relaxation coping skills training, they are described in the next chapter on coping skills training.

David Cognitive Concepts (End of Session Practice)

Therapist: *So, just to summarize, the focus of this session has been exploring the role of thoughts in creating and intensifying feelings. For some people, this is a new way of looking at the thought-emotion connection. The target exercise on the self-monitoring log for this week involves even more clearly identifying your anger increasing thoughts, including those related to any cravings for alcohol. If it's ok with you, let's fill in an entry on the self-monitoring log that happened in the last 24 hours to get you started.*

David: *Sure—this guy at work tried to blame me for his mistake. He copied some of my numbers for his report but he was using a different formula so the numbers didn't work. How is that my fault? He said I should have told him but what am I supposed to be, some kind of mind-reader? Just because he's lazy, I get blamed. I'm so sick of shit like this happening.*

Therapist: *What were some of your anger-increasing thoughts?*

David: *Ok... some of my thoughts: He's an idiot. He should have come up with his own damn numbers. Everybody I work with under the age of 30 is lazy and expects other people to hold their hand and do their work. Why me? I can't stand incompetence. How's that?*

Therapist: *Where do you see those on the anger increasing thoughts sheet?*

David: *Well, I definitely heard a 'should' in there... and labeling... and overgeneralizing... and magnification. Yikes—I got almost all of them.*

Therapist: *Again, these are common thoughts that increase anger emotions so you're not alone. What are some coping thoughts you could use for your situation at work?*

David: *I don't know. I still think I wouldn't get so upset if people just did their job.*

Therapist: *It would be ideal if everyone did that and made things easier for you. That's what we call an "elegant" solution—the world changes to fit your needs. Unfortunately, life rarely works that way. Which brings us to the need for a "practical" solution. If you can't change other people, how can you change yourself and the ways you react to them? What do you make of that, the idea of changing your reactions instead of waiting for the world to change for you?*

David: *I kind of see your point but does that mean I have to bite my tongue and settle for mediocrity?*

Therapist: *Not necessarily. What would be nice is for you to find something in between getting really angry and settling for mediocrity. Hopefully, staying calm and thinking clearly will help you find that middle ground more easily. For many people, learning to manage their anger emotions frees them up to problem-solve more creatively and to choose how, and even if, to respond. They often feel more in control of what happens and how they handle frustrating situations.*

David: *I'm an excellent problem solver unless I'm so mad I can think straight.*

Therapist: *Exactly. So learning to relax physically and cope more effectively with anger emotions are keys to that ability to think straight in provocative situations.*

David: *I'd like to be able to think straighter for sure.*

Therapist: *The next step in this process is to consider a few coping thoughts that could replace the anger increasing thoughts you were having at work the other day. Use the sheets if you want.*

David: *Ok—so he's not an idiot, he's just new to the job... I should be flattered that he used my numbers, even if it was stupid... Some under 30 workers don't totally suck, there was that one guy.... Incompetence is a fact of life, getting upset won't change that... It's just a hassle and I can cope with hassles...*

Therapist: *How did that feel?*

David: *Awkward and contrived but I get how this could help sometimes.*

Therapist: *You're starting to see that these skills could be useful for you. Are you willing to listen for these kinds of thoughts and track them on your self-monitoring log over the next week? I'd also challenge you to listen for sarcasm in both your anger thoughts and your coping thoughts. For many people, sarcasm can increase anger and it can turn a coping thought back into an expression of anger.*

David: *I'll try but I'm so used to sarcasm it might be hard to hear.*

Therapist: *Sarcasm can become a habit. Sometimes it's easier to recognize it by paying attention to how you feel when you say certain things and by listening to the tone of what you say. Other people's reactions can also be a good indicator of the message you're sending.*

David: *I guess I'll have to pay better attention to that kind of thing.*

Therapist: *We can talk more about it next week when we start practicing the skills in session. Which reminds me, on your self-monitoring log this week, please try to include one or two moderate intensity anger situations, somewhere between 40–60 on the scale. We'll need those for our practice run.*

David: *I can do that.*

Summary

Cognitive restructuring addresses the anger-increasing thoughts and cognitive distortions which function to increase anger to dysfunctional intensities and often leads to cravings for alcohol. We have outlined several steps, or phases, of cognitive restructuring including increased awareness of the influence of thinking on anger, identification of anger-increasing thoughts, and identification of coping thoughts. Our next chapter will describe the rehearsal of these coping thoughts within the context of relaxation exercises and their transfer to the real world.

The process of cognitive restructuring requires considerable therapist skill including distinguishing between thoughts and feeling and gently challenging the client to "think differently." These skills require establishment of strong rapport, trust, and, sometimes, humor.

Suggested Readings

Deffenbacher, J. L., Dahlen, E. R., Lynch, R. S., Morris, C. D., & Gowensmith, W. N. (2000). An application of Beck's cognitive therapy to general anger reduction. *Cognitive Therapy and Research, 24*, 689–697.

This study adapted Beck's cognitive therapy to a small group format for general anger reduction. The nine-session intervention led to significantly greater anger reduction and improved anger control compared to the control.

Hazaleus, S. L., & Deffenbacher, J. L. (1986). Relaxation and cognitive treatments of anger. *Journal of Consulting and Clinical Psychology, 54*, 222–226.

Research compared cognitive and relaxation coping skills interventions for general anger reduction. Both interventions were equally effective and superior to the control for improved anger management. Authors noted client resistance in early sessions of the cognitive intervention but not for the relaxation intervention.

Chapter 11

Coping Skills Rehearsal

Chapter Points

- Coping skills rehearsal blends relaxation skills and cognitive skills together as the client visualizes anger-related scenes in session.
- Over the course of multiple coping skills rehearsals, the intensity of the anger-related emotions increases from moderate anger scenes to high anger scenes to worst anger scenes.
- As the client's coping skill competency increases, therapist guidance is gradually faded.
- Transfer and use of these skills begin to occur between sessions. Experience and progress are described on the self-monitoring log.

Questions for Self-Reflection

- What makes you feel vulnerable in your work as a therapist?
- What makes you feel confident in your work as a therapist?

Anger Management Based Alcohol Treatment. DOI: https://doi.org/10.1016/B978-0-12-812709-4.00011-1

Logic and Goals of Coping Skills Rehearsal

The combined cognitive-relaxation coping skills approach described in this book has not only been effectively combined with alcohol-focused interventions for angry individuals with AUD (Walitzer et al., 2015) but has the greatest empirical support of any intervention for anger reduction (e.g., Deffenbacher et al., 1987, 1988, 2002; Deffenbacher, Thwaites, Wallace, & Oetting, 1994; Deffenbacher, Dahlen et al., 2000; Deffenbacher, Huff et al., 2000; Deffenbacher, Lynch, Oetting, & Kemper, 1996; Deffenbacher, Oetting, Huff, Cornell, & Dallager, 1996; McCloskey, Noblett, Deffenbacher, Gollan, & Coccaro, 2008; Novaco, 1975). Cognitive-relaxation interventions are effective for general anger, angry adolescents, angry drivers, and individuals with intermittent explosive disorder. Cognitive-relaxation coping skills interventions are as effective as relaxation, cognitive, and behavioral skills interventions. One study (McCloskey et al., 2008) found that individual and small group cognitive coping skills interventions were effective but that the individual format may be somewhat superior.

Being able to relax and having the capacity to counter cognitive distortions are rarely enough for reliable anger management. Clients need to practice these skills regularly to make sure that they can identify anger emotions and initiate relaxation and cognitive coping skills with a goal of anger reduction. Coping skills rehearsal is designed to provide this practice. In session, clients visualize personal anger scenes, experience anger arousal, and then use relaxation and cognitive coping skills to reduce the experienced anger. In this way, clients practice using coping skills in a controlled setting with the therapist's assistance. Clients are then supported as they begin to employ coping skills between sessions and the skills are transferred to their lives.

Two principles maximize success at in-session coping skills rehearsal. First, training begins with mild-to-moderate anger potential (i.e., 40–60 intensity level). Over time and with evidence of increased client control of anger, intensity of anger arousal is increased (i.e., generally about 10–15 units of increase). In the final sessions, clients visualize very high intensity scenes (i.e., 80–100 level), including their most angering situations. Second, the degree of therapist assistance in retrieving coping skills is modulated. In the beginning, the therapist provides a great deal of assistance by terminating the anger scene and actively instructing the client in both relaxation and cognitive coping skills. As the client's anger management skills increase, the degree of therapist assistance is faded. In the last few sessions, clients fully self-manage anger reduction. Clients visualize the scene and remain in the scene while actively initiating coping skills on their own. At this stage, the therapist primarily structures the process by providing instructions to turn scenes on and off, occasionally prompting for signals, and setting up the next rehearsal trial.

Coping skills rehearsal also provides guidance to ensure transfer of coping skills and anger management to real-life circumstances. Experiences at coping in real life situations are recorded on self-monitoring log 3. This log is reviewed at the beginning of each session, making adjustments in coping skill application as needed. The therapist also introduces a new worksheet called **Creating Coping Thoughts** (see Appendix II). Before starting the initial coping skills rehearsal, the therapist and client complete this worksheet together with two moderate level scenes, one on each side of the worksheet. After that, the client is asked to complete the worksheet between sessions to prepare for the upcoming rehearsals. The client uses this worksheet to describe two anger scenes, to identify the related anger–increasing thoughts, and to list the helpful coping thoughts for each scene. This sheet is reviewed and supplemented prior to each rehearsal.

Two procedures are employed to maximize success in transferring skills and to reduce client discouragement. First, clients are explicitly advised that initial efforts may not work completely, but that their efforts will improve with practice. A reference back to learning relaxation skills can be useful, noting that initially relaxation was long and cumbersome, but now they can relax easily on their own. Analogies to other types of skill acquisition (e.g., learning to ride a bike) can also be employed. Clients are reassured that using relaxation and cognitive coping skill in real life will become faster and easier with practice. Second, instead of the therapist offering suggestions, clients are asked for ideas on how they can improve their efforts and skills. This shift encourages client to take more responsibility for specific suggestions and strategies. Over time, the focus moves almost entirely to the client coming up with potential changes and improvements.

READY? SET? GO!

How does the therapist know when to initiate coping skills rehearsal? The answer is primarily based on client success in the use of relaxation and cognitive coping skills. This means that the client can self-initiate relaxation quickly using one or more relaxation coping skills, generally in 1–3 minutes. With regard to cognitive coping skills, the client should be reasonably capable of noticing thoughts, identifying what kinds of anger-increasing thoughts are involved, and constructing helpful coping thoughts to challenge the assumptions. When clients are able to do these things, coping skill rehearsal is ready to begin. This is typically about three to five sessions after the start of relaxation training.

Coping Skills Rehearsal Rationale

As with other portions of anger management based alcohol treatment, clients are told explicitly what to expect over the next few sessions. Successes in achieving relaxation, recognizing cognitive distortions, and developing coping thoughts are noted. Clients are told that the next sessions will be devoted to coping skills rehearsal. Rehearsal is described as visualizing scenes that provoke anger, experiencing anger arousal for a few moments (i.e., 30 seconds or so), and then relaxing and rethinking anger down. Rehearsals will start with lower anger levels and a lot of therapist help. As clients' anger management capacities increase, the degree of anger arousal from the scenes will increase and the degree of therapist help will decrease. Clients are told that they will start applying coping skills for anger in their everyday life. They are also advised that in the beginning, anger may not be fully reduced but that over time they will become much better at anger management. In the end, they will be able to identify angry situations, thoughts, and feelings and employ coping skills quickly to manage their anger and its impact on craving and/or drinking.

Giving such a rationale might go something like this:

> *You're doing well with relaxation and cognitive work. You're able to relax on your own in a minute or two by deep breathing and saying the word "relax"* (could be any other relaxation skill or combination). *You're also getting good at identifying your angry thoughts and developing coping thoughts.* (Check client understanding and see if he/she agrees.)
>
> *If you agree, I think we're ready to start practicing the relaxation and cognitive skills together. We talked about this back when we started, but let's review what we'll be doing. We'll develop and have you visualize anger scenes that generate anger emotions much like your relaxation scene helps you feel relaxed. In our sessions you'll begin by relaxing. Once you're relaxed, you'll visualize your anger scene, feel the anger for 30 seconds or so, and then relax and rethink your anger down. To make it easier, we'll start with scenes that only trigger mild to moderate anger, and I'll help you with your relaxation and cognitive coping thoughts. As you become more successful at anger management, we'll increase the level of anger in the scenes and decrease my coaching. At the end, you'll be coping with high anger on your own. As we go along, we'll have you practice relaxation and cognitive coping for anger in your everyday life. This may be a bit hard at first, but like everything else you've been doing, it'll become easier over time.*

Do you have any questions? Could you take a few moments and describe for me your understanding of what we'll be doing over the next few sessions? (Clarify client understanding as needed. This request is made because clients sometimes readily agree with therapist but do not fully understand processes for coming sessions. The summary provides a check on this possibility.)

Constructing Anger Scenes

During the coping skills rehearsal sessions, the therapist and client spend 10–15 minutes developing two anger scenes to be used for the rehearsals by writing scene details on the **Creating Coping Thoughts** worksheet (see Appendix II). As a target exercise from the prior session, clients were asked to identify two angering situations that elicited the range of anger arousal desired for the next session (moderate, high, worst). For example, before the first session of coping skills rehearsal, clients would be asked to identify two current or recent situations that elicited about a 40–60 level of anger. Further, they are asked to identify specific details of the situation and feelings, physical reactions, and thoughts that described the experience. In preparation for subsequent rehearsal session, clients are also asked to identify the cognitive distortions involved and to develop coping thoughts. If clients do not arrive with any anger situations prepared, the therapist can review log entries and use them to develop anger scenes.

IT'S ALL IN THE DETAILS...

Guidelines for anger scene development use the same principles as those for the relaxation scene, except that the focus is on anger arousal. As much as possible, the scene should include descriptions of the basic sensory experiences that make the scene real (i.e., sights, sounds, smells, motion, temperature-type details). The scene should also include relevant emotional (e.g., feeling mad, furious, really annoyed) and physiological detail (e.g., areas of tension, hot sensations, upset stomach, etc.). Physiological detail has added importance. Clients often can identify these internal cues more easily than emotional and cognitive cues and use them to trigger coping skills (e.g., use a clenched jaw or hot sensation in the face to initiate coping). Cognitive details are also emphasized, not only to aid anger arousal during scene visualization but also to frame the coping thoughts to be rehearsed. Clients often describe aggressive and other dysfunctional behavior. These are *not* included in the scene, because this would rehearse that dysfunctional behavior. Instead, behavior is addressed prior to initiating the behavior, when it is still a thought or urge. For example, instead of including examples of "yelling at them" or "shoving him," these might be phrased "you were having the urge to yell at them" or "you are at the point of wanting to shove or push him." This also applies to alcohol or drug use , that is, actual consumption is not used in the scene, but only the urge or desire to consume.

A general orientation to anger scene development might sound something like:

> *Thanks for bringing in the two situations in the 40–60 level of anger intensity. Let's go over them together to make sure we're clear on all the details including your feelings, physical sensations, and thoughts. We want to make the scene as real and specific as we can so it generates the anger emotions you experienced. The goal is to have you visualize the scene, feel the anger, and then practice relaxation and rethinking. The more realistic the better. So, please describe the situation as clearly as you can. I'm going to write everything down on a new worksheet called* **Creating Coping Thoughts**.

The therapist then uses open-ended questions and summaries to clarify and fill out the scene details (e.g., *What other sights or sounds stick out for you*? or *So, you were getting mad and had that warm sensation in your neck and face. What other physical reactions did you notice*?). When the client has fully described the situation and reactions, the therapist summarizes aloud and writes down these details. When the summary is complete, the client is asked if there are any other situational, emotional, physiological, and cognitive details that might have been missed or can make the scene clearer. Anything identified is added to the scene. These details are used later when the therapist asks the client to visualize the scene and experience anger arousal. After the scene is defined, therapist and client explore related anger–increasing thoughts and develop a written list of coping thoughts. The **Anger Increasing Thoughts** and **General Coping Thoughts** Worksheets (see Appendix II) can be useful in preparing these lists.

Four anger scenes from Stephan, David, and Tiffany are described below. They are presented from the lowest to highest anger intensity.

POKE THE BEAR?

A therapist new to anger management based alcohol treatment may have some trepidation about the construction of anger scenes and the client becoming angry during visualization. Our extensive experience in guiding clients through anger scenes is very positive. Clients begin visualization in a relaxed and comfortable state and, even when rehearsing the most intense anger scenes, we have seen no reason to be alarmed or concerned by this process. We have yet to see a client act out or lose control during a rehearsal session. Two other factors may offer reassurance to the therapist. First, the anger scene is experienced very briefly in session, usually less than 60 seconds, and is only activated after the client has signaled a state of relaxation. Second, by the time the clients are rehearsing their most angering situations, they have already been practicing the coping skills for several weeks or longer. The therapist has also had ample time to get to know the client and would most likely not have proceeded with this treatment if there were safety concerns.

Stephan's Moderate Anger Scene (55 Intensity Involving Rumination)

It was last Friday night at the end of my shift at the restaurant. Everyone was gone but me. I was out in the front part of the restaurant leaning on the bar thinking about the shift. (setting details) *I was the shift manager on Friday night, and I swear to god the entire staff was moving slow just to piss me off and get me in trouble with the big boss* (cognitive detail dealing with attributions). *I wanted to fire them all. My shoulders were really tight and the back of my neck was tense too. And there was a tight band around my head, like a headache coming on* (physiological detail). *I wasn't quite furious but I was pretty pissed* (emotional detail) *and I was thinking: My job sucks. My co-workers are resentful assholes. They're just jealous that the boss put me in charge and so they tried to make my night miserable. Why am I stuck working with these losers? I can't stand this pathetic f-ing job. I deserve better. I should be doing more with my life—this is a dead end. I need a drink. (cognitive detail)*

Stephan's coping thoughts:

- *I'm a good worker even at a sucky job.*
- *She picked me to be in charge so I must be doing something right.*
- *I can stay cool and not let them get to me.*
- *I'm not going to give them the satisfaction of seeing me all pissed off.*
- *I can't change them with anger. I only upset myself.*
- *Maybe that's the best they can do. Not very good, but their best.*
- *Getting mad sure doesn't make them move any faster.*
- *It's a hassle, and I've been dealing with hassles for years.*
- *I'll show them by staying calm.*
- *I need to get a new job.*

During the first rehearsal of this scene, Stephan noticed a strong urge to drink in addition to his anger. He remembered that, after work that night, he had gone home and drank almost two bottles of wine while replaying the work shift in his mind. He was surprised to realize how strongly his anger and craving for alcohol were connected for him in the scene rehearsal. He also recognized that coming up with coping thoughts while sober made the situation seem more manageable and his urge to drink in the repeated rehearsal was much less prominent.

David's High Anger Scene (80 Intensity)

It was last Wednesday after a long, stressful day at work. I walked into the kitchen and guess what I saw? All the lights were on, the cupboards were open, the garbage was overflowing, there were tons of dirty dishes in the sink... and there was a bonus. The dog threw up on the kitchen floor and it looked like it had been sitting there for hours. (situational details). *I was instantly pissed.* (emotional detail) *My jaw was so tight I could feel the tension in my face. My stomach hurt and I know my fists were clenched.* (physiological detail) *I was so pissed I wanted to yell or scream or throw something.* (behavioral urge detail) *I was thinking: This house is a disaster and no one seems to care. They do this just to piss me off. Why do I have to live with such lazy, incompetent, ungrateful slobs? Seriously! I deserve more respect. I pay the mortgage and all the bills. These people take me and my money for granted. This stuff drives me to drink. Why do we have this stupid fricking dog anyway?* (cognitive details including blaming as an explanation for his drinking)

David's coping thoughts:

- *Maybe they're all just busy and couldn't get to it.*
- *They know this stuff pisses me off, but I'm not 100% sure it's intentional.*
- *Am I using this as an excuse to drink? Probably. I'll have to think more about this.*
- *I do love them even though they do stuff that upsets me and I know they love me.*
- *It's not the dog's fault that he threw up.*

After visualizing this scene, David reported the following interesting observation. "*That was strange. While I was relaxing at the end I had an image flash through my mind. It was me living alone in a really clean apartment with all the cupboards closed. But I wasn't happy. It actually made me really sad because I was alone. Not even the dog was there. If I want a perfectly clean house, I'd probably have to live on my own but I'd miss my family.*" The therapist inquired about how this related to his anger and he added. "*It makes me think I'm pushing my family away by getting angry, drinking, and blaming the messy house. It makes me ask if it's worth it to get so mad.*"

Tiffany's High Anger Scene (90 Intensity)

It was late last week. I came home from work and found my mom outside my apartment building. She was drunk and asking to borrow money to pay her rent. (setting and interpersonal details) *I know she's drinking away all her money. I hate having to give her money but I CANNOT have her living with me if she gets evicted.* (more cognitive and interpersonal detail) *I was so mad, but it was kind of a sad-mad. You know where you're really mad, but also feel tired and stuck.* (emotional detail) *I noticed my stomach was all tight.* (physiological detail) *I was thinking: Why should I have to deal with her problems? I have enough on my own. She's the mom. She should be taking care of me. Why can't I get a break in life? I shouldn't have to support both of us. I'm working so hard while her life is just a party. She's the worst mom and I hate her.*

Tiffany's coping thoughts:

- *I can't expect people to act the way I want them to.*
- *Maybe I'm expecting too much from her.*
- *I've been taking care of her for years and I'm proud that I'm such a responsible person.*
- *At least I'm not as pathetic as she is.*
- *It's not worth getting so upset.*
- *I don't want to end up bitter and drunk like her.*
- *I will NOT let her drive me to drink!*
- *Getting all pissed off doesn't change anything.*
- *I don't hate her all the time. She's my mom.*

When debriefing the rehearsals, Tiffany said the first time through was tough; she felt really angry, it was hard for her to relax or find her coping thoughts, and she was glad the therapist was there to help her. The second time through the scene, she noticed herself feeling sad along with angry and that's when she decided to think about not letting her mom's problems become an excuse for her to drink. She said she also felt guilty for saying she hated her mom. The session ended with Tiffany admitting confusion about her relationship with her mom while also feeling more in control of her ability to calm down and think about her choices.

Tiffany's Worst Anger Scene (95 Intensity Involving Self-Directed Anger)

It was last Saturday around 7, still kind of light out. I was sitting alone on the couch in my living room just kind of staring at the wall where the TV sits. It wasn't on, but that's where I was looking. (setting details) *I was doing what I always do, sitting there being really, really mad at myself, really down on myself about how I look.* (emotional detail) *My body is disgusting and I think about it all the time. I was gross when I was fat and I'm just as gross now in a different way. I'll always hate my body. This is my own damn fault. Why me? My brothers can eat all day and never get fat. I can't stand looking in the mirror. I am one ugly bitch. No man will ever want to be with me once he sees me naked. I'm going to die alone.* (cognitive detail) *I'm trapped in this body and no one understands. I don't know what was going on physically. I just felt kind of numb.* (physiological detail)

Tiffany's coping thoughts:

- *I'm too hard on myself. I should lighten up and treat myself better.*
- *I get compliments on my clothes and hair all the time.*
- *I was even more miserable when I was fat; at least now I can buy clothes off the rack.*
- *There's a new guy at work and I think he's been checking me out so I can't be that disgusting.*
- *I look pretty good when I dress up.*
- *Weight loss isn't easy and I'm doing the best I can.*

There was enough time to go through three rehearsals of this scene which was a familiar one for Tiffany. These rehearsals were painful and challenging for her but also offered some hope. She was able to relax and find coping thoughts on her own and said she felt less angry and more in control by the third repetition. She knew her self-directed anger was leading her to drink and she knew her drinking would only make things worse for her, inside and out. She decided to start putting some of her alcohol money in a jar and save up for the skin surgery.

YOU DID IT!

It is important that the client and therapist recognize that the progress made by the client in learning, and using coping skills should be attributed to the client and not to the therapist. It is the client who retrieves relaxation and puts cognitive coping thoughts into use. Although this direction toward self-attributions is encouraged throughout treatment, more direct communication of this is helpful during coping skills rehearsals. As the client comes to accept that the progress toward change is made by him or herself, the transfer of these skills to the client's "real world" will be enhanced.

In-Session Coping Skills Rehearsal Using Anger Scenes

As previously mentioned, it is important to consider two principles that guide in-session training. First, anger-arousal capacity of scenes is arranged from moderate (40–60 level) upward to the clients' most angering situations (80–100 intensity). Second, degree of therapist assistance is faded from high to minimal or no assistance in coping skills retrieval. Change in scene intensity and level of therapist assistance are determined by client progress. As clients successfully negotiate the intensity level and degree of self-control built into the stage of coping skill rehearsal, anger intensity is increased and therapist assistance is decreased.

ACTING IT OUT...

In addition to verbally describing the anger-producing scene, it is imperative that the therapist includes voice tone, volume, and inflection, and the client's words and language, during the coping skills rehearsal. Without these critical components, clients are unlikely to experience in-session anger which is necessary to the success of the rehearsal.

Phase I: Moderate Anger and High Therapist Guidance

As described previously, each rehearsal begins with the collaborative development of the client's two anger scenes including specific details, anger cognitions, coping thoughts, and any related cravings. The therapist and client then discuss the methods of relaxation that have been working best for the client. Using a calm voice, the therapist begins by asking the client to get comfortable, with eyes closed, and then helps the client relax, reminding the client to signal when feeling relaxed. After acknowledging the client's signal, the therapist switches to a more intense tone of voice and instructs the client to visualize one of the prepared moderate anger scenes (40–60 intensity) and to reexperience the anger. The therapist asks the client to signal when feeling angry by raising a finger or hand. After the scene has been described and the client has signaled anger, the scene continues to be exposed for 20–30 seconds with an occasional therapist prompt to continue to experience the anger and focus on the anger-increasing thoughts. Then the therapist asks the client to switch off the scene and actively assists in the retrieval of relaxation. If the personal relaxation scene has been effective for the client, it is suggested that the relaxation scene be employed for the first couple of anger scene presentations. This way, the client can immediately switch from visualizing the anger scene to visualizing the relaxation scene which can be an easier transition from anger to relaxation. Instruction in a second relaxation coping skill (e.g., deep breathing) is then added to the rehearsal. The client is instructed to signal when feeling relaxed again. Once the client signals relaxation, the therapist reads aloud the client's prepared cognitive coping thoughts and asks the client to focus for a few moments on those and any other thoughts. The therapist then repeats the coping skills rehearsal with the second moderate anger scene. The two scenes are alternated and the procedures are repeated as time allows, hopefully for a total of four to six repetitions. After the first two or three rehearsals, any two relaxation coping skills can be employed if the client has demonstrated the ability to shift out of anger scenes. The session is ended with the backward counting procedure employed in relaxation training (5...4...3...2...1).

Instructions for initial coping skills rehearsal might be like:

> Close your eyes and take a few deep breaths...breathing out tension and breathing in a feeling of calm... *therapist continues to help the client relax and watches for the client's signal.* Good, I see your signal. Continue relaxing a little bit longer, enjoying the feeling of relaxation you've created. *In a moment, I'm going to have you turn on your anger scene involving (therapist provides a brief description and tone of voice changes). When I do, put yourself back into that situation like it's happening to you right now and signal me when you're in that scene and experiencing anger...So, right now, switch on that anger scene...Let yourself really be there...You are (therapist describes the scene using details and cues developed earlier)...(client signals anger)...Good, I see your signal...*(therapist continues describing the scene)...*Let the anger build...Notice how you experience the anger...Maybe it's the tension in your shoulders and neck, maybe in the clenching of your jaw, maybe that hot sensation in your face, maybe you're demanding that things be fair and right...Be right there, feeling that anger and listening to the thoughts* (therapist describes 2–4 angry thoughts)...(scene is exposed in this manner for approximately 30–60 seconds)...*Now switch off that anger scene and switch on your relaxation scene, signaling me when you're once again relaxed. So, put yourself right back into* (therapist describes relaxation scene in a calm voice)...(after relaxation is signaled, the therapist provides instruction for another relaxation coping skill)...*Now I want you to think about that anger situation you just visualized, but now thinking about it with the coping thoughts we identified earlier. So, you are thinking...(therapist reads several of the prepared coping thoughts slowly)...Good; you're reducing anger by relaxating and rethinking...Now we're ready for the second scene involving* (therapist makes brief reference). *We'll use the same procedure* (therapist briefly summarizes procedure to remind client of the steps)...*So, right now put yourself right back into...*(therapist describes scene and repeats procedure similar to that above)....

Occasionally, clients do not signal anger or relaxation. Two possibilities exist: either they are not experiencing anger or relaxation or they have experienced it but have forgotten to signal. This issue can be addressed by inserting a statement like, "*And signaling me when you're feeling angry (or relaxed).*" If the client signals, this is acknowledged and reflects he forgot to signal. If the client does not signal, indicating absence of the state, this is acknowledged, and the therapist continues activities to achieve that state (e.g., "*So, just continuing to say the word 'relax' slowly to yourself, relaxing more each time you say it, and signaling me when you're relaxed."*).

> **DOUBLE TAKE?**
>
> While we have been describing the process of rehearsing two distinct anger scenes in each session, this is not always possible. Sometimes, clients can benefit as much from the repeated rehearsal of one single scene as they can from two. This is especially true if the scene is something they frequently encounter (like their daily commute) or one that requires the client to employ more challenging coping skills (such as a heated argument with a friend). This repeated scene strategy can also be used if the client arrives unprepared or if there's limited time to formulate two scenes. Consequently, the repetition of a single anger scene, instead of two different situations, can be a useful alternative.

Scenes are presented in this manner as time permits. Allow 5–10 minutes at the end of the session to debrief the coping skills rehearsal experience. Note what made the scene vivid and anger-arousing (e.g., scene details and physiological and cognitive cues). Review relaxation experiences and identify the most effective methods. Review which coping thoughts worked best and which did not. Edit out thoughts that did not seem helpful and consider adding new coping thoughts.

If the coping skills rehearsal went well in the session, ask the client to identify two scenes at approximately 60–80 intensity for the next session using the **Creating Coping Thoughts** worksheet. Ask client to also complete self-monitoring log 3, with coping efforts, for next session. End the session with a goal of beginning to apply relaxation and cognitive coping skills in real life.

Phase II: High Anger and More Client Control

If, in a session or two, the client is handling higher intensity anger scenes, relaxation is being signaled quickly, and cognitive coping thoughts are effective, then rehearsal procedures shift toward increased client initiation of coping skills. The client starts the rehearsal by relaxing without help from the therapist. The therapist continues to turn anger scenes on and off, but after the anger scene is cleared, the client initiates relaxation and cognitive coping on his/her own. The therapist only provides general prompts, such as "*using whatever kind of relaxation works best for you*," "*changing those shoulds to wants*," "*staying with the reasonable negative*," or "*looking for alternative explanations*."

Instructions might be something like:

> *Things seem to be going pretty well in our sessions and are coming along outside as well. Does it seem that way to you?* (Therapist and client briefly review to make sure both have similar view.) *Given your progress, I want*

to changes things a bit today. Here's what I propose. We'll start by having you relax yourself in whichever way works best and then you'll signal me when you're feeling relaxed. I'll help you get into and out of your anger scenes like we've done before, but when you're out of the anger scene, I'll have you relax away anger and review the coping thoughts on your own. Ok with you? (discuss as needed and ask client to begin relaxation when ready). *Good, I see your signal. Stay with that feeling of relaxation you've created a little bit longer. In a moment, I'm going to have you visualize your scene involving* (brief reference to scene content). *So right now put yourself back into* (Procedures are the same as the prior session until the anger scene is terminated.)*. . .So, switch that scene off and start relaxing in whatever way works best for you, signaling me when you're once again relaxed. . .*(Therapist waits for signal and acknowledges it when seen. If no signal is apparent in 45–60 seconds, a prompt like, "And signaling me when you're relaxed," is added)*. . ..Ok, now start to rethink that situation using the coping thoughts we identified earlier. . .*(Every 10 seconds or so, the therapist may add a general cognitive prompt like, "Staying with what works best for you").

This procedure is repeated and alternated with the second prepared scene as time allows and then debriefed as in prior sessions. Attention is focused on client experience with self-initiation of relaxation and cognitive coping skills; the client's progress is affirmed and reinforced. Adjustments to relaxation and cognitive coping thoughts are made as needed. Target exercises and between-session goal application continue as before.

The notion of taking a mental or physical time out (i.e., distancing one's self from a frustrating situation in order to cope) can be a useful procedure for many people. If the client sees merit in this idea, several possibilities might be discussed in this session. All of these examples have in common that the person slows events down and makes time to apply coping skills for anger reduction. Sometimes these are combined with plans or strategies to address the frustration or provocation. Examples might include things like

- Physical separation from provocation—*Some angry, hurtful things have been said, and I don't want to contribute any more. I'm going to leave for a while so I can get my head together. We can talk about it later when I'm not so angry.* (Person applies cognitive and relaxation coping skills in the interim and develops a plan about addressing the situation.)
- Instructing self to physically separate when others may not be immediately involved—*I'm really pissed right now. I'm going to grab a pad of paper and go get some coffee. I'll relax and write some things down.* (followed by cognitive and relaxation coping skills)

- Seeking a delay in responding—*Let me think about that and I'll get back to you later.* (followed by coping skill application and development of a plan)
- Seeking a delay and alternative way of responding—*Let me think about that and I'll send you an email with my thoughts.* (followed by coping skill application and email)
- Self-instruction in thinking before responding—*Ok, slow down and think before you jump in...*(relaxation coping skill plus cognitive coping skills and calm, reflection on situation)
- Coping skill application in preparation for an event—Client identifies a time before a frustrating or provocative event to employ coping skills in order to be better prepared to deal with the event. *I'm dreading this meeting with my boss. I'm going to take a few deep breaths before I walk in there and try to stay calm and focused.*
- Coping skill application after some frustrating or angering event—Client has been through a stressful or angering situation and takes time out to apply coping skills in order to reduce residual anger and rumination about the event. *That meeting was frustrating and traffic was a nightmare. I think I'll sit in the car a few minutes and picture my relaxation scene before I walk in the house.*

Phase III: Worst Anger and High Client Control

As the client demonstrates success in Phase II and at least some success in external application, anger intensity of scenes moves higher (80–100 intensity), and therapist control is minimized so that the client takes an even more active role in reducing anger. To achieve this, procedures are changed in two ways. First, after the therapist switches on the anger scene, the client visualizes the scene, experiences anger, and then *stays in the scene* while applying relaxation and coping skills to reduce anger. This mimics real life, getting angry, and actively coping. Second, the signal system is modified so that the therapist knows when anger is both experienced and reduced. The client signals the experience of anger by raising a finger or hand and keeps the signal up until anger is reduced. The signal to the therapist that the client has managed the anger is the gentle lowering of the finger or hand. Then, the therapist clears the anger scene and prepares the client for the next scene.

During scene visualization, the therapist may provide a few general prompts (e.g., *really feeling the anger,"relaxing in the way that works best for you", listening for the 'shoulds'*). Many clients report that this helps keep them focused. Additionally, the therapist acknowledges signals and may need to provide a reminder to signal. Otherwise, the therapist provides little direct instruction.

Instructions for in-session coping skills rehearsal might sound like the following:

> *Good, I see your signal. Continue to enjoy that feeling of relaxation you've created. In a moment, I'm going to have you visualize your anger scene involving* (brief reference). *When I do, I want you to put yourself right back into it and experience that anger. Signal me by raising your finger when you are experiencing that anger, but this time keep your finger up as long as you're angry. Stay with the anger and let it build. When your anger is high, I want to stay in the scene and initiate your relaxation and coping thoughts to reduce your anger. That is, stay in the scene and cope with the anger, signaling me by lowering your finger when you've brought your anger under control. . ..So, right now put yourself into that situation* (therapist begins describing the scene.). . .(Some time later client raises finger.). . .*Good, I see your signal. Just let that anger build, really feeling the anger*. . .(20–30 seconds later). . .*And now using your favorite relaxation method. . .Perhaps challenging your demands that your co-workers must agree with you. . .Perhaps replacing your cursing with realistic negative thoughts and humor*. . ..(Client signals anger reduction by lowering finger). . .*Ok, I see your signal. Now, switch that scene off and notice how you feel about bringing your anger under control*. . .(5–10 seconds later the therapist orients the client to the next scene and presents in a similar manner).

As in prior sessions, the rehearsal with the new self-control approach is debriefed. Relaxation methods rarely need any adjustment at this point, but therapist and client collaboratively review the coping thoughts that work best and add and remove thoughts as needed. Target exercises remain the same. Between-session practice continues to focus on real-life application, monitoring those experiences, continuing to develop coping thoughts at home, and identifying new anger scenes for the next session.

As clients experience greater self-controlled anger reduction within and between sessions, two additional cognitive coping skills may be appropriate. The first is self-talk to initiate coping and the second is self-talk to reinforce progress. Clients' self-talk statements can be added to the general coping thoughts list and used as needed.

Self-talk to initiate best coping methods:

- *I'm starting to get angry. Take some deep breaths. . .Keep it real. No blowing things up.*

- *Time for relaxing. I'm just going to sit here for a few moments and turn on my relaxation scene.*
- *I hear the 'ought to, gotta' going off in my head. Focus now on how I'd like him to behave.*

Self-talk to reinforce effort and progress:

- *Cool. I handled that pretty well.*
- *I'm getting better at this anger management stuff.*
- *If they're doing this to piss me off, they're going to be so disappointed. I'm going to keep my cool by relaxing and trading in my catastrophes for real negatives.*
- *Way to go. You didn't get demanding. You didn't yell at anybody like you used to.*

IMPROVISE OR STICK WITH THE PLAN?

Sometimes, clients show up to sessions already feeling angry from a very recent situation; maybe a fight as they walked out the door, a last minute work conflict, or traffic. Ideally, these types of situations can be utilized in session without the need to "recreate" an anger scene from the past; the anger experience is happening in real time. The dilemma for therapists comes when the level of present anger is much higher than the level that was scheduled to be practiced in session. For example, the plan was to use a moderate level (40–60) scene but the client shows up with live anger in the 80–100 range. On the one hand, assuming the client is new to anger management skills, the progression of skill acquisition is designed to be gradual in order to build skills and confidence over time. On the other hand, the opportunity to rehearse anger management in real time provides a unique opportunity and one more consistent with "real life." Using the presenting anger also serves to meet the clients where they are and to help them address a situation practically in the moment. Therefore, we leave the final decision to the therapist's best clinical judgment, balancing the needs of the client, and the comfort of the therapist.

Transfer of Coping Skills Rehearsal to Real Life

When in-session coping skill training begins, clients are encouraged to start applying cognitive and relaxation coping skills to deal with anger and alcohol use in everyday life. As noted before, clients are reminded that the skills will become more effective with time and practice. As therapy progresses, clients spend part of each session reviewing the self-monitoring log with the therapist, identifying challenges in daily skills use, and noting situations in which they were successful using the skills to manage anger and avoid alcohol.

When the client demonstrates improved anger control and has made changes in alcohol use, the last two or three sessions may be stretched out to 2 or 3 weeks apart. This keeps the client involved in continued practice without loss of therapy contact, providing a partial bridge to maintenance and relapse prevention (see Chapter 12: Relapse Prevention).

OVER AND OVER AGAIN...

Sometimes clients begin to notice that certain types of situations repeat in their lives. An additional task may be for clients to make an anger coping plan for such situations. The plan should include the type of situation, relaxation coping skills to be used, and list of common cognitive distortions followed by three to five specific coping thoughts. Clients may also list specific behaviors they want to include (e.g., listening carefully and summarizing what person is saying before expressing an opinion, identifying ways to respectfully disagree, taking a time out, problem-solving, using drink refusal skills). Clients are encouraged to review and adjust plans as time goes on. Clients are also encouraged to set aside two or three times a week to review the situation and their plans going forward.

Clients may have identified certain cognitive coping thoughts that address issues best. These can be summarized in list of best coping thoughts, which are rehearsed and added to over time. Some categories and examples are listed below:

Cool thoughts

- *That's it. Three big deep breaths and chill on each one out.*
- *Be cool. Just be cool.*
- *Easy does it. No flaming tempers today.*

Reducing catastrophes

- *It's a deal, but not a horribly big deal.*
- *It's a hassle, not the end of the world.*
- *Its happened. I don't like it but can stand it.*
- *All hell's breaking loose. Now there's a funny image.*

Seeing the big picture

- *Look for exceptions.*
- *Stop being so negative. Find some positive.*
- *Stop judging the person. Look at and react to behavior only.*

Dealing with should, got to, have to, need, must

- *They don't have to do what I want. They're free to choose what they want.*
- *Nobody appointed me king. Just stay with my preferences and only for me.*
- *My values are important to me but aren't rules for others to live by.*

Blame and punishment

- *They're doing the best they can.*
- *They made a mistake, but they're probably just scared (hurt, depressed, overwhelmed, confused, misinformed, etc.).*
- *Cut 'em some slack. I mess up sometimes and hope they'd give me a break.*
- *Nobody appointed me judge, jury, and executioner.*

Escape routes

- *I can always walk away rather than lose it or do something dumb.*
- *I'm going to let my feet do the talking, not my fists.*
- *Nobody's going to push me into anything. I'll walk first.*

Problem-solving

- *It's not a disaster, just a problem to be solved. So, how do I want to approach it?*
- *Develop a plan. So, the first step is....*
- *It's a complicated problem. Break it down into smaller parts and deal with each one at a time.*

No good solutions

- *Not everything has a good solution. No need to get all pissed off because I can't find one.*
- *Looks like I'm stuck. I'm going to chill and use my skills. Maybe it'll look different later.*
- *No need to yell or beat on it, just because I can't solve it. Everyone has bad days.*

Self-efficacy thoughts

- *I'm getting better at this anger management stuff.*
- *Now I can hang in there and cope.*
- *I'm handling things now, not yelling like the old days.*

Time outs

- *Rarely do things have to be done right now. I can take a time out, relax, and rethink it before I deal with it.*
- *Great coaches take strategic time outs. That's what I'm going to do right now. Take a time out.*
- *Back away. Rethink things. It'll probably look better then.*

Sober thoughts

- *I know drinking is just going to make things worse.*
- *I don't need to drink, I have other ways to handle things.*
- *I'm not going to use my anger as an excuse to drink anymore.*
- *I've come too far to slip up now. I can do this!*

Summary

In-session practice of relaxation skills and cognitive coping skills is the basis for anger management based coping skills rehearsal. The client becomes skilled and confident at managing anger emotions in session and gradually transfers this skill set to daily life. This can be a rewarding part of therapy; clients may actually begin to report difficulty experiencing anger during sessions because of immediate application of relaxation and coping skills. Ideally, with time and practice, these skills will become the client's automatic response to frustrating situations. Our next chapter discusses the critical topic of maintenance of both sobriety skills and anger management improvements.

Suggested Readings

Deffenbacher, J. L., & McKay, M. (2000a). *Overcoming situational and general anger: Therapist protocol.* Oakland, CA: New Harbinger.

Deffenbacher, J. L., & McKay, M. (2000b). *Overcoming situational and general anger: Client protocol.* Oakland, CA: New Harbinger.

The therapist manual provides information to therapists about how to conduct a cognitive-relaxation coping skills approach for working with clients with general or situational problem anger. The client protocol is to provide angry clients with general understanding of anger and parallel activities in therapy.

Deffenbacher, J. L., Thwaites, G. A., Wallace, T. L., & Oetting, E. R. (1994). Social skills and cognitive-relaxation approaches to general anger reduction. *Journal of Counseling Psychology, 41*, 386–396.

Research compared cognitive-relaxation coping skills and social communication skill approaches for anger reduction. Both interventions were equally effective and superior to the control condition for general anger reduction.

McCloskey, M. S., Noblett, K. L., Deffenbacher, J. L., Gollan, J. K., & Coccaro, E. F. (2008). Cognitive-behavioral therapy for intermittent explosive disorder: A pilot randomized clinical trial. *Journal of Consulting and Clinical Psychology*, *76*, 876–886.

This research compared individual and small group cognitive-relaxation coping skills training for the reduction anger and impulsive aggressive behavior in individual with intermittent explosive disorder. Both coping skills training formats led to superior outcomes compared to the control. Some evidence suggested that the individual format may have been superior to the small group format.

Chapter 12

Relapse Prevention

Chapter Points

- A difficult truth in addiction treatment is that many clients who have made substantial gains while in treatment will subsequently experience a "lapse" or "relapse".
- It is important for the therapist and client to consider what could lead to a lapse or relapse in either drinking, anger management, or both.
- Making a plan to get back on track if a relapse happens is essential for long-term success.
- We outline client strategies and therapist strategies for avoiding and proactively preparing for drinking and anger management lapses and relapses.

Questions for Self-Reflection

- Why do you think relapse happens for many people?
- When you've made a behavior change in your life, how did you maintain it?

Anger Management Based Alcohol Treatment. DOI: https://doi.org/10.1016/B978-0-12-812709-4.00012-3

Therapist: *We're nearing the end of the program. You've made a lot of changes in both your drinking and in managing your anger emotions. I'd like to spend time today talking about how to maintain your progress and avoid going backwards.*

David: *That's what I've been thinking about too. I'm feeling great; I'm sober, I'm more productive at work without the foggy head and the constant feelings of irritation, I'm getting along better with my family, and I'm not letting the little stuff bug me as much. I still get mad but I'm able to recognize what's happening and calm myself down before I react. I want to keep this going and I can't afford to go back. I have too much to lose.*

Therapist: *You're a different person that you were a few months ago, sober, more in control and you want to keep it that way. A helpful way to think about this is something called "relapse prevention." Basically, relapse prevention has two goals: identifying high-risk situations and identifying the skills needed to manage those situations. We can talk about relapse prevention in terms of both alcohol and anger and also look at some ways to maintain your successes.*

David: *That makes a lot of sense. I've been doing a good job avoiding alcohol and managing my anger but I'm worried about the future. And I know all about relapse. I've been sober before for a couple years but ended up going back. I can't let that happen again. I'm running out of chances.*

For any individual client, predicting, preventing, and coping with posttreatment relapse is a difficult and challenging, but critically important, therapeutic task. Many factors, intrapersonal, intrapersonal, and situational, can bring about a high-risk situation and influence a client's response to it. The therapist and client have the goal, often discussed in the latter phase of treatment, of preparing the client for these posttreatment challenges.

The Relapse Prevention Model

The relapse prevention model is a conceptual and theoretical system that provides insight into the process of addictive behavior relapse. Relapse, loosely defined as a return to a previously problematic behavior such as drinking, is an unfortunately common posttreatment occurrence. As most recently described and elaborated upon by Witkiewitz and Marlatt (2004) and Hendershot, Witkiewitz, George, and Marlatt (2011), the relapse prevention model incorporates three dynamic and interactive constructs: the contextual factors of the high-risk situation (e.g., the intrapersonal, interpersonal, environmental characteristics that serve as triggers for relapse), tonic processes (i.e., stable characteristics that serve as risk or protective factors for relapse such as family history of addictions, personality traits, physical dependence), and phasic responses (i.e., transient and fluid reactions and responses such as affect and coping behaviors that serve as risk or protective factors for relapse). Fig. 12.1 describes the relationships between these constructs, which interact in both unidirectional and bidirectional effects. Tonic processes influence longer term risk for relapse as these processes are trait-like personal characteristics. Witkiewitz and Marlatt (2004) describe tonic process as those that "often accumulate and lead to the instigation of a high-risk situation, proving the foundation for the possibility of a lapse" (p. 230). Phasic responses, in contrast, change and flow as the individual experiences affect, cognitions, and behaviors. The authors describe phasic responses as "the cusp, or turning point, of the system, where behavioral responding may lead to a sudden change in substance use behavior" (p. 230).

The relapse prevention model spawned relapse prevention (RP) therapy in the mid-1980s. Broadly speaking, RP has two central goals: identify the problem drinker's triggers and enhance coping skills to address them. Relevant coping skills, cognitive-behavioral in nature, may include assertiveness training, communication skills, couples and family therapy, negative mood management,

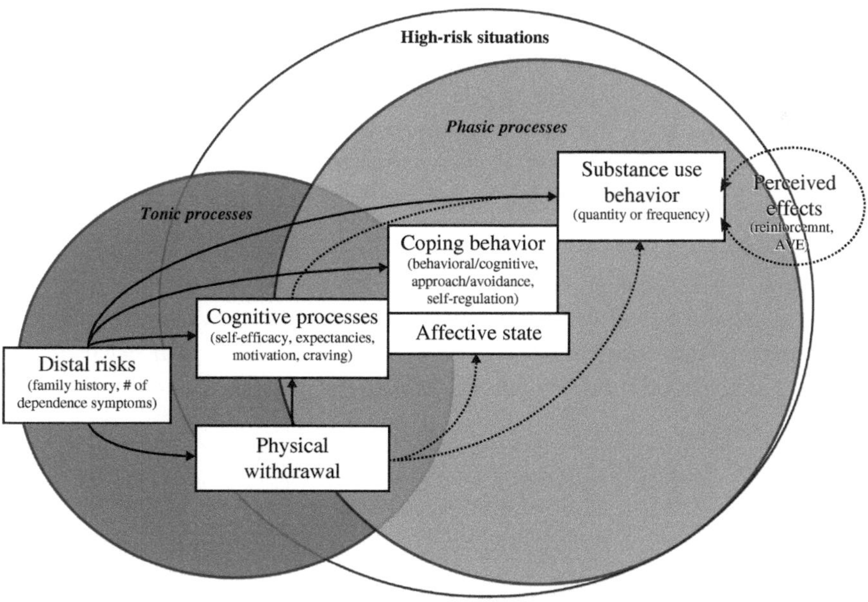

Figure 12.1 The dynamic model of relapse proposed by Witkiewitz and Marlatt (2004) and Wikiewitz et al. (2007).

relaxation training, problem solving, and urge surfing. RP treatment content is flexible, adaptable, and individualized. It may be implemented as a treatment protocol in and of itself or in combination with other therapeutic approaches, as an individual therapy or group therapy, in outpatient or inpatient settings. Let's take a closer look at several components of the model.

THE RP MODEL

Three overarching constructs are proposed to contribute to and to protect from drinking relapse: (1) *contextual factors* such as the presence of high-risk triggers and/or protective elements in the environment; (2) *stable individual characteristics* that are protective or risk factors for relapse (e.g., impulsivity, family history of addiction, supportive family, economic stability, and resources); and (3) *fluid factors* that have moment-by-moment changes and transient influences that are protective or risk factors (e.g., affect, cognitions, coping behaviors).

Substance Use

With regard to drinking, alcohol consumption is often assessed as the frequency of consumption (e.g., times per day, days per week) and the quantity (i.e., number of standard drinks consumed in a single drinking event or day). Important, however, is the distinction between a "lapse" and a "relapse" with regard to posttreatment drinking. Steckler, Witkiewitz, and Marlatt (2013) describe this distinction: "The initial transgression of a problem behavior after a quit attempt, herein defined as a 'lapse,' could eventually lead to continued transgressions of the problem behavior to a level that is similar to the prequit level of behavior, which is often defined as a 'relapse.'" (p. 125). A common axiom which utilizes this distinction is "Don't let a lapse become a relapse!"

> Therapist: *That brings up something else I'd like to discuss. Of course it'd be ideal if you never go back to your old ways, but it's important to consider what you would do if you noticed that starting to happen. It's like a fire drill. You do what you can to prevent the fire, you hope it never happens, but you need to have a plan in place, and practice that plan, in case there is a fire.*
>
> David: *I know what you mean. I've had a few drinking relapses in my time and for me, it's like a slippery slope rather than a dramatic event. I get lazy, I get complacent, and I think "it'll be different this time," but it never is.*
>
> Therapist: *You're not alone in that experience; relapse to drinking is common. If it's ok with you, let's focus first on drinking relapse and then we can talk about relapse in terms of anger emotions.*

David: *Sure. I guess what's happened in the past is that I get away from what's been working and I decide that "one drink won't hurt." Of course it's not that one drink that hurts, it's the hundreds that come after that one. Sometimes I find myself saying, "Well, I already blew it, might as well finish the bottle and quit again tomorrow." That doesn't work either.*

Therapist: *It might be helpful to think about a "lapse" as something a little different than a "relapse." A lapse is when you find yourself in that high-risk situation and may have already taken a drink. You can't undo taking the drink, but what you do next determines whether this is truly a lapse or if it becomes a full relapse into old behaviors. Lapses can be learning experiences and a chance to refocus your energy on abstinence. Relapses...*

David: *are horrible. I end up back where I was but it's even worse and more disappointing because I was doing well.*

Therapist: *Let's take a look at this sheet* ***(What to do if a Lapse Happens).*** *It has some ideas on managing a lapse, learning from it, and preventing it from becoming a relapse.*

David: *This seems so obvious but I like the way this handout breaks it down and makes it sound manageable. If this happened to me, I'd need to not finish the bottle and not beat myself up. I would also need to think seriously about how I let myself get to this point.*

Cognitive Processes

Cognitions—specifically, thoughts and expectations about drinking behavior and sobriety—contribute importantly to the process of relapse. Central cognitive constructs include self-efficacy and self-confidence (thoughts regarding changing drinking behavior), outcome expectations (thoughts regarding alcohol's and sobriety's effects on the individual), the "abstinence violation effect" (thoughts regarding continuing to drink after a brief lapse), motivation (thoughts regarding the desire and need to change drinking behavior), and craving (thoughts regarding wanting and needing alcohol). These alcohol-related cognitions are placed in the relapse prevention model within the overlap of the tonic stable processes and the phasic fluid responses. As such, these cognitive constructs have both a stable and enduring effect emanating from the individual's general cognitive beliefs as well as a malleable and plastic effect emanating from upon the individual's moment-to-moment experiences.

Goals of cognitive therapy as it pertains to RP include identification of, insight into, and modification of an individual's maladaptive thoughts and ideas as they relate to achieving sobriety and avoiding relapse. Cognitive therapy seeks to identify and challenge maladaptive thoughts and ideas such as *I can never be 100% sober, the stress of my job makes me drink, if I only felt better and less stressed I would be able to stop drinking. Therapy also supports and encourages positive protective thoughts and ideas such as sobriety is hard and I will work hard to get there, but it is much better than the alternative, drinking used to be fun, now it just causes me problems, and I can do this if I take it one day, one moment at a time.*

Affective States

Emotion and affect are closely related to relapse. Depression, anxiety, anger-related emotions, and combinations are closely and bidirectionally related to the experience of maladaptive cognitions and risk for relapse. These emotions are worthy of therapeutic attention when experienced at both a clinical intensity (e.g., depression and/or anxiety disorders) as well as at a subclinical level (feeling sad, annoyed, or stressed).

Why is negative mood such a predictable trigger for drinking? For many (if not most) individuals —both nonproblem drinkers and problem drinkers alike — alcohol consumption regulates and alleviates negative emotional states. Negative affect, such as depression, anxiety, and anger-related emotions, is often regulated, or coped with, by drinking. This negative reinforcement loop is an important factor in both social drinking and problematic drinking. Drinking to cope with negative emotions typically yields this short-lived benefit, and this relatively quick mood improvement associated with alcohol consumption is a potent reinforcer for drinking for many individuals.

Experiencing positive mood states may also be a trigger for relapse. It is not incompatible that individuals also find that positive moods such as being happy, relaxed, and excited can be triggers for drinking. Why? Enhancement of a positive affect state is also an important positive reinforcer for alcohol consumption. Drinking to celebrate, because one "deserves it," to enhance socializing with others, and to enhance relaxation are examples of drinking's positive reinforcement value. Although clinically speaking, drinking to enhance positive mood states may be a less frequent problem among most clients, it is important to recognize that the experience of both positive affect and negative affect may serve as a relapse risk to clients.

Cognitive-behavioral therapies and emotion regulation training are effective treatments for addressing negative affect and the maladaptive links between negative affect and risk for relapse. Behavioral activation strategies, cognitive therapies, relaxation skills, and negative affect tolerance are examples of therapeutic strategies to alleviate and manage negative affect. A focus of RP therapy is identifying what, if any, positive and/or negative moods are relapse risks for an individual and then developing strategic behavioral plans to cope with mood-related high-risk situations.

Coping Behaviors

The ability to cope with life's problems and challenges is a central component of the relapse prevention model. The success or failure to cope with difficulties and complications in life is proposed to have a direct, although variable, impact on the likelihood of relapse. A wide variety of cognitive-behavioral coping strategies have been proposed and studied including interpersonal skills (e.g., assertiveness, communication), stress coping, affect regulation skills, problem solving (such as the SOBER model described earlier), relaxation skills (e.g., deep breathing, body scan), and alcohol-specific coping skills (e.g., "urge surfing"). Although closely associated with cognitive constructs such as self-efficacy, an individual's ability to successfully cope and address life problems is protective against relapse to drinking.

YOU WOULD DRINK TOO...

Clinical intuition suggests that the experience of negative life events (e.g., job loss, relationship dissolution, and financial difficulties) often triggers heavy drinking among previously sober problem drinkers. Krenek, Prince, and Maisto (2017) report that, in a sample of 417 alcohol dependent treatment-seeking individuals, distal negative life events (i.e., life problems occurring the year before treatment) predicted proximal negative life events (i.e., life problems occurring during treatment) which then predicted the frequency of heavy drinking. This pattern of findings underscores the importance of teaching active and proactive coping techniques during treatment to both stabilize life functioning and decrease posttreatment relapse.

Therapist: *You're determined to make your changes stick. Essentially, you've been putting together a "toolbox" of coping skills and using them to stay sober and to manage your anger emotions. I want to take some time to review those tools and talk about how you can keep them sharp. But first, let's spend a minute reviewing the high-risk situations you included on your worksheet* ***Coping with High Risk Situations*** *(see Appendix II).*

David: *Sure. Having alcohol in the house is a big one. Another is letting myself getting too stressed out. Thinking 'I can have just one' is also risky.*

I included social events but those aren't as common. For anger, high risk situations are everywhere, especially dealing with other people.

Therapist: *So let's talk more about the coping skills or tools you have to manage your drinking and your anger emotions.*

David: *Ok. I was skeptical at first but the relaxation skills have been really helpful. My favorite is still the deep breathing and I find myself using it every day. I've used it when I'm angry and I've used it when I've had a craving. It helps me slow down and think things through. I have to admit, I've gotten away from the regular practice of the other skills, like the full body relaxation and the scene, even though I liked doing them. Maybe I should get back to that.*

Therapist: *You've found the relaxation helpful and you want to continue practicing it. How could you make sure that happens?*

David: *Well, I know how to do it, I just need to set aside some time and remind myself to do it. Maybe I can set a reminder on my phone.*

Therapist: *Ok. What other skills are in your toolbox?*

David: *I was always a good problem solver but I realize I'm even better when I'm sober and not feeling angry all the time. Having a clear head makes me feel like I can solve any problem—at work and at home.*

Therapist: *Your problem solving skills were always there; you've found a way to make them stronger. What else?*

David: *Changing my thinking has been huge. I had no idea how many problems I was creating for myself just in the way I thought about things. I still have high standards but I can hear my "shoulds" and I can hear my sarcasm. I can even laugh at myself sometimes when I hear those kinds of thoughts. My family has noticed a difference and a co-worker recently commented on how much more I'm smiling. I've also changed the way I think about drinking. I no longer "need" alcohol to relax. It was more trouble than it's worth.*

Therapist: *You've come a long way in recognizing the role of your thinking in both your anger and your drinking. How can you keep doing that?*

David: *In some ways, it's become a habit; I automatically catch myself making demands on the world and other people. I also realize I've had to think about all this to prepare for these sessions so I'm worried that I'll start to get lazy and slip back after I'm done here. I think I'll make a list of my favorite anger-increasing thoughts and maybe some of my favorite coping thoughts and put them in my desk drawer and maybe somewhere at home so I can't escape seeing them.*

Therapist: *Some of the change in your thinking has become automatic but seeing your favorite thoughts in writing each day will help provide another reminder. What other skills will be useful?*

David: *I've used the drink refusal skills a couple of times and it's really not too hard, especially if I'm with my wife. What I need to take from that is the part about saying "no" to myself first. After all, who was pouring the drinks most days? It was me; no one was forcing me to drink.*

Therapist: *Ok, so we've covered the SOBER problem solving, the drink refusal skills, the relaxation skills, and the cognitive skills, otherwise known as the changes in your thinking. What other things have been working for you lately?*

David: *Definitely walking in the woods and I've even started doing a little running. I feel healthier and more grounded when I'm physically active, especially outdoors. I'd also say talking to my wife. We're communicating more and really trying to be supportive of each other. I feel like she's on my side now and that feels great.*

Therapist: *Physical activity, time outdoors, and support from your wife are other essential tools to have in your box.*

David: *For sure. I know I can do this and, like I said, I can't afford to slip backwards.*

Relapse Prevention Model and Anger-Related Emotions

RP targets maintenance of anger management progress. As with alcohol lapse and relapse, posttreatment anger lapses and relapses are a function of high-risk contextual factors (e.g., changes in family such as marriages, birth of children, or divorces, changes in economic conditions or employment), tonic processes (e.g., stable individual characteristics such as propensity for anger, beliefs about how life should be, and family history of anger emotions and expression), and phasic responses (fluid factors such as state anger, use of coping strategies, stress, negative affect, and self-efficacy for anger management). The relapse prevention model applied to anger-related emotions is complex and difficult to apply, in whole, to any given individual. However, salient components of the model may be identified for any particular client and will provide important and helpful insights into the prevention of anger-related emotion lapse and relapse.

Nearing the end of treatment, anger management skill practice will have successfully increased the client's awareness of anger-provoking situations and the internal cues of anger arousal. This awareness allows the client to apply coping skills to proactively manage these situations and cues. However, as with drinking, clients are also vulnerable to post-therapy "lapses," individual angry overreactions, and "relapses," returning to angry responding and related dysfunctional behavior.

As with RP for drinking, the importance of maintaining posttreatment anger management into the future is discussed openly in the final sessions. The notion of experiencing a "lapse" to anger (e.g., a poor effort at anger reduction) is described as a common posttreatment issue. This normalizes the notion of a lapse. It is important to identify and develop concrete strategies to help the client prevent a lapse from becoming the first in a long line of lapses (relapse) and a rationalization for giving up (e.g., "*There I go again. Anger management is all shot to hell. I'm back where I started.*").

ANOTHER DIET...

The analogy of weight loss is often helpful in addressing RP for anger. Weight loss is useful because nearly everyone is familiar with the experience of losing weight, only to find the weight has returned 6 months to a year later. When asked why they regained the weight, people generally describe a gradual return to old eating habits. When asked what should be done to keep the weight off, people typically provide two types of responses. First, instead of being used as an excuse to give up on the diet, an episode of overeating or eating high caloric food, such as a piece of cake (a lapse), can instead be seen a signal to get back on track with healthy eating. Second, people who are successful with weight loss usually stay on a maintenance diet (i.e., a modification of the original dieting approach). Anger management treatment can thus be likened to weight loss. The increased awareness of anger and the coping skill training are like the diet. During treatment, the client lost a great deal of the "weight of anger." Now the job is keeping the weight of anger off (maintenance and RP). The client need not let a lapse lead to relapse but can return to the principles and 'diet' of anger management concepts.

Client-Based Strategies for Relapse Prevention

Memory Support Strategies

A variety of strategies may be implemented by the client to support positive posttreatment functioning. These are discussed with the client as part of RP therapy. One of the most common reasons people do not maintain behavioral changes (in this case, sobriety and anger regulation) is because they do not continue the strategies and skills they used to attain these changes. Clients can do many things that help them remember and focus on key steps of anger management based alcohol treatment. The goal is to keep these strategies present and salient in the client's world.

With regard to maintaining sobriety, clients can:

- Write out a list of the "pros" of sobriety and the "cons" of drinking to keep a focus on the benefits of change.
- Continue or consider attending a mutual-help group, such as Alcoholics Anonymous, for ongoing social sobriety support and reminders to "work the program."
- Use the SOBER model of problem solving when a difficult challenge arises, detailing the situation, brainstorming options, being aware of their consequences, evaluating the effectiveness of each to make a choice, and reviewing the results.
- Be appreciative of the changes made for sobriety and the positive consequences of sobriety.
- If comfortable, use the serenity prayer or any other meditative practice to maintain feelings of self-comfort, self-worth, and self-awareness.

THE SERENITY PRAYER: (REINHOLD NIEBUHR [1892–1971])

God, grant me the serenity to accept the things I cannot change,

Courage to change the things I can,

And wisdom to know the difference.

With regard to maintaining anger management, clients can:

- Write out a description of the personal relaxation scene to make it easy to review and use.
- Schedule, using a calendar or smart phone reminders, three daily practices of relaxation coping skills to keep them fresh and easy to use.
- Write out a list of coping thoughts and review several each day.
- Identify frequently occurring activities (e.g., washing hands, turning on/off a computer) and employ a relaxation coping skill when doing that activity. This routine moment of relaxation can identify and prevent the subtle rise of anger and tension throughout the day.
- Write out the most effective cognitive and relaxation coping skills and review before any anticipated conflict.
- Develop routine times for anger scanning (e.g., upon waking, at breakfast, just after arriving at work, midmorning, at lunch, midafternoon, just before leaving

work for home, or an hour or two before bedtime) and make a commitment to apply an effective coping skill to address any anger present.

- Note specific cognitive successes (e.g., "*That was tough, but I kept my cool by taking those deep breaths and saying 'relax' while she yelled at me. I feel good about that.*" or "*I was angry at myself for missing that assignment, but I thought my way through it and didn't put myself down and blame myself. I didn't like it, but I kept it real.*").
- Consider using external reinforcers (e.g.,*Great. I coped and didn't get pissed. I'm allowing myself a treat tonight.* or *I'll put a dollar in a jar for each time I calm down and cope. I'll save up for something fun!*).

Self-Monitoring

Ongoing monitoring is important. Continuing attention and self-observation will identify future patterns of triggers and behaviors and how they may be related to urges or lapses not only in drinking but also in anger management. Clients are strongly encouraged to continue ongoing monitoring and conduct periodic reviews of their cravings, any drinking or anger lapses that may occur, and ongoing sobriety skills and anger reduction efforts.

With regard to self-monitoring alcohol-related issues, clients can:

- Record on a self-monitoring log, calendar, app, or journal, occurrences of craving, urges to drink and, if any, drinking lapses. Whether occasionally or daily, make efforts to maintain self-awareness of the ongoing progress toward sobriety goals.
- Keep a journal about the journey to sobriety, commenting on personally-relevant components of the relapse prevention model. These reflections might include cravings to drink, thoughts about drinking and sobriety, the connections between anger emotions and cravings, other negative emotions, and ongoing use of sobriety skills.
- Make a commitment with a close friend to check in periodically to maintain self-awareness.

With regard to self-monitoring anger management-related issues, clients can:

- Continue to employ self-monitoring log 3 at the end of every day or use the journal idea above with a primary focus on managing anger.
- Set up a routine 15–20 minutes of time to review ongoing efforts at anger management. For example, set up a time every week to review anger management efforts, look for difficult situations in the coming week, and identify and practice coping skills for those situations.

- Identify a friend who is willing to discuss anger management every couple of weeks and review continued progress efforts.
- If the weight loss analogy was helpful, decide to "step on the anger scales" every week or so. If added "anger pounds" are noted, develop a plan for returning to "healthier anger loss strategies."

Planning for High-Risk Situations

Clients are encouraged to be aware of and anticipate situations that are high risk for possible drinking and anger. Many people are aware of situations that "set them off" and trigger both cravings and anger. Clients are encouraged to identify these specific triggers and to develop concrete plans for coping with them.

- Each week, identify upcoming high-risk drinking triggers (e.g., celebration or social event, increasing stress at work, extra free time on a holiday or vacation) and potential anger-provoking events (e.g., dealing with adolescent's request to use the family car, discussion of family budget with spouse, dealing with a difficult supervisor at work). Review and rehearse specific sobriety skills and coping skills strategies to effectively manage the situations.
- Consider a 3–6-month preview of drinking triggers (e.g., weddings and celebrations, vacation, upcoming life and family changes), anger events (e.g., brother's visit in the summer, potential layoffs at work), and identify and practice sobriety skills and coping skills strategies.
- Anticipate events or times of the year that may trigger anger or drinking (e.g., holidays). Develop a plan for identifying specific anger and drinking triggers along with the skills needed to address them.

Preparing for Lapses

Clients should be prepared for the possibility of drinking and/or anger-related emotion lapses. Instead of punishing themselves for a lapse, clients are encouraged to learn from experience so that the lapses will be less likely in the future. In the final sessions, lapses are discussed and clients are encouraged to identify and rehearse specific sobriety skills and cognitive and relaxation coping strategies.

- Use a prior lapse to learn from, prepare for, and prevent future lapses. Clients can recall what the salient drinking or anger triggers were and consider how to handle the trigger more effectively should it recur.
- Rehearse sobriety and anger management skills to get back on track.
- Recall the dangers of the abstinence violation effect: Don't let a lapse become a relapse!

Therapist-Based Strategies for Relapse Prevention

The client is ultimately responsible for maintaining progress after treatment. As such, the client's ongoing monitoring and practice of therapy skills and strategies are important for minimizing posttreatment lapse and relapse. The therapist, however, may be able to offer support to clients in the following ways:

- Spreading out the last several treatment sessions by a month or so allows the client independence in his or her environment followed by a therapy session to review progress. These sessions can be devoted to discussion of maintenance, addressing lapses, and minor tuning of skills. Clients often report that it is very helpful to know that they will be talking with the therapist again and that it keeps them focused on continuing their efforts for sobriety and anger reduction.
- Encourage clients to journal and/or to continue to complete self-monitoring logs. In some cases, these completed logs can be sent to the therapist for review and feedback. These activities will help clients maintain self-awareness for alcohol cravings and anger triggers.
- Several brief, posttreatment phone contacts can be scheduled on a monthly or weekly basis. These phone conversations can address lapses, adapt skills, review self-monitoring logs, and reinforce successes. The frequency and duration of the phone contacts can be faded as client feedback suggested continued progress.
- Allow clients to return for short-term "booster sessions" (e.g. three or four sessions) of anger management based alcohol treatment as the need arises. Not all problems or issues can be anticipated and brief periods of therapy may be needed to address them in the future.

Therapist: *Getting back on track after a drinking relapse isn't easy but it's possible, and it can help you learn and maybe even add more tools to the toolbox. I'm wondering how you see this relating to the progress you've made in managing your anger more effectively.*

David: *In some ways it feels different to me. Picking up a drink would be a potential catastrophe for me and that's not an exaggeration. I still get angrier than I need to once in a while, but it's not the end of the world as long as I don't drink. I can stop and relax and get myself under control. I guess it's the same in that I have to look back and figure out what happened to set me off, but the consequences don't seem as severe. If I went back to being so pissed off all day, it could be a problem but still not as dramatic as the drinking. Plus, I still have to deal with incompetence and messes and bad drivers every day; I don't have to deal with alcohol every day.*

Therapist: *So there are clear differences but also some similarities.*

David: *Yeah, and I have more chances to practice with the anger stuff every day. But I do know they're connected so I think a serious relapse in one might lead to a relapse in both. Again, I have too much to lose to let that happen.*

Therapist: *You can see a future where you're sober, clear-headed, managing anger more effectively, and connected to your family.*

David: *And let's throw in running a 5k and getting a promotion at work!*

Therapist: *You've got ambitious plans! There's one more idea that can be helpful on this journey: the idea of "Progress, not Perfection." What does that mean to you?*

David: *Yeah, that's probably true. I've certainly had to let go of some of my perfectionism so the idea of focusing on progress makes sense. In a lot of ways it feels like this program saved my life, or at least my marriage and my job. I'm really grateful.*

Therapist: *I appreciate how hard you've worked to make these changes. You're giving yourself a chance to live the life you deserve.*

Summary

Anger, drinking, and anger-related alcohol use are typically overlearned and consistently reinforced cognitive–emotional–behavioral processes. Preparing a client for posttreatment challenges and high-risk situations is critical for long-term maintenance of treatment gains (as well as long-term ongoing improvement in these skills). With regard to anger management lapse, this treatment has instilled both relaxation and cognitive coping skills to manage posttreatment anger-related emotions that naturally occur as part of life experiences. With regard to drinking lapse, anger management based alcohol treatment has increased awareness of and ways to address problematic anger, especially as it relates to craving and drinking. It has also enhanced the client's repertoire of sober coping skills. Therefore, maintenance and ongoing behavior change need daily attention and application of skills. During treatment, both the client and the therapist can actively engage in strategies to support the client's positive changes long after treatment is over.

Suggested Readings

Bowen, S., Witkiewitz, K., Clifasefi, S. L., Grow, J., Chawla, N., Hsu, S. H., et al. (2014). Relative efficacy of mindfulness-based relapse prevention, standard relapse prevention, and treatment as usual for substance use disorders: A randomized clinical trial. *The Journal of the American Medical Psychiatry*, *71*, 547–556.

Bowen et al. report the relative efficacy of two forms of RP treatment (cognitive-behavioral RP and mindfulness-based RP) as compared to a treatment-as-usual intervention. Findings include that both RP approaches significantly reduced relapse during the year following treatment. In addition, the mindfulness approach provided added benefit at 12-month posttreatment with regard to reduced drug use and heavy drinking. Specific mindfulness strategies may provide the ability for clients to monitor and cope with discomforts associated with craving and relapse.

Hendershot, C. S., Witkiewitz, K., George, W. H., & Marlatt, G. A. (2011). Relapse prevention for addictive behaviors. *Substance Abuse Treatment, Prevention, and Policy*, *6*, 1–17.

This review article describes the changes to and advancements of the relapse prevention model occurring during 2000–10. This time period was characterized by the reformulation of this model to incorporate dynamic and fluctuating risk factors, advanced scientific techniques to support the model, incorporation of additional individual characteristics that serve as risk factors, and the application of mindfulness–based therapy techniques into RP treatment.

Krenek, M., Prince, M. A., & Maisto, S. A. (2017). Life events and alcohol use disorder clinical course: Modeling the dynamic association. *Drug and Alcohol Dependence*, *180*, 137–143.

This study found that, in a sample of 417 Alcohol Use Disorder treatment-seeking individuals, negative life events (e.g., divorce, deaths, legal problems, illness, injuries, etc.) that occurred in the year before treatment predicted more current negative life events; current negative life events predicted increases in heavy drinking. Clinical implications include the importance of enhancing coping strategies addressing both older and more current negative life events.

Steckler, G., Witkiewitz, K., & Marlatt, G. A. (2013). Relapse and lapse. In P. Miller (Ed.), *Principles of addiction: Comprehensive addictive behaviors and disorders* (Vol. 1, pp. 125–132). New York: Elsevier Press.

The authors describe distinguishing characteristics and interplay of an addiction "lapse" and "relapse." Components of the RP model and the research support for the treatment approach are reviewed. Conclusions include that RP treatment is more effective that no treatment and as effective as or more effective than other addictions treatments.

Witkiewitz, K., & Marlatt, G. A. (2004). Relapse prevention for alcohol and drug problems: That was Zen, This is Tao. *American Psychologist*, *59*, 224–235.

This important article describes the reconceptualization of the process of relapse that was proposed by G.A. Marlatt in 1985. This dynamic model incorporates distal risks, defined as stable predispositions increasing the likelihood of relapse, and proximal risks, defined as immediate precipitants that predict the likelihood of relapse. Tonic processes are state-like characteristics that contribute to the overall likelihood of relapse; phasic responses are the day-to-day, moment-to-moment fluid actions and reactions that are the turning point for the instigation of relapse.

Chapter 13

Putting It All Together

Chapter Points

- The progress of our three case study clients is presented with assessment results.
- A detailed progression of 12-session anger management based alcohol treatment is outlined.
- High quality clinical supervision is essential when using this treatment.

Questions for Self-Reflection

- How do you think you will incorporate this treatment approach in your work?
- What is your opinion about having a structured plan for each session in treatment?

We begin this chapter with our three case studies, David, Tiffany, and Stephan. We have included details about their progress and what was happening for each of them as they completed 12 weeks of anger management based alcohol treatment. We have also included charts comparing their assessment measure results pre- and posttreatment (see Fig. 13.1).

Anger Management Based Alcohol Treatment. DOI: https://doi.org/10.1016/B978-0-12-812709-4.00013-5

This chapter concludes with 12 outlines that describe the suggested content, flow, and materials for each session of anger management based alcohol treatment. These outlines provide our recommendations as to how the treatment skills, rehearsals, and sobriety skills described in this book may be presented in a standardized 12-session format. It is our hope that these outlines pull together the information provided throughout the book and can be used as a guide in planning and implementing this treatment approach with your clients. These outlines describe the specific steps of each session as well as indications of where to locate more comprehensive information within the previous chapters.

We cannot stress enough our belief in the absolute necessity of quality clinical supervision when doing this type of work. There are numerous formats of supervision available including individual, group, peer, long distance, phone, and online. Effective supervision, especially with some level of direct observation (such as audio- or video-recorded sessions), provides opportunities to improve skills, process clinical issues, encourage therapist self-care, seek help in managing challenging situations, and receive supportive feedback.

This program can also be adapted to include additional sober coping skills, enhanced focus on mutual-help group involvement, and recommended treatment medications for alcohol use disorder, such as Naltrexone and Acamprosate. The pace of the treatment can be determined by the client's needs, skills acquisition, and treatment setting. We recommend that modifications to the treatment be made collaboratively, with input from the client, the therapist, and the therapist's clinical supervisor. We encourage you to consider how these recommendations and outlines can be most effectively and appropriately presented and adapted to the unique circumstances of any given client.

The End (is Just the Beginning)...

David

At the final session, David was sober and much less irritated in his daily life. He noticed improvements at home with his wife and children as well as at work where he was feeling more productive without the foggy head and constant feelings of irritation. Quitting alcohol and managing his anger made him a better employee, husband, and father, and important people in his life wanted to spend time with him. He still got angry, but said he was able to recognize what was happening and calm himself down enough to decide how to handle the situation. For David, the intersection of alcohol and anger was clear and consistent. Making changes in both areas together brought him closer to his goals, and in his words, it may have saved his life. He was amazed and pleased that the skills he was using had changed his life so profoundly.

On the posttreatment assessments, David's results reflected his self-reported improvements in drinking and anger management. On the QDS (Quick Drinking Screen), he reported no drinking over the past 30 days which was a drastic change from the 11 drinks a day, 7 day a week pattern that brought him into treatment. His PACS (Penn Alcohol Craving) score dropped from a 4.4 average to a 1.6. He was still experiencing occasional cravings but was using his coping skills and had been abstinent for almost 3 months. His scores on the SIP (Short Inventory of Problems) dropped dramatically from 26 to 5. Because he was sober and managing his anger more effectively, he was noticing a considerable reduction in related problems.

David's anger-specific score on the SIP fell from 5 to 0. His score on the DAR (Dimensions of Anger Reactions) dropped from 14 to 9, indicating that he was reacting differently to triggers and coping better with anger emotions when they did present themselves. His PANAS (Positive and Negative Affect) scores also changed notably. His anger score dropped to 1.2 or "a little" in terms of how he'd been affected by anger emotions recently, down from the 3 or "quite a bit" range. His negative affect average fell by more than half, from 3.0 to 1.4, while his positive affect score increased from 2.1 to 3.2. All these results were consistent with the way he described his feelings about his life; he was feeling more optimistic, more confident, and more in control of himself and his reactions.

When filling out the CSQ (Client Satisfaction Questionnaire) at the end of the program, David was enthusiastic in his responses. He rated the quality of the services as "excellent" and said he "definitely" got the kind of services he wanted. He reported that "most" of his needs were met by the program and said he would "definitely" recommend it to a friend. He was "very satisfied" with the amount of help he received and thought the services helped him deal more effectively with his drinking and his anger. He was overall "very satisfied" with the program and would "definitely" come back if he needed help in the future. He added a comment saying, "I'm grateful for this program. It probably saved my marriage and maybe even my life."

Therapist Thoughts

David's progress in treatment was remarkable. He left the program looking and sounding like a different person. His physical appearance had changed with sobriety—his blood pressure was lower and his face was no longer red. His initial reluctance about anger management had been transformed; he came to realize that there was power in being able to calm himself, rethink, and choose his reactions. For the therapist, the careful use of reflections and open questions throughout treatment had helped David make his own arguments for changing his behavior and his thinking. Maintaining a focus on David's autonomy and keeping a collaborative spirit in session were also a key to keeping him engaged in the process. David felt confident using the skills after leaving treatment, and he would also benefit from future check-in or booster sessions to refresh his commitment. David's past experience with relapse could pose a concern. He said his greatest obstacle in the past was the thought, *"I can handle a couple drinks now and then."* He said he needs to stay focused on how confident and healthy he feels when he's sober and not let himself forget how bad things get when he relapses.

TIFFANY

Tiffany's final coping skills rehearsal was once again focused on her physical appearance. Tiffany was able to relax on her own and then reexperience the intense thoughts and emotions about her body. She was also able to relax and find the identified coping thoughts without help. However, while debriefing the exercise, she became teary and voiced doubt that she will ever feel satisfied with her body or be able to let go of her deep anger. She had come to realize that not all the anger was self-directed; some of the anger was at her cousin for sexually abusing her as well as at her mom who should have done more to protect her or at least have noticed what was going on. These were painful topics for Tiffany and more than could be addressed in the program, so her therapist offered appropriate support in session and talked to Tiffany about a referral for ongoing counseling.

At the final session, Tiffany reported her first completely sober week of treatment; she felt proud of herself and motivated to stay focused on abstinence for now. She also noticed that she was letting fewer things bother her. The therapist reinforced the idea that this was due to the positive changes Tiffany was making rather than any transformation in the world around her. As usual, Tiffany seemed to appreciate the encouragement and support. She was surprised that she actually felt more powerful when she was able to manage her anger emotions and then decide how to express them. Along with the changes in her drinking, this made her feel more in control of her daily life. She was spending time with certain friends and talking with them more openly. She was at the gym more consistently, was focused on improving her eating habits to continue her weight loss, and had started saving money for skin-removal surgery in the future. She recently had a positive work review and was recommended for a management training course offered at her job. She agreed that she would probably benefit from additional therapy to deal with the past abuse and neglect in her life. She was given a list of referral options and said she would call for an appointment.

On the posttreatment assessments, Tiffany's score changes were consistent with her self-reported progress and her continued struggles. Her QDS showed a decrease in alcohol consumption in both frequency and amount, from 6 drinks 6 days a week to 4 drinks 4 days a week. She averaged 3 days a week of no alcohol use, up from less than 1, and the greatest number of drinks in a day dropped from 8.5 to 6. Her PAC score fell slightly from 3.0 to 2.6 which indicated an ongoing experience of cravings, consistent with her gradual reduction in alcohol use. She felt good about her completely abstinent week and was hoping for more like that. Her SIP score dropped from 27 to 17; she was noticing a steady decrease in alcohol-related problems as she reduced her drinking.

Tiffany's SIP anger score was half of what it was at the beginning, falling from 6 to 3, indicating a notable decrease in anger-related alcohol problems. Her DAR score dropped from 16 to 12, and her average score on the PANAS anger scale fell from 3.7 ("extremely") to 2.5 (between "moderately" and "quite a bit"). She was still experiencing anger but at a relatively lower level. Also on the PANAS, her negative affect average dropped from 3.4 to 2.7, while her positive affect score bumped up from 1.6 to 1.9. She was identifying with more positive emotions and fewer negative ones.

On the CSQ, Tiffany's responses were mixed. She rated the quality of the services as "fair" and said she "generally" got the kind of services she wanted out of the program. She felt that "only a few" of her needs were met by the program, and she would recommend it to a friend. She was "mostly satisfied" with the amount of help she received and believed the program "somewhat" helped her deal more effectively with her drinking and her anger. Overall, she was "mostly satisfied" with the program and thinks she would come back if she needed help again. At the end, she commented, "It was good and I got some stuff out of this but I'm still not where I want to be."

Therapist Thoughts

Tiffany saw gradual and genuine improvement while in the program and for her, ongoing supportive therapy will be important. One central goal for Tiffany is to find a way to balance the motivating and activating aspects of her anger with the debilitating and limiting parts. For example, she and the therapist talked about using her anger emotions as a cue to set boundaries, especially with her family members. Tiffany was determined to stop allowing other people to take advantage of her and saw these new skills as a way to accomplish that goal without hurting herself in the process. Her struggle with sobriety, her complicated family issues, unresolved past abuse, and her self-directed anger pose significant risks for relapse. At the same time, she is strong, competent, and driven. Hearing the therapist affirming and reflecting those qualities was beneficial, and she was beginning to do some of that for herself by the end of treatment. She had become especially proficient at relaxation; she was able to relax easily, quickly, and effectively almost anytime. She was using the cognitive skills to catch herself being self-critical and was able to refocus her thoughts on her strengths and trying to accept herself. She ended the program pleased with her progress, not quite where she wants to be in her life, but with a clearer vision of where she is headed.

Stephan

At the final session, Stephan announced that he had actually been less reactive in traffic lately, which he never believed could happen. He was amazed that he was sober, practicing relaxation, coping with his anger in different ways, and yet did not at all feel like a lazy doormat. He seemed to understand that this change was due to his efforts and he felt confident about the future. Michael had agreed to couples' counseling and said he was proud of Stephan for the changes he was making. Stephan had applied for a new job and was planning to take a college class in the fall. He said he was even considering getting back in touch with his parents since he heard they were experiencing more serious health problems. He was glad he took a chance on the program despite his early doubts.

On the posttreatment assessments, Stephan's scores reflected the changes he had made while in the program. His QDS numbers went from 6 drinks daily to none; he had quit drinking and smoking marijuana more than 2 months before. He was especially surprised about the cannabis use which he had not originally intended to quit. He said he might consider smoking again in the future but wants to have his mind sharp when he goes back to school. His PAC average score went from a 2.2 to 1 indicating very little experience of craving. His score on the SIP dropped from 22 to 4. He still had a few problems, but they were less often related to his drinking.

His SIP anger score dropped from 6 to 0, and his DAR went from 12 to 7, indicating he was experiencing less intense and less frequent anger. On the PANAS, his average score on the anger scale dropped from 3 ("quite a bit") to 1.7 (between "a little" and "moderately"). At the same time, his positive affect score rose from 2.7 to 3.4, while his negative affect number fell from 2.9 to 1.2. He was feeling more positive about the changes he was initiating in his career and in his marriage.

When filling out the CSQ, Stephan was generally positive in his feedback. He rated the quality of the services as "good" and felt he "generally" got the kind of service he wanted. He said "most" of his needs were met, and he would "definitely" recommend the program to a friend. He reported being "mostly satisfied" with the amount of help he received and believed the services he received helped him a "great deal" in dealing more effectively with his drinking and anger. Overall, he was "mostly satisfied" and would "definitely" come back if he needed help in the future. In the comment section he wrote, "I thought it was impossible to change my anger but I really have been able to feel a difference. Quitting drinking was easier than I thought. Thanks for the help."

Therapist Thoughts

Stephan made several important changes while in treatment and was determined to keep his forward momentum, so relapse prevention was an important concept for him. He was planning to continue tracking his anger emotions in a daily journal and wanted to carry on his relaxation practice along with spending more time in his garden enjoying life. He and the therapist talked about ways he could remind himself to do those things, and he gave Michael permission to tell him if he was getting off track. Notably, he had let go of his belief that anger management and relaxation were signs of weakness. He surprised himself by finding strength in being able to manage his anger. While sessions with Stephan were often full of humor, the therapist's gentle reflections helped him become more aware of his sarcastic responses and how he used his humor to deflect and attack. While he was not ready to let go of the sarcasm altogether, he started using it sparingly and found out he was often funnier without the biting edge. Returning to school and starting a new job could add more stress to his life in the short term and pose a relapse risk. However, he was certain that these changes would put him on a much better path for the future. He felt confident and secure in himself but promised to not get overconfident or "preachy" to others.

Outcome Tables (Fig. 13.1)

Case Study Assessment Tables

Dimensions of anger reactions (DAR-5)

	Pre	Post
Name	Score/25	Score/25
David	14	9
Tiffany	16	12
Stephan	12	7

Penn alcohol craving scale (PACS)

	Pre	Post
Name	Average score/6	Average score/6
David	4.4	1.6
Tiffany	3	2.6
Stephan	2.2	1

Short inventory of problems (SIP+anger)

	Pre	*Post*	Pre	*Post*
Name	Total score/57	Total score/57	Anger/12	Anger/12
David	26	5	5	0
Tiffany	27	17	6	3
Stephan	22	4	6	0

Positive and negative affect scale (PANAS+anger)

	Pre	Post	Pre	Post	Pre	Post
Name	Negative affect average score/4		Positive affect average score/4		Anger affect average score/4	
David	3.0	1.4	2.1	3.2	2.5	1.2
Tiffany	3.4	2.7	1.6	1.9	3.7	2.5
Stephan	2.9	1.2	2.7	3.4	3	1.7

Figure 13.1 Case studies assessment tables—pretreatment and posttreatment scores.

Case Study Assessment Tables

QDS

Pretreatment

Name	Average drinking days per week	Average number of drinks per day	Number of drinking days above 4 (women) 5 (men) drinks	Greatest number of drinks consumed in one day	Average days per week with no alcohol use	*Total number of days abstinent (if<1 day per week)*
David	7	11	30/30	17	0	0/30
Tiffany	6	6	20/30	8.5	<1	3/30
Stephan	7	6	23/30	13	<1	1/30

Posttreatment

Name	Average drinking days per week	Average number of drinks per day	Number of drinking days above 4 (women) 5 (men) drinks	Greatest number of drinks consumed in one day	Average days per week with no alcohol use	*Total number of days abstinent (if<1 day per week)*
David	0	0	0/30	0	7	N/A
Tiffany	4	4	10/30	6	3	N/A
Stephan	0	0	0/30	0	7	N/A

Figure 13.1 (Continued).

Bold font indicates worksheets, forms, and handouts that are available in Appendix I and II.

First Session: **Assessment and Introduction to Treatment**

1. Administer the assessment instruments prior to starting the session (Chapter 5)
   ___ **DSM-V (AUD Checklist)** ___ **SIP**
   ___ **QDS** ___ **PANAS**
   ___ **PACS** ___ **DAR**
2. Opening question and exploration: "Please tell me what brings you here today?"
3. Present general guidelines/program overview
4. Complete general alcohol and psychosocial assessments (Chapter 5)
   ___ Psychosocial (agency specific)
   ___ **Brief Drinking History Assessment** (if not already included in psychosocial)
5. Introduce the anger/alcohol connection (Chapter 4)
6. Complete the initial anger assessment (Chapter 5)
   ___ **Brief Anger Assessment**
7. Introduce self-monitoring as a useful tool (Chapter 7)
8. Assign Target Exercise (fill in one client example) and ask for client commitment
   ___ **Self-Monitoring Log 1** (Chapter 7)
9. Discuss upcoming week plans, goals, and challenges
10. Answer questions and schedule next session

THERAPIST TIP
Rapport is established right from the start of the session with the opening question. Continue to build rapport by encouraging client elaboration throughout the assessment process using open-ended questions and reflections.

Second Session: **Rationale for Treatment and SOBER Problem-Solving**

1. Review previous week
   - ___ Alcohol use/cravings ___ Anger
   - ___ Abstinence ___ Mutual-help groups
2. Review assessment measure results if indicated (Chapter 5)
   - ___ **DSM-V** ___ **SIP**
   - ___ **QDS** ___ **PANAS**
   - ___ **PACS** ___ **DAR**
3. Review Target Exercise (Chapter 7)
   - ___ **Self-Monitoring Log 1** entries (fill in if not complete)
4. Discuss rationale for anger management based alcohol treatment (Chapter 4)
   - ___ Link between anger, alcohol use, and relapse
   - ___ Two components of anger (physiological and cognitive) to manage
   - ___ Goal of program is to develop and practice new coping skills
   - ___ Use client examples to enhance understanding
5. Introduce new log version and assign Target Exercise (fill in one example)
   - ___ **Self-Monitoring Log 2** (includes thoughts)
6. Explain and practice sobriety skill—**SOBER Problem Solving** (Chapter 8)
   - ___ **S**top and see the problem
   - ___ **O**rganize your options
   - ___ **B**e aware of consequences
   - ___ **E**valuate options and choose the best one(s)
   - ___ **R**eview the results
7. Provide and explain Target Exercise
   - ___ **Sober Problem Solving Worksheet**
8. Ask client to think of a personal relaxation scene for next session (Chapter 9)
9. Discuss upcoming week plans, goals, and challenges
10. Answer questions and schedule next session

THERAPIST TIP

Presenting and discussing the rationale for anger management based alcohol treatment and self-monitoring are critical in this session. Support client participation by asking for opinions and checking for understanding. Include client experiences and examples as much as possible.

Third Session: **Initial Relaxation Practice**

1. Review previous week (alcohol use, cravings, anger, abstinence, sober skills, mutual-help groups)
2. Review Target Exercises
   ___ **Self-Monitoring Log 2** entries (or fill in if not complete)
   ___ **SOBER Problem Solving Worksheet** (Chapter 8)
3. Introduce new log and assign Target Exercise (fill in one client example if needed)
   ___ **Self-Monitoring Log 3** (includes coping efforts)
4. Discuss the benefits of relaxation (Chapter 9)
5. Develop *personal relaxation scene* in detail (take notes)
6. Describe the process and demonstrate tension and release relaxation sequence
7. Address minor issues (glasses, jewelry, areas of pain)
8. Begin relaxation training (ask client to *signal* with hand or finger)
   ___ Deep breathing
   ___ Tension and release (include muscle group reviews)
   ___Therapist "turns on" relaxation scene and describes details (*signal*)
   ___ Therapist "turns off" scene while client continues relaxation
   ___ Repeat relaxation scene as time permits
   ___ Count backwards from 5
   ___ Debrief together
9. Provide and explain relaxation log and handout (ask for commitment to practice)
   ___ **Relaxation Log**
   ___ **Home Practice of Relaxation I Handout**
10. Discuss upcoming week plans, goals, and challenges
11. Answer questions and schedule next session

THERAPIST TIP

Setting a comfortable, positive environment and expectation for relaxation training is essential. Remember to use a calm, slow voice during the relaxation exercises. Encourage regular home relaxation practice and problem solve any barriers to practice.

Fourth Session: **More Relaxation Practice and Drink Refusal Skills**

1. Review previous week (alcohol use, cravings, anger, relaxation, abstinence, sober skills, mutual help)
2. Review Target Exercises
   ___ **Self-Monitoring Log 3** entries (or fill in if not complete)
   ___ **Relaxation Log**
3. Provide blank self-monitoring log
   ___ **Self-Monitoring Log 3**
4. Introduce and practice sobriety skill: Drink Refusal Skills (Chapter 8)
   ___ Say "No" first
   ___ Use assertive body language
   ___ Suggest an alternative activity
   ___ Change the subject
   ___ Have a nonalcoholic drink in hand
   ___ Ask the person to stop offering
   ___ Avoid vague excuses
   ___ Minimize feelings of guilt
5. Describe new relaxation concepts and skills (Chapter 9)
   ___ Relaxation without tension (based on client's success with home practice)
   ___ Relaxation phrase ("relax," "chill," "calm," "control," "peace," etc.)
6. Begin relaxation training (cover minor issues: glasses, jewelry, areas of pain)
   ___ Deep breathing
   ___ Relaxation without tension
   ___ Relaxation scene *(signal)*
   ___ Relaxation phrase
   ___ Repeat as time permits
   ___ Self-attribution (affirm client's use of skills)
   ___ Count backwards from 5
   ___ Debrief together
7. Provide relaxation handout and Target Exercises (commitment to practice)
   ___ **Home Practice of Relaxation II Handout**
   ___ **Relaxation Log**
   ___ **Drink Refusal Skills Worksheet**
8. Discuss upcoming week plans, goals, and challenges
9. Answer questions and schedule next session

THERAPIST TIP

As relaxation training continues, it's important to begin attributing the relaxation state to the client, not the therapist. Model self-attribution statements such as, "Noticing those calm feelings you've been creating and that you'll use to reduce feelings of anger and stress."

***Fifth Session:* Cognitive Model Introduction + Optional Sobriety Skill**

1. Review previous week (alcohol use, cravings, anger, relaxation, abstinence, sober skills, mutual help)
2. Review Target Exercises
   ___ **Self-Monitoring Log 3**
   ___ **Relaxation Log**
   ___ **Drink Refusal Skills Worksheet**
3. Provide blank logs
   ___ **Self-Monitoring Log 3**
   ___ **Relaxation Log**
4. Introduce Cognitive Model (Chapter 10)
   ___ **A (activating event) → B (BELIEFS/THOUGHTS) → C (consequences)**
   ___ Explore thoughts that increase anger and reinforce drinking
   ___ Describe angry driver example
   ___ Include client examples from logs
5. Provide and review in session:
   ___ **Anger Increasing Thoughts Handout**
   ___ **General Coping Thoughts Handout**
6. Describe the plan for next session: rehearsing the skills together (Chapter 11)
   ___ Ask client to prepare two moderate (40–60 level) anger scenes for next session
7. As appropriate, consider introducing another sobriety skill, practicing relaxation skills, or talking about mutual help group involvement
8. Discuss upcoming week plans, goals, and challenges
9. Answer questions and schedule next session

THERAPIST TIP

Deeply involve the client in understanding and accepting that thoughts mediate the causal relationship between triggers, cravings, and the experience of anger. This is foundational to cognitive change. Remember to remain patient; clients will grasp these concepts at different rates.

Sixth Session: **Moderate Anger Scene Rehearsal With High Therapist Guidance**

1. Review previous week (alcohol use, cravings, anger, relaxation, abstinence, sober skills, mutual help)
2. Review Target Exercises
   ___ **Self-Monitoring Log 3**
   ___ **Relaxation Log**
3. Introduce and use **Creating Coping Thoughts** worksheet: (Chapter 11)
   ___ Recreate two moderate (40–60 level) anger scenes from client log
   ___ Ask about specific details (sights, sounds, smells, other emotions)
   ___ Identify anger increasing thoughts (use handout)
   ___ List related coping thoughts (use handout)
4. Explain the rehearsal process in detail and cover minor problems (glasses, pain, jewelry)
5. Begin Coping Skills Rehearsal... (high therapist guidance)
   ___ *Therapist* relaxes client (*signal relaxation*)
   ___ *Therapist* "turns on" anger scene (*signal anger emotions*)
   ___ *Therapist* "turns off" anger scene
   ___ *Therapist* "turns on" relaxation scene (*signal relaxation*)
   ___ *Therapist* "turns off" relaxation scene
   ___ *Therapist* further relaxes client
   ___ *Therapist* reviews coping thoughts
   ___ Repeat with other prepared scene (alternate scenes and repeat as time permits)
   ___ Count backwards from 5
   ___ Debrief the exercise together
6. Assign Target Exercises
   ___ **Self-Monitoring Log 3**
   ___ **Relaxation Log**
   ___ **Creating Coping Thoughts**: Prepare two additional moderate anger scenes (40–60 level)
7. Discuss upcoming week plans, goals, and challenges
8. Answer questions and schedule next session

THERAPIST TIP

Developing client anger scenes in substantial detail is the key to success in the rehearsals. Use the **Anger Increasing Thoughts and General Coping Thoughts** handouts to identify multiple anger-increasing thoughts as well as coping thoughts. Remember to vary your tone of voice to reflect the anger and relaxation segments of the process.

***Seventh Session:* Moderate Anger Scene Rehearsal With Some Client Control**

1. Review previous week (alcohol use, cravings, anger, relaxation, abstinence, sober skills, mutual help)
2. Review Target Exercises
   - ___ **Creating Coping Thoughts**
   - ___ **Self-Monitoring Log 3**
   - ___ **Relaxation Log**
3. Prepare two moderate (40–60 level) anger scenes from worksheets
   - ___ Identify anger increasing thoughts
   - ___ List related coping thoughts
4. Explain the rehearsal process in detail and cover minor problems
5. Begin Coping Skills Rehearsal... (some client control)
   - ___ *Therapist* relaxes client (or client relaxes self if ready) (*signal relaxation*)
   - ___ *Therapist* "turns on" anger scene (*signal anger*)
   - ___ *Therapist* "turns off" anger scene
   - ___ *Therapist* helps client retrieve relaxation (*signal relaxation*)
   - ___ *Therapist* reviews coping thoughts
   - ___ Repeat with other scene (alternate scenes and repeat as time permits)
   - ___ Self-attribution (reinforce client's use of the skills)
   - ___ Count backwards from 5
   - ___ Debrief exercise together
6. Assign Target Exercises
   - ___ **Self-Monitoring Log 3**
   - ___ **Relaxation Log**
   - ___ **Creating Coping Thoughts**: Prepare two high-anger scenes (60–80 level)
7. Discuss upcoming week plans, goals, and challenges
8. Answer questions and schedule next session

THERAPIST TIP
Some clients may be ready to take a more active role in retrieving relaxation and coping thoughts during the rehearsal in this session. Others may still need more therapist assistance. Continue to emphasize home practice of skills and genuinely affirm client progress.

Eighth Session: **High Anger Scene Rehearsal With Increased Client Control**

1. Review previous week (alcohol use, cravings, anger, relaxation, abstinence, sober skills, mutual help)
2. Review Target Exercises
    ___ **Creating Coping Thoughts**
    ___ **Self-Monitoring Log 3**
    ___ **Relaxation Log**
3. Prepare two high (60–80 level) anger scenes from worksheets
    ___ Identify anger increasing thoughts
    ___ List related coping thoughts
4. Explain the rehearsal process in detail and cover minor problems
5. Begin Coping Skills Rehearsal… (increased client control based on client skill level)
    ___ *Client* relaxes self with therapist help only if needed (*signal*)
    ___ *Therapist* "turns on" anger scene (*signal*)
    ___ *Therapist* "turns off" anger scene
    ___ *Client* retrieves relaxation with therapist help only if needed (*signal*)
    ___ *Client* reviews coping thoughts with therapist help if needed
    ___ Repeat with other prepared scene (as time permits)
    ___ Self-attribution
    ___ Count backwards from 5
    ___ Debrief exercise together
6. Assign Target Exercises
    ___ **Self-Monitoring Log 3**
    ___ **Relaxation Log**
    ___ **Creating Coping Thoughts**: Prepare two additional high anger scenes (60–80 level)
7. Discuss upcoming week plans, goals, and challenges
8. Answer questions and schedule next session

THERAPIST TIP

Encourage clients to relax on their own and review coping thoughts with only minimal assistance. Facilitate self-attribution of coping efforts through comments like "*Noticing how you reduced your anger by relaxing and thinking about things differently.*"

***Ninth Session:* High Anger Scene Rehearsal With High Client Control**

1. Review previous week (alcohol use, cravings, anger, relaxation, abstinence, sober skills, mutual help)
2. Review Target Exercises
   ___ **Creating Coping Thoughts**
   ___ **Self-Monitoring Log 3**
   ___ **Relaxation Log**
3. Prepare two high (60–80 level) anger scenes from worksheets
   ___ Identify anger increasing thoughts
   ___ List related coping thoughts
4. Explain the rehearsal process in detail and cover minor problems
5. Begin Coping Skills Rehearsal... (high client control)
   ___ *Client* relaxes self (*signal*)
   ___ *Therapist* "turns on" anger scene (*signal*)
   ___ *Therapist* leaves anger scene on (*signal stays up*)
   ___ *Client* retrieves relaxation
   ___ *Client* reviews coping thoughts (*signal goes down*)
   ___ *Therapist* "turns off" anger scene
   ___ *Therapist* reviews general coping thoughts
   ___ Repeat with other prepared scene (as time permits)
   ___ Self-attribution
   ___ Count backwards from 5
   ___ Debrief exercise together
6. Assign Target Exercises
   ___ **Self-Monitoring Log 3**
   ___ **Relaxation Log**
   ___ **Creating Coping Thoughts**: Prepare two worst anger scenes (80–100 level)
7. Discuss upcoming week plans, goals, and challenges
8. Answer questions and schedule next session

THERAPIST TIP

Keeping the anger scene "on" while the client relaxes and reviews coping thoughts is new to this session. The signal system changes as well; the signal stays up in the scene and goes down when coping is achieved. Repetition of scenes is important for ensuring client success and self-efficacy.

***Tenth Session:* Worst Anger Scene Rehearsal With Highest Client Control**

1. Review previous week (alcohol use, cravings, anger, relaxation, abstinence, sober skills, mutual help)
2. Review Target Exercises
   ___ **Creating Coping Thoughts**
   ___ **Self-Monitoring Log 3**
   ___ **Relaxation Log**
3. Recreate two worst (80–100 level) anger scenes from worksheets
   ___ Identify anger increasing thoughts
   ___ List related coping thoughts
4. Explain the rehearsal process in detail and cover minor problems
5. Begin Coping Skills Rehearsal... (highest client control)
   ___ *Client* relaxes self (*signal*)
   ___ *Therapist* "turns on" anger scene (*signal*)
   ___ *Therapist* leaves anger scene on (*signal stays up*)
   ___ *Client* retrieves relaxation
   ___ *Client* reviews coping thoughts (*signal goes down*)
   ___ *Therapist* "turns off" scene
   ___ Repeat with other prepared scene (as time permits)
   ___ Count backwards from 5
   ___ Debrief exercise together
6. Assign new Target Exercises to prepare for final sessions (Chapter 12)
   ___ **Coping with High Risk Situations**
   ___ **Best Coping Thoughts**
7. Provide blank copies of **Self-Monitoring and Relaxation Logs**
8. Discuss upcoming week plans, goals, and challenges
9. Answer questions and schedule next session

THERAPIST TIP

In this final rehearsal session, the client is in control of almost the entire process, and the level of anger scene is at its highest intensity. Staying in the anger scene while coping mirrors real life. Continue to reinforce client success and start to prepare for the end of treatment.

***Eleventh Session:* Relapse Prevention**

1. Review previous week (alcohol use, cravings, anger, relaxation, abstinence, sober skills, mutual-help groups)
2. Review Target Exercises
   ___ **Coping with High Risk Situations**
   ___ **Best Coping Thoughts**
   ___ **Self-Monitoring Log 3**
   ___ **Relaxation Log**
3. Introduce Relapse Prevention and identify client's high risk situations for anger and drinking (Chapter 12)
   ___ Current high risk situations
   ___ Anticipated future high risk situations
4. Summarize coping strategies using client worksheets:
   ___ **Best Coping Thoughts**
   ___ **Coping with High Risk Situations**
5. Discuss ways to maintain progress in anger management
   ___ **Anger Emotion Management Plan**
6. Review **"What to do if a Lapse Happens"** handout
7. Discuss upcoming plans, goals, and challenges
8. Answer questions and schedule next session
9. Ask client to complete the **posttreatment assessment** measures if applicable
   ___ PACS ___SIP ___PANAS ___DAR ___QDS

THERAPIST TIP

This session focuses on critical strategies to maintain change and prevent relapse for anger and drinking. Key strategies are to identify high-risk situations, preplan coping strategies for managing these challenges, and to discuss the notion of "not letting a lapse become a relapse."

Final Session: Bringing Treatment to a Close

1. Review and discuss client's progress in both alcohol use and anger management
2. Review and discuss client's plan to avoid relapse and maintain skills
3. Reinforce/Affirm client for ongoing progress and effort
4. Problem-solve any specific upcoming high-risk situations
5. Review assessment measure results and compare with first session results if completed
6. Talk about and schedule a booster session, in person, by phone or email, if available
7. Ask client to complete **Client Satisfaction Questionnaire (CSQ)** before leaving

THERAPIST TIP

At the final session, two points are critical. First, the client should "own" the progress made during treatment. Even if the client thinks that the progress is not yet complete, coping skills learned along the way can and should be attributed to changes made by the client with only guidance from the therapist. In effect, these coping skills are now part of the client. Second, if at all possible, booster contact(s) several weeks hence should be scheduled. Even with positive self-attribution, clients often report feeling concerned regarding their ability to continue the skills without therapist help. A check-in (or two) allows the therapist to reinforce successes and offer support for challenges.

Section IV

OTHER TOPICS AND ISSUES

Chapter 14

Client Diversity

Chapter Points

- Important differences exist between men and women with regard to alcohol use, consequences of drinking, and barriers to treatment.
- Men and women report similar intensities of anger-related emotions.
- Men report greater levels of physical aggression; women report greater levels of indirect aggression.
- A therapeutic stance of cultural humility with regard to client diversity is critical for the working alliance and positive treatment outcomes.

Questions for Self-Reflection

- How do you interact with clients who are different than you in terms of, as examples, race, ethnicity, religion, age, and gender?
- How do you demonstrate openness and acceptance when working with your clients?
- What does cultural humility mean to you?

Anger Management Based Alcohol Treatment. DOI: https://doi.org/10.1016/B978-0-12-812709-4.00014-7

Human diversity is an ever-present fact of life. In this chapter, our primary focus is on gender differences and the implications for gender-informed anger management based alcohol treatment. In addition to gender, a vast array of diversity is present between clients and between the individual therapist and any given client. Cultural and individual differences impact the expression and interpretation of anger-related emotions and behaviors; we, as therapists, should aspire to a principle of cultural humility to address this diversity in anger management based alcohol treatment.

Gender, Drinking, and Alcohol Use Disorder

Important differences exist between men and women with regard to drinking, binge drinking, and alcohol use disorder. Biologically, men and women are affected by alcohol consumption differently. Drink per drink, women tend to experience higher levels of intoxication and blood alcohol content (BAC) relative to same-sized men. This is in part because alcohol is more dilute in men's bodies (resulting in a relatively lower BAC) and more concentrated in women's bodies (resulting in a relatively higher BAC), corresponding to differences in average water content in men's and women's bodies. The National Institute on Alcohol Abuse and Alcoholism low-risk drinking limits differ between sexes, in part, because of this. Women are advised to have no more than three standard drinks in a single day and no more than seven standard drinks per week; the limits for men are no more than four standard drinks in a single day and no more than 14 standard drinks per week.

Overall, women drink less frequently and less heavily than men, across cultures and nationalities (see Erol & Karpyak, 2015). Research also shows that drinking, heavy drinking, and binge drinking among women have been increasing in recent years. Women, relative to men, experience greater risks for medical problems (e.g., severe liver problems, cardiomyopathy, cognitive dysfunction, and brain loss) and psychiatric problems (specifically mood and anxiety symptoms and disorders) associated with problematic drinking. An additional sex-specific concern, drinking during pregnancy, can be harmful and put the fetus at risk for physical, cognitive, and behavioral problems. Gender-specific "telescoping," the more rapid progression from drinking initiation into drinking problems and dependence among women compared to men, appears to be evident among individuals in treatment for alcohol disorders but not evident among individuals in the general population (Alvonzo et al., 2011).

Women, as compared to men, are thought to face more barriers and challenges to initiating and participating in addictions treatment. Recent research by Verissimo and Grella (2017) examined what barriers individuals faced that hindered their entry into alcohol treatment. The majority of men and women in the study reported that concerns such as embarrassment, pessimism that treatment would help, and fear of what treatment would entail were barriers for treatment for alcohol problems; these attitudinal barriers were more widespread in women of all races/ethnicities (about 85% of women reported these barriers) relative to men (about 75%). Additionally, approximately 25% of both men and women reported that challenges such as time, transportation, childcare, and lack of information held them up from getting alcohol treatment. These findings indicate that addressing barriers to ease entry into and participation in alcohol treatment are needed for both women and men and especially efforts that address negative beliefs about alcohol treatment among women. These efforts may include promoting alcohol treatment as helpful and positive, destigmatizing women (and men) who can benefit from treatment, and educating the public about what alcohol treatment does and does not entail.

Implications for Anger Management Based Alcohol Treatment

As discussed earlier, women in treatment for alcohol use disorder may benefit from attention to important gender differences with regard to drinking. First, providing information on higher levels of intoxication and heightened risk for alcohol-related medical and psychiatric problems can be therapeutic. Second, acknowledging and problem-solving individual barriers and challenges to treatment engagement may be necessary. Focusing attention on intrapersonal concerns such as shame and embarrassment about having a drinking problem may be especially helpful; addressing these feelings can help engage the client in treatment as well as strengthen the therapeutic alliance. Finally, exploring the client's confidence in the ability to stop drinking, address high-risk situations, and achieve sobriety may be uniquely important. As women are more likely to be pessimistic regarding the impact of treatment and the ability to recover, gently normalizing these concerns and supporting self-efficacy may reduce these obstacles to treatment participation. These common barriers to treatment should also be explored with male clients, but special attention and support for female clients seems warranted.

Gender, Anger, and Aggression

The Experience of Anger-Related Emotions

Cultural stereotypes and clinical lore would lead us to believe that there are important differences in anger-related emotions between genders. Early theories of gender and anger suggested that women exhibited emotions more openly with the exception of anger; for women, anger was suppressed and inhibited. In contrast, these theories suggested that men generally inhibited emotional expression except for anger; anger was displayed more openly. As reviewed by Sharkin (1993), in this early theoretical perspective, anger was considered the "primary male emotion" and the "masculine" emotion. Women's expression of anger, however, was considered "unfeminine" and "unthinkable." Sharkin's literature review of the empirical research at that time, in contrast to these more historical stereotypes, concluded that there were few, if any, significant gender differences in anger.

Research on gender differences in the experience and expression of anger has flourished. In the 10 years after Sharkin's review, Archer (2004) reported the results of a major meta-analytic review of the research examining gender differences in anger and aggression. As with Sharkin's review, Archer concluded that there were no differences in self-reported anger between men and women. This absence of a systematic gender difference was the case across the 11 countries contained within the meta-analysis (including the United States, United Kingdom, New Zealand, Singapore, and Australia) and between age categories (ranging from 6 years of age through 55 years). This consistent finding suggests that the self-reported emotional experience of anger is similar between men and women.

WHAT IS A META-ANALYSIS?

Literature reviews can be described as narrative systematic reviews or meta-analytic reviews. Both types of reviews are meticulous and thorough examinations of the empirical literature on a given topic and are highly respected for their integration of research findings across populations, assessments, and methodologies. A meta-analytic review additionally combines the statistical analyses presented in each individual article to calculate effect sizes. These effect sizes are then quantitatively combined across studies to further understanding of the vast literature on a particular topic.

Aggressive Behaviors

The Archer (2004) meta-analysis also evaluated gender differences in aggression. Three distinct forms of aggression were studied: physical aggression, verbal aggression, and indirect aggression. Of these, physical aggression (e.g., hitting another person, breaking things) evidenced the strongest gender difference, with males evidencing greater physical aggression relative to females. Of note, this gender difference was found across ages and the nationalities included in the review. Subjects' self-reports of physical aggression evidenced the greatest magnitude of gender differences; men self-reported engaging in physical aggression to a greater extent than women. In contrast, for laboratory studies and observational studies, the gender difference was not as strong, but still present.

Similarly, verbal aggression (e.g., swearing, yelling, name-calling, insulting) followed the same gender difference effects as physical aggression, but the differences between men and women were smaller and less consistent. As with physical aggression, this finding of men engaging in more verbal aggression relative to women was consistent across age or nationalities. Interestingly, this gender difference was most pronounced in peer reports; other individuals observing the verbal behaviors of men and women detected the greatest magnitude of a gender effect. Self-reports and observational studies of verbal aggression reveal less of a gender difference.

Finally, Archer (2004) evaluated gender differences for indirect aggression (e.g., spreading rumors, social exclusion, making insults "behind the back"). Although men were more likely to engage in physical aggression and verbal aggression relative to women, the reverse was true for indirect aggression, which women displayed more relative to men. This gender difference—relatively small—was most evident in studies that used observational measures rather than self-report. Studies using self-report and peer-report yielded smaller-to-absent estimates of gender differences for indirect aggression.

Our three case study clients appeared to follow these general gender patterns. David reported instances of verbal aggression with his family members, sometimes screaming at them when the cupboards were left open. Stephan's physical aggression had resulted in smashed dishes and his own fingers broken after punching a wall. Both David and Stephan were also prone to biting sarcasm and body language that was intended to intimidate others (cold stares, crossed arms, clenched fists). Tiffany, on the other hand, frequently talked about using social media as a way to get back at her ex-boyfriend and other friends when she was mad at them, a more indirect form of aggression. Interestingly, both David and

Stephan reported a greater likelihood of direct aggressive behaviors (yelling, breaking things, attacking sarcasm) when they were angry and drunk simultaneously. Tiffany, when both angry and drunk, felt powerful enough to act more directly and verbally aggressive; that's when she would call people and yell at them in addition to trashing them on social media.

Implications for Anger Management Based Alcohol Treatment

There is a dearth of research on the implications of gender differences in anger management treatment and the usefulness of gender-specific treatment content. In our experience, the skills presented in this book have been equally effective for men and women. Based on Archer's descriptions of gender differences (and lack thereof), however, we have identified two potential therapeutic implications regarding how women and men may respond differently to the anger management approach described in this book.

- Men's self-reports of angry physical and verbal aggression should be considered, assessed carefully, and reviewed weekly via the self-monitoring logs. Although in our experience, extreme forms of physical and verbal aggression are rare, men should be viewed at higher risk for direct aggression throughout the intensity spectrum.
- Women, more likely to engage in indirect aggression, may require more in-session exploration and discussion about this form of aggressive behavior, as it may not be readily apparent on the self-monitoring logs. Therapists' awareness of women's tendency to engage in indirect forms of angry behavior may come from a more detailed in-session weekly review.
- The physical relaxation exercises and strategies may be of extra importance to men. We speculate that the ability to calm the body and muscles when angry may have extra benefit in protecting from direct physical anger expression.
- The cognitive relaxation exercises and strategies may be of extra importance to women. We speculate that calming the mind and minimizing anger-increasing maladaptive cognitions may have extra benefit in protecting from indirect anger expression.

Diversity-Based Considerations

Tiffany*: There's no f-ing excuse for racism and don't try to tell me there is. All these years later and we're still fighting to be treated fairly -- that's bullshit. You have no idea what it's like to be followed around a store like a criminal just because of your skin color. That's something I refuse to just* *roll over and accept. Shit like that will always make me angry and, in my opinion, it damn well should.*

Important and meaningful differences exist between genders, sexes, races, ages, ethnicities, sexual orientations, socioeconomic statuses, religions, and spiritualties, just to name a few. Despite the differences present between any therapist and any client, we must find a way to successfully work with people different from ourselves. This effort requires empathy, sensitivity, and cultural competency. We propose that we, as therapists, should aspire to a principle of cultural humility to appreciate and address the breadth of human diversity and apply this principle to our treatment. Cultural humility is based on the ability to admit what we do not know and the curiosity to learn from and understand others. We need a willingness to "walk in their shoes," if only for a few moments. As described by Hook, Davis, Owen, Worthington, and Utsey (2013), cultural humility...

> *involves the ability to maintain an interpersonal stance that is other-oriented (or open to the other) in relation to aspects of cultural identity that are most important to the client. Cultural humility is especially apparent when a therapist is able to express respect and a lack of superiority even when cultural differences threaten to weaken the therapy alliance... therapists who are more culturally humble approach clients with respectful openness and work collaboratively with clients to understand the unique intersection of clients' various aspects of identities and how that affects the developing therapy alliance. (p. 354)*

Tiffany's statement above is one that pleads for cultural humility and openness. As with any client, it is important for the therapist to work toward clearly and deeply understanding the implications of Tiffany's situation and her reaction to it. The therapeutic goal is not to eliminate or invalidate Tiffany's anger at her experience of racism but to help her to manage anger-related emotions so that she can make choices about how she wants to respond.

Therapist: *Being unfairly judged, especially based on your skin color, is one thing you just won't put up with.*

Tiffany: *Of course not! That shop owner is an ignorant racist bitch and doesn't deserve my business. I would've spent some money there too if she hadn't been so stupid. People like her shouldn't be allowed to get away with shit like that.*

Therapist: *You really feel strongly about what happened to you in that store.*

Tiffany: *No shit! And it's not just at that store, it happens all the time.*

Therapist: *You're fed up.*

Tiffany: *I am. I deserve to be treated with respect. I never stole anything in my life.*

Therapist: *She got you totally wrong and that made you really angry.*

Tiffany: *She doesn't know me! I glared at her as I stomped out of that store but I wanted to scream in her stupid f-ing face. Who the hell does she think she is judging me like that?*

Therapist: *I'm wondering if you're willing right now to practice this scene using the coping skills we've been working on.*

Tiffany: *I don't know. I don't need anybody telling me to calm down. I think I have a right to be mad about this. If I calm down, isn't that just accepting her racist bullshit?*

Therapist: *Well, as we've been talking about, learning to manage anger doesn't mean making anger go away. For a lot of people, it means getting the anger down to a level that lets you decide what to do with it. A certain amount of anger can tell you that things aren't right and actually push you to do something or change something.*

Tiffany: *So you're saying I calm down enough to decide how to get back at that bitch?*

Therapist: *Possibly. At least calming down enough to consider some of your options. When you're really pissed off like you were in that store, what usually happens?*

Tiffany: *Sometimes I do stupid shit or say things I regret. Sometimes I'm just so mad I do nothing but go home and drink and think about it over and over.*

Therapist: *It sounds like you feel pretty out of control or powerless when that happens.*

Tiffany: *I guess that's true. I hate letting people get to me. That bitch ruined my weekend.*

Therapist: *So maybe for you, calming down enough to stay in control and not giving your power away to other people could be a goal.*

Tiffany: *That kind of makes sense. All I thought about the whole weekend was her stupid face. It's like I let her take over my life.*

Therapist: *You want to be in charge of your own life and choices.*

Tiffany: *Absolutely. I'm a strong black woman and proud of it!*

Therapist: *It seems to me that a lot of social change starts with feelings of anger. The goal is to use the energy of that anger to motivate rather than to get stuck.*

Tiffany: *So I can still get mad but maybe calm down enough to do something useful with it. That sounds like a better idea. Let's practice.*

How, specifically, do we work toward a position of cultural humility? The dialog above reflects the therapist's focus on the client (clarifying her experience), understanding of her emotional and behavioral reactions (through reflections), and a nondefensive and nonjudgmental stance (being open and accepting).

Based on Hook et al. (2013), working toward cultural humility involves:

- Engaging each client with an attitude of humility, respect, and lack of cultural superiority.
- Continuously self-evaluating and displaying openness to learn from others.
- Maintaining a focus on the unique beliefs, values, and worldviews of the client.
- Avoiding the assumption of understanding the client's cultural background and experiences based on previous knowledge or training.
- Collaborating with the client to explore the beneficial and harmful aspects of cultural background and experiences.
- Expressing curiosity and genuine interest in the client's cultural identity and its impact on current life issues.
- Asking sincere questions to enhance understanding and using reflective listening to communicate empathy and acceptance.

Summary

A comprehensive review of dimensions of human diversity that could potentially affect anger, Alcohol Use Disorder, and anger management based alcohol treatment is not feasible in this book. In fact, a comprehensive review would be so extensive that it simply may not be possible. Instead we propose that we, as therapists, should aspire to a principle of cultural humility to appreciate and address this diversity in anger management based alcohol treatment. A humble, respectful, empathic, and nonjudgmental stance is critical for successfully working with clients different than ourselves. Whether the diversities between client and therapist are gender, sexual orientations, races, ethnicities, religions, and/or nationalities, we encourage a stance of humility and respect for the client's unique situation and experiences.

Suggested Readings

Archer, J. (2004). Sex differences in aggression in real-world settings: A meta-analytic review. *Review of General Psychology*, *8*, 291–322.

This meta-analysis studied anger emotion, physical aggression, verbal aggression, and indirect aggression with regard to gender differences, age differences, and nationality differences. Findings include the absence of a gender effect for anger emotions but gender effects for physical and verbal aggression (men reported more) and indirect aggression (women were observed to have more). These findings were generally consistent across ages and nationalities. Findings are reviewed in the context of sexual selection theory and social role theory.

Erol, A., & Karpyak, V. M. (2015). Sex and gender-related differences in alcohol use and its consequences: Contemporary knowledge and future research considerations. *Drug and Alcohol Dependence*, *156*, 1–13.

This chapter reviews 266 research articles including studies from multiple nations and cultures in order to describe sex and gender differences in drinking and drinking problems. Findings support the hypotheses that women, relative to men, are more often lifetime abstainers, drink less, and are less likely to meet diagnostic criteria for alcohol use disorder. Women who drink heavily however are more likely to develop alcohol-related medical and psychiatric problems relative to heavily drinking men. Recent research indicates that gender differences in drinking behaviors may be decreasing.

Hook, J. N., Davis, D. E., Owen, J., Worthington, E. L., Jr., & Utsey, S. O. (2013). Cultural humility: Measuring openness to culturally diverse clients. *Journal of Counseling Psychology*, *60*(3), 353–366.

Cultural humility is described as having an "other" viewpoint as opposed to a "self" viewpoint with regard to an individual's background and life experiences. Appreciation of the multicultural diversity of the human experience is critical to a positive working alliance and successful outcomes.

Verissimo, A. D. O., & Grella, C. E. (2017). Influence of gender and race/ethnicity on perceived barriers to help-seeking for alcohol and drug problems. *Journal of Substance Abuse Treatment*, *75*, 54–61.

The authors examined barriers and challenges to alcohol treatment entry among men and women not currently in treatment. The strongest set of barriers identified was related to beliefs and attitudes about alcoholism and its treatment. Greater than 75% of the sample reported concerns such as embarrassment, fear, and pessimism hindered consideration of and entry into treatment. These attitudinal barriers were greater among women relative to men. Implications include the need to tailor treatment interventions to address these barriers to increase access to alcohol treatment.

Chapter 15

Broader Applications and Final Thoughts

Chapter Points

- Addressing anger-related emotions has the potential to help smokers quit.
- Relaxation and cognitive coping skills and coping skills rehearsals may be effectively applied to linkages between other negative emotions and drinking.
- Anger management based alcohol treatment, described here in an individual outpatient context, may be adapted to a counseling group setting.

Questions for Self-Reflection

- How confident do you feel using this treatment?
- What would make you feel more confident?
- How do you see this treatment method being useful in other areas of your practice?

Anger Management Based Alcohol Treatment. DOI: https://doi.org/10.1016/B978-0-12-812709-4.00015-9

Application of Anger Management Therapy to Smoking Cessation

In addition to its relevance to the treatment of alcohol use disorder, the strategies and tools of anger management based treatment may have relevance to other addictions. The strongest rationale for inclusion of anger management techniques with other addiction treatments is for smoking cessation. Extant empirical literature documents a strong link between anger-related emotions and smoking behaviors, nicotine withdrawal, and relapse following a quit attempt. Cougle et al. (2013) reviewed this literature and provided data on over 5600 adults recruited via a national representative survey; the results of this paper are strongly consistent with the hypothesis that anger is strongly, and problematically, associated with smoking behavior. Remarkably, the experience of anger-related emotions was linked with every smoking-related aspect they assessed including daily smoking, nicotine dependence, heavy smoking, and a history unsuccessful quit attempts, leading the authors to conclude that "problematic anger experience may be a crucial variable to consider when assisting with smoking cessation" (p. 300).

In initial exploration of the application of anger management treatment to smoking cessation, we treated nine clients with a combination of nicotine replacement therapy (NRT) transdermal patch and anger management therapy sessions (Rath, Walitzer, and Deffenbacher, 2016). In order to be consistent with therapy duration in the smoking cessation field, we redesigned anger management therapy to six sessions. This abbreviated treatment protocol contained assessment and therapy rationale (one session), relaxation skills (one session), cognitive skills (one session), and coping skills rehearsal (three sessions). All nine clients received a 12-week course of NRT; quit date was set as session 3. These clients completed research assessments at intake, at the end of anger management therapy, and at end of NRT. All nine clients completed treatment. As described in Rath et al. (2016), at the end of 12 weeks of anger management therapy and NRT, three clients had quit smoking, three clients had reduced substantially and were still in the quitting process, and three clients had reduced smoking. Importantly, the client feedback on the Client Satisfaction Questionnaire was very positive; client attendance and satisfaction demonstrated feasibility for future smoking cessation treatment outcome research.

Multiple differences between cigarette smoking and problematic drinking exist; these differences should be considered in future treatment research on anger management based smoking cessation. First, relative to drinking episodes, cigarette smoking is more likely to occur multiple times throughout the day as the smoker goes from cigarette to cigarette. Second, smoking behavior is very often strongly habitual and cue triggered. Daily, and multiple times each day, behaviors and activities such as morning cup of coffee, driving, speaking on the phone, scheduled smoke breaks, and having an alcoholic beverage may be repeatedly associated with smoking behavior. Therefore, in addition to linkages with anger and other negative emotions, smoking behavior may have many powerful associations with cues and triggers experienced multiple times each day. In an abbreviated treatment protocol, relaxation and cognitive coping skills and coping skills rehearsals must broadly address this complex environment of the smoking context.

ELAINE: ANGER MANAGEMENT THERAPY FOR SMOKING CESSATION

A 10-cigarette per day smoker, Elaine, was strongly motivated to quit because of her young daughter; specifically she wanted to eliminate her daughter's exposure to second-hand smoke as well as to improve her own health and reduce her risk for smoking-related illness and death. She was a nurse, working the night shift in an emergency department (ED). The majority of her smoking was just before, during, and just after her demanding work shift, although she regularly had several cigarettes at home. Elaine's triggers were emotional and included stress and the "adrenaline rush," referring to the emotional and physiological state associated with the Level II Trauma Care that she and her colleagues provided. Cognitions associated with smoking included both needing the smoke to cope with and "come down from the jitters" and the agitation she experienced in the ED, as well as "deserving" the smoke after the emotional stresses of her work. Given the importance of physiological arousal (the adrenaline rush, agitation, and jitters) as a component of her triggering emotions, the therapist spent an extra session on relaxation coping skills so that Elaine could reliably, quickly, and confidently relax in her busy work environment. Cognitive coping skills include identifying the arousal-increasing thoughts (e.g., "*I need a smoke to calm me down; when I'm jittery, smoking re-focuses me.*") and developing and implementing cognitive coping thoughts (e.g., "*I can use my relaxation skills to focus my mind and energy on what is important.*"). Additional coping thoughts reflected Elaine's desire to be healthy for her daughter and herself. Half way through her sessions, Elaine added transdermal patch NRT to her therapy plan to take the edge off the jitters and uncomfortable feelings she was experiencing from nicotine withdrawal. At the end of her sessions, Elaine was 4 weeks smoke-free. She felt very positive about her quit attempt and her initial success. She also felt encouraged by her new-found skill to quickly relax and focus in the ED environment and felt that she was providing better emergency care as a result.

Applications to Negative Moods Other Than Anger

In addition to anger, our case study clients described further negative emotions that they were experiencing both during anger episodes and independently. This is generally true; clients will often present with other negative emotions (e.g., anxiety, fear, shame, guilt, depression) that have a negative impact on their lives and, likely, lead to their alcohol consumption. Clients may experience these negative emotions to a problematic degree and may or may not meet diagnostic criteria (e.g., major depression, generalized anxiety disorder). With or without a formal diagnosis, it may be appropriate, and necessary, to focus on these additional negative emotions. This typically would take place toward the end of anger management based alcohol treatment after the relaxation and cognitive coping skills directed toward anger were in place.

To address these negative emotions, the client would analyze them within the same type of framework. The client would self-monitor the situations in which the problem emotion was experienced, along with the physical reactions, thoughts, images, and behaviors involved. Cognitions would be assessed for distortions and alternative coping thoughts would be developed. Then relaxation and cognitive coping skills would be rehearsed. As the client would already be experienced with relaxation and familiar with coping skills rehearsal format, it would be possible to start with the second or third training format and with somewhat higher levels of emotional arousal (e.g., level of 60–80 to start). Only the content of the scenes and the specific nature of the cognitive coping skills would change.

PAUL: COPING SKILLS REHEARSAL WITH ANXIETY

A client, Paul, experienced significant social anxiety and embarrassment in dealing with his friends since quitting drinking. In turn, this interfered with consistent application of drink refusal skills. That is, Paul would become anxious, make weak, ambivalent refusals, and then cave to repeated offers to drink because he did not want to look bad in front of his friends. Anxiety intensities were often around 60–70 and spiked to 90 if attention was focused directly on him or if his friends were making fun of him. Paul quickly understood and accepted that his anxiety was interfering with his ability to refuse drinks. Relaxation to combat anxious feelings also made ready sense to him. Exploration of cognitions revealed numerous catastrophes about how bad it was if his friends did not like and approve of him and overgeneralizations regarding both his self-worth and fears of being rejected by his friends. Cognitive coping skills focused on these issues and on questioning how strong Paul's friendships were if his friends could not accept him without a drink in his hand. Three anxiety scenes were developed (levels 70, 80, and 90). Over portions of three sessions, Paul visualized the scenes, experienced anxiety and embarrassment, and then actively coped with those feelings, employing both the relaxation (i.e., relaxing more on each of six deep breaths) and anxiety-focused cognitive coping skills. Paul reported that while he still did not like to have attention focused on him, he was learning to cope with the anxiety which was now much lower. He felt proud of himself because he could openly refuse drinks. He also reported that he had taken on a new role as the designated driver.

LUCY: COPING SKILLS REHEARSAL WITH SELF-MEDICATION OF CHRONIC PAIN

A client, Lucy, became aware of using alcohol to self-medicate chronic, moderate pain stemming from arthritis. She was particularly vulnerable to this when she was home alone for extended periods of time. Cognitions were marked by a low sense of self-efficacy at coping (e.g., thoughts about not being able to handle the pain and about becoming dependent on drinking). A series of coping thoughts around the ability to endure uncomfortable, painful feelings were developed, along with cognitive reminders of the importance of not mixing alcohol with other medications. Three scenes involving being home alone and experiencing 5, 6, and 8 levels of pain. A 0–10 scale was employed because that was the way in which Lucy had learned to code pain. Relaxation and new cognitive coping skills were rehearsed in the self-control format. In addition, a new relaxation image that involved greater sensations of warmth and comfort was developed and employed as an active coping skill at home. Lucy reported improved capacity to deal with pain and broke the alcohol/pain reduction link.

Adapting Anger Management Based Alcohol Treatment to a Group Setting

The intervention as described has been for individuals with a mixture of anger and alcohol issues. Individual therapy provides the opportunity for greatest individualization of procedures. However, group intervention provides greater economy and efficiency, and much of the research on the anger portion of the protocol has been successfully conducted in a group context. With a few modifications, this treatment can be adapted to groups. Here are some suggestions for that transition to a group format.

- Consider a group of six to eight individuals. This allows for significant group interaction and discussion while being small enough for individual attention.
- Consider a mixed gender group. This provides for an easier, fuller discussion of gender-related issues involved in anger and alcohol.
- Consider using a single therapist. This leads to greater efficiency, and there is no obvious benefit to more than one therapist.
- Consider lengthening the session to 75–90 minutes. This provides extra time for addressing the concerns of all and for individualizing material within a group format (e.g., developing anger and relaxation scenes).
- Consider lengthening the duration of treatment by a session or two. This provides the opportunity for all members of the group to complete the components of treatment.
- Assess treatment readiness and engage in preparation activities prior to the client entering the group. If members are at significantly different places in

terms of readiness, the change-focused nature of the group may be at odds with where some clients are and impasses and difficulties are likely to ensue.

- Be careful in mixing "mandated" individuals into a group with people who join on their own volition. Individuals who are mandated to attend may have issues that diverge from other group members.
- Address issues of confidentiality early. We suggest that these topics be covered in the first session right after the therapist introduces him or herself. Guidelines for when the therapist is required to break confidentiality (e.g., danger to self or others, suspected child abuse) should be outlined. These issues should be linked to state laws and professional ethical guidelines.
- Although complete confidentiality in group treatment settings cannot be guaranteed, rules regarding clients not sharing information outside of group should be discussed. Members are encouraged to share issues within the group, and the confidentiality of those communications should be respected and not shared outside the groups.
- Certain procedures need to be modified somewhat:

    Relaxation scenes and anger scenes might be referred to "your relaxation scene" or "your first (second) anger scene," because the individual referents cannot be included for all members.

    The therapist can develop a relaxation or anger scene with two or three people modeling how detailed they should be. Then he or she can check generally to make sure that everyone has a clear scene.

    The length of anger scene exposure might be increased by 30 seconds or so. This will allow more time for all group members to visualize their scenes and ensure sufficient anger arousal for coping skill rehearsal.

    Signal systems need to be visible to the therapist. If group members are seated in a circle, the therapist may want to make the instruction something like, "*Signal me by raising your hand closest to me.*"

    If certain group members only have one scene prepared or if one of their scenes is not working, then they are told to ignore the instructions regarding first and second scenes and to just visualize their one scene.

Final Words

We have written this book to address a gap in the treatment of anger- and alcohol-involved individuals. Hopefully, it provides practitioners with hands-on practical knowledge and skills. Practitioners, however, may benefit from additional training, supervision, and demonstrations. For example, training workshops and materials could be developed and delivered. Training videos could be created to demonstrate specific intervention components such as developing relaxation scenes, presenting anger scenes, or working with a client to identify types of cognitive distortions and develop new coping thoughts related to the distortions. Guidelines could be established for locating qualified supervisors and for the provision of supervision of intervention components (most likely addressing anger) with which staff are least likely to be familiar. Web-based materials might be developed for practitioners, so they can easily access materials and video demonstrations. Web-based materials might also be developed for individuals with anger and alcohol issues. People could access sequenced, self-help modules that address these issues.

The three case studies we presented each had generally positive outcomes in our anger management based alcohol treatment. Even with a variety of challenges, these three clients attended all sessions, completed worksheets, and made improvements in their drinking and management of anger. You may be left with questions such as, "Is this the norm? Is this a realistic expectation? Will I get similar results?" We would love to say "Yes! Absolutely!" But alas, no treatment method is 100% successful or even close to that in the real world. In our experience, this treatment proved to be as successful as other evidence-based approaches and the clients who participated made significant changes in their lives. Ideally, the availability of anger management based alcohol treatment provides another option to further tailor treatment interventions to the specific characteristics of clients who may benefit.

There are always those clients who drop out, sporadically participate, or decide they are not yet ready to change. Ambivalence is universal in behavioral health care. We have intentionally chosen to include these relatively successful and cooperative case studies to demonstrate the effectiveness of this treatment and to offer clear examples of how clients can progress through this program. We sincerely believe this treatment is meaningful, worthwhile, and rewarding. We hope that attitude is evident and contagious, and we hope you decide to incorporate anger management based alcohol treatment into your clinical portfolio.

Suggested Readings

Cougle, J. R., Zvolensky, M. J., & Hawkings, K. A. (2013). Delineating a relationship between problematic anger and cigarette smoking: A population-based study. *Nicotine & Tobacco Research, 15*, 297–301.

Results from this large population sample demonstrate important relationships between problematic anger and numerous aspects of smoking behavior. The authors conclude "efforts to improve smoking cessation outcomes may be aided through integrated smoking cessation and anger reduction strategies" (p. 300).

Rath, M. S., Walitzer, K. S., & Deffenbacher, J. L. (2016). Anger management-based smoking cessation treatment: Three case studies. *Clinical Case Studies, 15*, 157–173.

In this case study article, anger management therapy is integrated in smoking cessation treatment. Three case studies are presented, purposely with varying outcomes. Content for a six-session protocol is described.

Appendix I: Assessment Interviews and Questionnaires

Appendix I Preface: “The following Assessment Interviews and Questionnaires are in the public domain and can be copied and used without permission by the authors.”

Date:________ **Adapted DSM-V Checklist** **Name:**________

Instructions: Please answer "yes" or "no" to following questions based your drinking over the PAST 12 MONTHS:

	Yes or No
1. Have you often had times when you ended up drinking more, or for longer, than you intended?	
2. Have you persistently wanted or tried to cut down or stop drinking but couldn't?	
3. Have you spent a lot of time getting or using alcohol, or recovering from drinking?	
4. Have you had cravings for alcohol or had strong urges to drink alcohol?	
5. Have you found that drinking—or being sick from drinking—often interfered with taking care of your family or your house? Or it often caused problems at work or school?	
6. Have you continued to drink despite persistent problems, or worsened problems, with family or friends?	
7. Have you given up or cut back on activities that were important or interesting to you in order to drink?	
8. Have you more than once gotten into situations during or after drinking that put you at more risk of getting hurt (such as driving, swimming, using machinery, walking in a dangerous area, or having unsafe sex)?	
9. Have you continued to drink even though it was making you feel anxious, depressed, making a health problem worse, or after having a memory blackout?	
10a. Have you had to drink much more than you used to in order to get the effect you want?	
10b. Or have you found that your usual number of drinks had much less of an effect than before?	
11a. Have you found that when the effects of alcohol were wearing off, you had withdrawal symptoms, like sleep trouble, shakiness, restlessness, nausea, sweating, or a racing heart?	
11b. Have you taken a drink to avoid these withdrawal symptoms?	

Date:_______ **Brief Drinking History Assessment** **Name:_______**

1. **Why are you here for treatment now?**

2. **Describe your drinking history** (how did you start? at what age? when did it become a problem?).

3. **Describe your typical drinking pattern** (how many? how often? with whom? where? recent changes?).

4. **Tell me about any other substances you use** (drugs, tobacco).

5. **Describe the situations and emotions that are connected with drinking for you** (triggers).

6. **What kinds of problems have you had because of drinking** (family? work? health? legal?)

7. **What do the important people in your life think about your drinking? Do you have support?**

8. **Explain any medical issues, especially those related to drinking** (including medications).

9. **Tell me about any periods of abstinence** (how long? how? relapse issues? withdrawal?).

10. **Talk about any previous treatment experience** (where? when? result?).

11. **Have you ever attended Mutual Help Group meetings like AA? What was your experience like?**

12. **Tell me about past successes in making behavior changes in your life** (i.e. smoking? weight loss?)

13. **How important is for you to stop drinking? (0-10 scale)**

14. **How confident are you that you can quit drinking? (0-10 scale)**

15. **What needs to change in your life right now in order for you to stop drinking?**

Date:____________ Quick Drinking Screen (QDS) Name:____________

Alcohol Use

The next few questions focus on the 30-day period before you last use of alcohol. When was the last time, before entering treatment, that you used alcohol?

Date of Last Alcohol Use _____/_____/_____ Date of 30 Days Earlier ____/____/____

OK. So the 30-day period that we'll be talking about runs from [day and date] to [day and date]. Take a moment and get that period of time clear in your mind. Do you have a clear picture of it?

Now, the first few questions are about any alcohol use in this 30-day period. For these questions on alcohol consumption, we ask people to report their drinking in terms of what we call STANDARD DRINKS. For example, one Standard Drink is equal to:

One 12-ounce bottle/can of regular beer or wine cooler, OR
One 5-ounce glass of regular (12%) wine, OR
1.5 ounces of hard liquor (80 proof) either straight or in a mixed drink, OR

1. In this 30-day period, on average how many days per week did you drink ANY alcoholic beverages?
   ________ days per week

   1a. If Q1 is answered as "less than 1 day per week," that is, you drink but not weekly, then how many days out of this 30-day period did you drink any alcohol?
   ________ # days drank alcohol in 30-day period

2. On average, on days when you did drink, how many standard drinks did you drink in a day?
   ________ drinks

3. In this 30-day period, how many days did you drink [for men: 5 or more standard drinks; for women: 4 or more standard drinks] in one day?
   ________ days

4. In this 30-day period, what was the greatest number of standard drinks you consumed in one day?
   _______ drinks

ADDITIONAL QUESTIONS:

5. The next questions are about days when you were totally abstinent, that is, days in which you consumed no alcohol. Again, the period in question runs from [day and date] to [day and date]. In this 30-day period, on average, how many days per week were you totally abstinent from alcohol?
   ________________ days/weeks

   5a. If Q5 is answered as "less than 1 day per week" that is you were totally abstinent on some days but less than 1 day per week then how many days out of the 30-day period were you totally abstinent from alcohol?
   _____________ # days totally abstinent in this 30-day period

Date:__________

Short Inventory of Problems (SIP)

Name:__________

Instructions: Here are a number of things that drinkers sometimes experience. Please mark the appropriate answers:

DURING THE PAST 3 MONTHS, how *often* has this happened to you?	Never (0)	Once or a few times (1)	Once or twice a week (2)	Daily or almost daily (3)
1. I have been unhappy because of my drinking.				
2. Because of my drinking, I have not eaten properly.				
3. I have failed to do what is expected of me because of my drinking.				
4. I have felt guilty or ashamed because of my drinking.				
5. I have taken foolish risks when I have been drinking.				
6. When drinking, I have done impulsive things that I regretted later.				
7. When drinking, I have broken or smashed something.				
8. I have gotten into a physical fight while drinking.				
9. I have felt irritable or angry as a result of my drinking.				
10. While drinking, I have said harsh or cruel things to someone.				
DURING THE PAST 3 MONTHS, how *much* has this happened to you?	Not at all (0)	A little (1)	Somewhat (2)	Very much (3)
11. My physical health has been harmed by my drinking.				
12. I have money problems because of my drinking.				
13. My physical appearance has been harmed because of my drinking.				
14. My family has been hurt by my drinking.				
15. A friendship or close relationship has been damaged by my drinking.				
16. My drinking has gotten in the way of my growth as a person.				
17. My drinking has damaged my social life, popularity, or reputation.				
18. I have spent too much or lost a lot of money because of my drinking.				
19. I have had an accident while drinking or intoxicated.				

Intrapersonal: #1, 4, 16 Interpersonal: # 14, 15, 17 Social: # 3, 12, 18 Impulse: # 5, 6, 19 Physical: # 2, 11, 13 Anger: # 7, 8, 9, 10

Penn Alcohol Craving Scale (PACS)

Circle the most appropriate number for each item. The questions apply to the ***past week****.*

1) How often have you thought about drinking or about how good a drink would make you feel?

Never (0)
Rarely (1)
Occasionally (2)
Sometimes (3)
Often (4)
Most of the time (5)
Nearly all of the time (6)

2) At its most severe point, how strong was your craving?

Not at all (0)
Slight urge (1)
Mild urge (2)
Moderate urge (3)
Strong urge (easily controlled) (4)
Strong urge (difficult to control) (5)
Strong urge (unable to control) (6)

3) How much time have you spent thinking about drinking or about how good a drink would make you feel?

None at all (0)
Less than 20 minutes (1)
21-45 minutes (2)
46-90 minutes (3)
90 minutes – 3 hours (4)
Between 3 – 6 hours (5)
More than 6 hours (6)

4) How difficult has it been to resist taking a drink?

Not difficult at all (0)
Very mildly difficult (1)
Mildly difficult (2)
Moderately difficult (3)
Very difficult (4)
Extremely difficult (5)
Not able to resist (6)

5) Keeping in mind your responses to the previous questions, please rate your *overall average* alcohol craving.

Never (0)
Rarely (1)
Occasionally (2)
Sometimes (3)
Often (4)
Most of the time (5)
Nearly all of the time (6)

Date: ________ **Brief Anger Assessment** **Name**__________

1) **What makes you feel frustrated or angry?** (situations, people, driving, etc.)

2) **How often do you feel frustrated and/or angry?**

3) **How intense are your anger emotions? On a scale from 0-100?** (Celsius thermometer)

4) **What kind of words do you use to describe your anger emotions?** (mad, pissed off, furious)

5) **What happens in your body when you get angry?** (pounding heart, seeing red, clenched fists, headache, blood pressure, stomachache, etc.)

6) **What other emotions do you notice when you're angry?** (sadness, disappointment, fear, etc.)

7) **What thoughts and/or images run through your mind when you're angry?** (imagine a small microphone or a camera in your head)

8) **How do you act when you're angry?** (hold it in, yell, use sarcasm, drive aggressively, throw things, swear, slam doors, hit people etc.)

9) **What good and/or bad things happen when you're angry?** (short term/long term)

10) **How do important people in your life react when you're angry?**

11) **What do you do to calm down when you're angry?** (effective and less effective coping)

12) **Describe how anger and alcohol are connected for you** (Anger → Alcohol → Anger)

Dimensions of Anger Reactions (DAR)

Thinking *over the* ***past 4 weeks***, circle the number under the option that best describes the amount of time you felt that way.

	None or almost none of the time (1)	A little of the time (2)	Some of the time (3)	Most of the time (4)	All or almost all of the time (5)
I found myself getting angry at people or situations					
When I got angry, I got really mad					
When I got angry, I stayed angry					
When I got angry at someone I wanted to hit them					
My anger prevented me from getting along with people as well as I'd have liked to					

Date:_________ Positive and Negative Affect Schedule (PANAS) Name:_________

Instructions: **Here are of a number of words that describe different feelings and emotions. Read each item and mark the appropriate answer in the box next to the word. Indicate to what extent you felt this way during the PAST WEEK.**

		Not at all/ very slightly (0)	A little (1)	Moderately (2)	Quite a bit (3)	Extremely (4)
1	Interested					
2	Distressed					
3	Excited					
4	Angry					
5	Upset					
6	Strong					
7	Guilty					
8	Scornful					
9	Scared					
10	Hostile					
11	Enthusiastic					
12	Proud					
13	Irritable					
14	Alert					
15	Ashamed					
16	Inspired					
17	Disgusted					
18	Nervous					
19	Determined					
20	Attentive					
21	Jittery					
22	Loathing					
23	Active					
24	Afraid					

POS = #1,3,6,11,12,14,16,19,20,23 NEG = #2,5,7,9,10,13,15,18,21,24 ANG = #4,8,10,13,17,22

Date:_________ Client Satisfaction Questionnaire (CSQ) Name:_________

Instructions: Please answer the following questions based on your experience with our treatment program. We are interested in your honest opinions, whether they are positive or negative.

1. How would you rate the quality of the services you received?
   Poor   Fair   Good   Excellent

2. Did you get the kind of service you wanted?
   No, definitely not   No, not really   Yes, generally   Yes, definitely

3. To what extent do you feel your needs were met by this program?
   None of my needs were met   Only a few of my needs were met
   Most of my needs were met   All of my needs were met

4. If a friend were in need of similar help, would you recommend this program?
   No, definitely not   No, I don't think so   Yes, I think so   Yes, definitely

5. How satisfied were you with the amount of help you received?
   Very dissatisfied   Mostly dissatisfied   Mostly satisfied   Very satisfied

6. Do you think the services you received helped you deal more effectively with your drinking?
   No, they made things worse   No, they didn't really help
   Yes, they helped somewhat   Yes, they helped a great deal   N/A

7. Do you think the services you received helped you deal more effectively with your anger?
   No, they made things worse   No, they didn't really help
   Yes, they helped somewhat   Yes, they helped a great deal   N/A

8. In an overall, general sense, how satisfied were you with the program?
   Very dissatisfied   Mostly dissatisfied   Mostly satisfied   Very satisfied

9. If you were to seek this help again, would you come back to this program?
   No, definitely not   No, I don't think so   Yes, I think so   Yes, definitely

10. Other comments: ____

____

____

Appendix II: Client Handouts and Worksheets

Appendix II Preface: "The following Client Handouts and Worksheets can be copied and used without permission by the authors."

Self-Monitoring Log 1

Date/ Time	Frustration situation	Emotion intensity 0–100	Alcohol related? If yes, how?	Craving 0–10	Number of drinks?

Self-Monitoring Log 1

TRACKING—Observing and logging your anger emotions, cravings, and any alcohol use will help increase awareness of patterns.

1. Record at least once per day. If you experience no anger emotions, record "none."
2. Fill out the entry just after the frustrating event, if possible.
3. Describe the Frustrating Situation with details.
4. Record the intensity of your anger emotions (0–100).
5. Record any physical symptoms you notice.
6. Record a "yes" if the entry was alcohol related and describe how.
7. Record the intensity of any craving experienced (0–10).
8. Record any alcohol drank, in standard drinks (1 standard drink = 12 oz. beer, 5 oz. wine, 1.5 oz. liquor).

Log 1 Example

Date/ Time	Frustration situation	Emotion intensity 0–100	Physical symptoms	Alcohol related? If yes, how?	Craving 0–10	No. of drinks
8/20 7:00 p.m.	*Stupid drivers on the way home from work slowed me down and I missed my daughter's big game. My wife was really upset*	85	*Gripped wheel*	*I had to get away from my wife*	9	10
8/21 7:00 p.m.	*Home late from work, my son never mowed the lawn, someone left a sink full of dishes, and all the lights were on in the house*	90	*Stomach*	*Drank as soon as I walked in the door*	10	9
8/22 6:00 p.m.	*Crappy day. Late for work, missed a meeting, boss was pissed, wife was nagging, and spilled coffee on my new shirt*	75	*Stomach*	*Started a bottle on the way home*	10	9

Self-Monitoring Log 2

Date/ Time	Frustration situation	Thoughts	Emotion intensity 0–100	Alcohol related? If yes, how?	Craving 0–10	No. of drinks?

Self-Monitoring Log 2

TRACKING—Observing and logging your anger emotions, cravings, and any alcohol use will help increase awareness of patterns.

1. Record at least once per day. If you experience no anger emotions, record "none."
2. Fill out the entry just after the frustrating event, if possible.
3. Describe the Frustrating Situation with details.
4. **Describe your thoughts during the situation.**
5. Record the intensity of your anger emotions (0–100).
6. Record a "yes" if the entry was alcohol related and describe how.
7. Record the intensity of any craving experienced (0–10).
8. Record any alcohol drank, in standard drinks (1 standard drink = 12 oz. beer, 5 oz. wine, 1.5 oz. liquor).

Log 2 Example

Date/ Time	Frustration situation	Thoughts	Emotion intensity 0–100	Alcohol related? Yes? How?	Craving 0–10	No. of drinks?
10.23 11:00 a.m.	*Running errands. Every stupid driver was on the road and I hit all the red lights too*	*Some of these moronic asses shouldn't even have licenses*	55	*The wine store was on the list of errands*	7	10
10.24 all day	*Woke up feeling awful. Decorated the house for Halloween with no help from Michael*	*Why am I the only one who cares about taking care of this house?*	75	*Drank all day because I was alone and pissed*	9	10
10.25 11:00 p.m.	*Hungover, slept all day, went to work. The chef was in a nasty mood*	*I can't stand this job anymore! He's an asshole*	80	*Drank at work and at home*	9	6

SOBER Problem Solving

S: Stop and See the problem—*recognize that there is a problem and describe the problem as accurately as possible.*
O: List your Options—*consider a variety of ways to solve the problem. Brainstorm as many ideas as you can from all different angles.*
B: Be Aware of Consequences—*consider the positive and negative effects of each option. Think about the short and long term aspects too.*
E: Evaluate and select the best options—*choose one or more ideas that have the best chance of working for you. Try them out.*
R: Review the Results—*give your solution a chance and then check to see if it's working. If it is—great! If not, go back to an earlier step and try again.*

Practice Exercise

S: The Problem ____

O: Options	**B:** Positive Consequences	**B:** Negative Consequences

E: Best Option ____

E: Next Choice____

R: How do I know it's working? ______________________________

____

Self-Monitoring Log 3

Date/ Time	Frustration situation	Thoughts	Coping efforts	Emotion intensity 0–100	Alcohol related? If yes, how?	Craving 0–10	No. of drinks?

Self-Monitoring Log 3

TRACKING—Observing and logging your anger emotions, cravings, and any alcohol use will help increase awareness of patterns.

1. Record at least once per day. If you experience no anger emotions, record "none."
2. Fill out the entry just after the frustrating event, if possible.
3. Describe the Frustrating Situation with details.
4. Describe your thoughts during the situation.
5. **Describe your coping efforts for the situation**.
6. Record the intensity of your anger emotions (0–100).
7. Record a "yes" if the entry was alcohol related and describe how.
8. Record the intensity of any craving experienced (0–10).
9. Record any alcohol drank, in standard drinks (1 standard drink = 12 oz. beer, 5 oz. wine, 1.5 oz. liquor).

Log 3 Example

Date/ Time	Frustration situation	Thoughts	Coping efforts	Emotion intensity 0–100	Alcohol related? How?	Craving 0–10	No. of drinks?
11/07 6:00 p.m.	*Every day I come home to an empty apartment*	*I can't stand being alone. Why me? My life is a hot mess*	*Tried to do some deep breath-ing but it didn't work*	80	*Yes I drank*	10	5
11/08 3:00 p.m.	*My mom wonders if I'll ever give her grandbabies*	*She says shit like that just to piss me off*	*I left her and went to the gym*	65	Drank the rest	7	3.5
11/09 7:00 p.m.	*Sore from the gym and dis-gusted with my body*	*No one will ever want to be with me I'm gross*	*Called my friend but he wasn't home*	95	*Drank a whole bottle*	10	8.5
11/10 6:00 p.m.	*Some days I absolutely hate my job*	*I wish I could just quit. Why didn't I stay in college?*	*Did relaxation and actually calmed down a little bit*	70	*Didn't drink*	4	0

Relaxation Log

Please put a check mark under all relaxation exercises completed on each date.

Date	Progressive Relaxation		Deep breathing	Relaxation scene	Relaxation phrase
	With tension	Without tension			

On at least **5** days this week try out these tools for relaxation:

Relaxation *Without* Tension—Focus on relaxing your muscle groups *without* tensing

Deep Breathing—Focus on deep abdominal breaths

Relaxation Scene—Imagine a relaxing scene and place yourself in it

Relaxation Phrase—Relaxing more each time you say the word “relax” to yourself

Relaxation *With* Tension—Focus on relaxing your muscle groups by first tensing them

Home Practice of Relaxation I

Practice of relaxation is a very important part of our process. It is a skill that develops with practice. You are asked to practice it regularly, say 5 out of every 7 days. Practice more if you can. Make your relaxation experience at home parallel closely your experience in the session. Choose a place that is quiet and where you can be undisturbed for approximately 30 minutes. Pick a place where your body will be supported and as tension-free as possible. Beds, couches, and comfortable chairs generally work well. If you find a good system, stay with it. If you are uncomfortable or fall asleep, change your position and/or time of day. If you practice in the later afternoon or evening, you may experience a kind of "second wind" a few minutes to an hour or so later. If this happens, make it work for you. However, make sure that you do not get this "second wind" just at the time when you want to drift off to sleep. So, do not practice relaxation within the last hour or so before you go to bed.

Follow the tension-release procedures you learned in the session (see list of muscles and ways of tensing them below). Tense each muscle group hard for 5–10 seconds, but not to the point of pain or cramping. Then let that muscle group go quickly and spend 20–30 seconds focusing on letting the tension go and attending to the contrast between tension and relaxation. If an area is still tense, repeat the tension-release exercise. At various points (see below), you should go back over an area and review the muscles and let them relax a bit more without tensing them up. When you are finished, arouse yourself by counting backwards from 5 to 1. On 4, move your arms and legs gently. On 2, open your eyes and look around. On 1, feel alert and refreshed.

Muscles and How to Tense Them

1. **Hands** by clenching them into fists
2. **Lower arms** by holding them out straight with wrists held at a 90° angle
3. **Upper arms** by holding arms in front, 45° angle, while making fists
4. **Shoulders** by shrugging them, pulling shoulder blades back and together

   (Review the shoulders, arms, and hands)

5. **Forehead** by lifting the eye brows upward, or frowning
6. **Eyes and bridge of nose** by closing eyes tightly
7. **Cheeks, jaws, and lips** by grinning from ear to ear with lips pressed together
8. **Chin and neck** by pressing and burying chin into chest

   (Review head and neck area)

9. **Chest and upper back** by arching the back, taking a deep breath, holding it and releasing it
10. **Stomach** by hardening the stomach muscles; continuing to breathe

    (Review chest, back and stomach)

11. **Thighs** by lifting the feet slightly off the floor and clenching the thighs and upper legs firmly
12. **Legs** by stretching and trying to touch your toes to your knee caps
13. **Feet** by pointing the toes downward and away

    (Review lower body)

Drink Refusal Skills

- Get a nonalcoholic drink ahead of time
- Say "no" first (to yourself and then to others)
- Use your body language:
  - Use a clear, firm, unhesitating voice
  - Make direct eye contact
- After saying no, change the subject
- Suggest something else to eat, drink, or do:
  - *No thanks. How about seeing a movie?*
  - *No thanks, but let's meet for coffee.*
- Ask the person to stop offering you a drink
- There's no need to use excuses or feel guilty:
  - You have the right <u>not</u> to drink!

Practice Exercise

Listed below are some people who might offer you a drink in the future. Give some thought to how you will respond to them, and write your responses under each item.

Someone close to you who knows about your drinking problem: ________________

____

Boss/Coworker: ____

____

New acquaintance: ____

____

Waitress/Waiter with others present: ______________________________________

____

Relative at a family gathering: ____

____

Other: ____

____

Home Practice of Relaxation II

Practice of relaxation continues to be a very important part of our process, and you should attempt to practice it regularly, at least 5 out of every 7 days. Practice more if you can. In the previous session, two kinds of changes were made. The biggest change was dropping out the tensing of the muscles.

The second change involved saying a word like "relax" or "calm" slowly, relaxing more every time you say the word. Try to make your relaxation experience at home as similar as possible to your experience in the session. Choose a place that is quiet and where you can be undisturbed for about 15 minutes. Pick a place where you will be comfortable and as tension-free as possible. You should start each time with Relaxation *without* Tension and then practice each of the others at least once. You can sequence the other three in any order that you wish.

Relaxation Without Tension:

Start the relaxation practice by closing your eyes and going through the body, relaxing the muscles without tensing them up. Start with the hands and work up your arms. Then go to the head and work down to your feet. Focus on the areas you tensed last week, but this week just focus there and let a wave or flow of relaxation increase in that area. Do that for a short time, and then focus on the next area and let that sense of relaxation increase there. Keep moving through the body until you just let remaining tensions flow right out the end of your toes. This generally takes people about 5–8 minutes. If you find yourself distracted for a moment, that is fine. Just focus back on the last place you relaxed and continue. This list can help you remember sequence of muscles from last week: hands; arms; shoulders; forehead; eyes and bridge of nose; cheeks, jaws, and lips; chin and neck; chest and upper back; stomach and lower back; thighs; lower legs; and feet.

Relaxation Scene:

Visualize your relaxation scene. Put yourself right into it. Be there and let the scene develop clearly and the relaxed feelings increase. Do this for a minute or so, and then switch it off. If you want to, you can switch it back on again a time or two before you finish practicing relaxation.

Relaxation Phrase:

This involves relaxing more each time you say the word "relax," or another word you like to use such as "chill" or "peace." Repeat the word slowly to yourself 10–15 times. Let yourself relax more each time you say the word. Some people find it helpful to say the word each time they breathe out regularly and slowly. If that works for you, then do it.

Deep Breathing:

This involves relaxing each time you take a deep breath. So, practice taking a deep breath and relaxing more each time. Repeat this 3–5 times.

Anger Increasing Thoughts

Our thoughts play a key part in both generating anger emotions and increasing them. Below are listed several types of thoughts that commonly increase anger emotions. Following each are some alternative ways of thinking that help manage emotion and deal more helpfully with emotion-provoking situations.

Magnification

This is making things worse than they really are. Events are often described as "awful," "terrible," "disgusting," or "horrendous." When you magnify, you are more likely to respond angrily or even go on the attack, as if things are actually as bad as your magnification makes them seem.

Examples

This is the worst thing that's ever happened.
My job is totally screwed up.
I can't stand the way that he or she is talking to me.

Coping Thoughts

It's not the end of the world. It's just frustrating.
It's just not worth getting all bent out of shape about.
Hang in there. It'll be over soon.

Overgeneralization

You can make a problem seem bigger than it is by using words such as " always," " all," " every," "never," " total," " everybody," "nobody," and so on. These go way beyond what is really true. These terms make an event that happened a few times feel like something that's continuous and bigger than life.

Examples

You never got home on time.
Everybody was totally unhappy.
You pick a fight with me every day.

Coping Thoughts

Be accurate. How many times has this really happened?
Sometimes things go a lot better than this. I'm going to think about that, too.
No need to get upset. I'll think about exceptions when _____acted a lot better than this.

Anger Increasing Thoughts

Shoulds/Oughts

This is the tendency to make your "wants" into demands for yourself or the rest of the world. Shoulds are typically couched as "ought to," "have to," "need to," "gotta," "expect," and "must" kinds of thoughts. Anger emotions are often triggered by a judgment based on a set of rules about how people should and should not act. People who behave according to the rules are right, and those who break the rules are wrong and bad. You might think that others know and accept your rules, but the people with whom you feel frustrated rarely agree with you. Your perception of the situation leaves you feeling blameless and justified.

Examples

He or she should have known that would hurt my feelings.
They should not have done that.
He isn't being fair; he needs to listen to me once in a while.

Coping Thoughts

So what if I don't get what I want? Sometimes I do and sometimes I don't.
There's no guarantee. No reason to blow up about it. Stay cool.
People do what they want to do, not what I want them to do.
This is disappointing, and I would prefer things to be different, but I can cope and make the best of it.

Global Labeling

A global label makes sweeping, negative judgments. Typical global labels include the terms like "stupid," "selfish," "jerk," "loser," "liar," and so on. Global labels fuel your anger by turning the target into someone who is totally bad and worthless. Instead of focusing on a particular behavior, you indict the entire person.

Examples

That salesperson is an idiot.
That liar can't be trusted.
Why are you so selfish?

Coping Thoughts

He or she is not scum, just a person with whom I have a disagreement.
No one's bad—people do the best they can.
Children make mistakes. That's their job.

Anger Increasing Thoughts

Jumping to Conclusions

This is about mind reading. When people hurt or annoy you, it's easy to imagine that it was deliberate and meant to upset you. You jump to conclusions and assume you know someone else's motives. Rather than thinking about the multiple reasons for why things could happen the way they did, you focus on a single negative explanation.

Examples

He or she is doing that to get to me.
They wouldn't have done that if they were my friends.
He corrected what I said to make me look stupid.

Coping Thoughts

Don't jump to conclusions. Check out the facts.
Where is my evidence that this is the only reason?
Don't second guess the motives of others.

Blaming

Blaming comes from a belief that the other person did it to you, often on purpose, and that he or she shouldn't be allowed to get away with it. While blaming feels very good at times, it also leaves you feeling helpless. The power to solve a problem always seems to lie with others. You keep waiting for them to change their bad behavior, but they rarely do.

Examples

You want breakfast in the morning and that always makes me late.
I could enjoy this vacation if it weren't for your constant negativity.
This house looks like a pigsty because you never lift one finger to clean or fix it.

Coping Thoughts

I'm not helpless; I can take care of myself in this situation.
I'll make a plan to deal with this myself.
I may not like it, but they are doing the best they can.

General Coping Thoughts

Serenity Prayer:
God grant me the serenity to accept the things I cannot change;
courage to change the things I can;
and wisdom to know the difference.

- Take a deep breath and relax.
- Getting upset won't help.
- Just as long as I keep my cool, I'm in control.
- Easy does it—there's nothing to be gained in getting irritated.
- I'm not going to let him/her get to me.
- I can't change him/her with anger; I'll just upset myself.
- I can find a way to say what I want to without frustration.
- Stay calm—no sarcasm, no attacks.
- I can stay calm and relaxed.
- No one is right, no one is wrong. We just have different needs.
- Stay cool, make no judgments.
- No matter what is said, I know I'm a good person.
- I'll stay rational—getting upset won't solve anything.
- Let them look all foolish and upset, I can stay cool and calm.
- His or her opinion isn't important—I won't be pushed into losing my cool.
- I'm in control. I can always leave rather than say or do something I'll regret.
- Take a time-out. Cool off, then come back and deal with it.
- Some situations don't have good solutions. Looks like this is one of them.
- No use getting all bent out of shape.
- If they're trying to make me angry, boy, are they going to be disappointed.
- It's just a hassle. Nothing more, nothing less. I can cope with hassles.
- Break it down. Frustration often comes from lumping things together.
- I got angry, but kept the lid on saying dumb things. That's progress.
- It's just not worth it to get so upset.
- Irritation means it's time to relax and cope.
- I can manage this; I'm in control.
- I can't expect people to act the way I want them to.
- I don't have to take this so seriously.
- I have a plan to relax and cope.
- This is funny if you look at it that way.

Creating Coping Thoughts

Between Session Practice: Please complete both sides and bring to the next session.

Describe an anger emotion scene (circle level): MODERATE (40–60) HIGH (60–80) WORST (80–100)

____

____

____

____

Anger Increasing Thoughts:

a. ____

b. ____

c. ____

d. ____

Helpful Coping Thoughts:

a. ____

b. ____

c. ____

d. ____

Creating Coping Thoughts

Describe an anger emotion scene (circle level): MODERATE (40–60) HIGH (60–80) WORST (80–100)

____

____

____

____

Anger Increasing Thoughts:

a. ______________________________________

b. ______________________________________

c. ______________________________________

d. ______________________________________

Helpful Coping Thoughts:

a. ______________________________________

b. ______________________________________

c. ______________________________________

d. ______________________________________

Coping with High Risk Situations

On the left side of this form, list your potential high-risk situations. Then, on the right side list the coping strategies you will be able to use to deal with each of these high-risk situations.

High-Risk Situation	Coping Strategies
* ______________________	* ______________________
______________________	______________________
* ______________________	* ______________________
______________________	______________________
* ______________________	* ______________________
______________________	______________________
* ______________________	* ______________________
______________________	______________________
* ______________________	* ______________________
______________________	______________________
* ______________________	* ______________________
______________________	______________________

Best Coping Thoughts

"I Believe in Myself" Thoughts

"I can handle this, I've done it before."
"I'm hanging in and coping."
"I have what it takes to get through this hassle."

Your coping thought example:

____

Keep Cool Thoughts

"Just stay cool-getting all wound up won't help."
"It's just not worth it. Take a few deep breaths and chill out."
"This too shall pass. Others have to deal with this kind of stuff without getting crazy."

Your coping thought example:

____

Problem-Solving Thoughts

"It's okay to feel annoyed, but it's just a challenge to be dealt with."
"Develop a plan. So, the first thing I would want to do is ..."
"Break the frustration down. I can deal better with it that way."

Your coping thought example:

____

Escape Routes

"It's okay to take time out. Move away, get your act together, then come back and deal with it later."
"Better to walk away than to be a screaming idiot."
"Bottom line, I'll walk before I hit or do something dumb."

Your coping thought example:

____

Reframing Thoughts

"They're probably just (scared, overwhelmed, not understanding, hurting, etc.)."
"Cut them some slack. I'd hope they'd do the same for me if I was having a bad time."
"It's just that time in the day (year, season)."

Your coping thought example:

____

Best Coping Thoughts

See the Whole Picture
"Look at the other side."
"There are exceptions. For example…"
"Time to look for some of the good for a change."

Your coping thought example:

____

Getting Accurate
"Cut the angry crap. Tell it like it is."
"Just focus on the facts."
"Tell it simple and straight."

Your coping thought example:

____

Preferences, Not Shoulds
"It doesn't have to be my way, I just prefer it."
"What I want and what has to be are two different things."
"Nobody appointed me supreme ruler. So give it up."

Your coping thought example:

____

People Doing Their Best
"They're only doing what they know how to do."
"They're coping the best they can, all things considered."
"I don't know why they do it, but they're just trying to survive."

Your coping thought example:

____

Other Favorite Coping Thoughts:

____

____

____

Anger Emotion Management Plan

Memory strategies (reminder hints) I have in place that will help me remember to cope during upcoming situations:

____

____

Coping behaviors: What can I say or do that will calm things down?

____

____

____

____

Problem solving: Is there a way to solve this problem and avoid conflict?

____

____

____

What to Do if a "Lapse" Occurs

1. Renew your commitment to abstinence;
   "don't allow a lapse to become a relapse."

2. Use the lapse as a learning experience.

3. See the lapse as a specific, unique event.

4. Examine the lapse openly in order to reduce the amount of guilt and/or shame you feel (those thoughts can lead to feelings of hopelessness and continued drinking).

5. Analyze the triggers for the lapse.

6. Examine what the expectations about drinking were at the time
   (what did you anticipate drinking would accomplish in that situation?)

7. Plan for dealing with the aftermath/consequences of the lapse.

8. Make immediate plans for recovery—don't hesitate—do it now.

9. Attend a self-help group (e.g., Alcoholics Anonymous, SOS)

10. Contact your therapist.

References

Archer, J. (2004). Sex differences in aggression in real-world settings: A meta-analytic review. *Review of General Psychology, 8*, 291–322.

Alvanzo, A. A. H., Storr, C. L., La Flair, L., Green, K. M., Wagner, F. A., & Crum, R. M. (2011). Race/ethnicity and sex differences in progression from drinking initiation to the development of alcohol dependence. *Drug and Alcohol Dependence, 118*, 375–382.

Bowen, S., Witkiewitz, K., Clifasefi, S. L., Grow, J., Chawla, N., Hsu, S. H., et al. (2014). Relative efficacy of mindfulness-based relapse prevention, standard relapse prevention, and treatment as usual for substance use disorders: A randomized clinical trial. *The Journal of the American Medical Psychiatry, 71*, 547–556.

Cougle, J. R., Zvolensky, M. J., & Hawkings, K. A. (2013). Delineating a relationship between problematic anger and cigarette smoking: A population-based study. *Nicotine & Tobacco Research, 15*, 297–301.

Dahlen, E. R., & Deffenbacher, J. L. (2000). A partial component analysis of Beck's cognitive therapy for the treatment of general anger. *Journal of Cognitive Psychotherapy, 14*, 77–95.

Deffenbacher, J. L. (2009). Angry drivers: Characteristics and clinical interventions. *Mexican Journal of Psychology, 26*, 5–16.

Deffenbacher, J. L., Dahlen, E. R., Lynch, R. S., Morris, C. D., & Gowensmith, W. N. (2000). An application of Beck's cognitive therapy to general anger reduction. *Cognitive Therapy and Research, 24*, 689–697.

Deffenbacher, J. L., Demm, P. M., & Brandon, A. D. (1986). High general anger: Correlates and treatment. *Behaviour Research and Therapy, 24*, 481–489.

Deffenbacher, J. L., Filetti, L. B., Lynch, R. S., Dahlen, E. R., & Oetting, E. R. (2002). Cognitive-behavioral treatment of high anger drivers. *Behaviour Research and Therapy, 40*, 895–910.

Deffenbacher, J. L., Huff, M. E., Lynch, R. S., Oetting, E. R., & Salvatore, N. F. (2000). Characteristics and treatment of high anger drivers. *Journal of Counseling Psychology, 47*, 5–17.

Deffenbacher, J. L., Lynch, R. S., Oetting, E. R., & Kemper, C. C. (1996). Anger reduction in early adolescents. *Journal of Counseling Psychology, 43*, 149–157.

Deffenbacher, J. L., & McKay, M. (2000a). *Overcoming situational and general anger: Therapist Protocol*. Oakland, CA: New Harbinger.

Deffenbacher, J. L., & McKay, M. (2000b). *Overcoming situational and general anger: Client Protocol*. Oakland, CA: New Harbinger.

Deffenbacher, J. L., & McKay, M. (2000c). *Overcoming situational and general anger: A protocol for the treatment of anger based on relaxation, cognitive restructuring and coping skills training (therapist protocol)*. Oakland, CA: New Harbinger Publications, Inc.

Deffenbacher, J. L., Oetting, E. R., Huff, M. E., Cornell, G. R., & Dallager, C. J. (1996). Evaluation of two cognitive-behavioral approaches to general anger reduction. *Cognitive Therapy and Research, 20*, 551–573.

Deffenbacher, J. L., Oetting, E. R., Thwaites, G. A., Lynch, R. S., Baker, D. A., Stark, R. S., et al. (1996). State-trait anger theory and the utility of the Trait Anger Scale. *Journal of Counseling Psychology, 43*, 131–148.

Deffenbacher, J. L., & Stark, R. S. (1992). Relaxation and cognitive-relaxation treatments of general anger. *Journal of Counseling Psychology*, *39*, 158–167.

Deffenbacher, J. L., Story, D. A., Brandon, A. D., Hogg, J. A., & Hazaleus, S. L. (1988). Cognitive and cognitive-relaxation treatments of anger. *Cognitive Therapy and Research*, *12*, 167–184.

Deffenbacher, J. L., Story, D. A., Stark, R. S., Hogg, J. A., & Brandon, A. D. (1987). Cognitive-relaxation and social skills interventions in the treatment of general anger. *Journal of Counseling Psychology*, *34*, 171–176.

Deffenbacher, J. L., Thwaites, G. A., Wallace, T. L., & Oetting, E. R. (1994). Social skills and cognitive-relaxation approaches to general anger reduction. *Journal of Counseling Psychology*, *41*, 386–396.

Demirbas, H., Ilhan, I. O., & Dogan, Y. B. (2012). Ways of problem solving as predictors of relapse in alcohol dependent male inpatients. *Addictive Behaviors*, *37*, 131–134.

Denson, T. F., Moulds, M. L., & Grisham, J. R. (2012). The effects of analytical rumination, reappraisal, and distraction on anger experience. *Behavior Therapy*, *43*, 355–364.

Dolan, S. L., Rohsenow, D. J., Martin, R. A., & Monti, P. M. (2013). Urge-specific and lifestyle coping strategies of alcoholics: Relationships of specific strategies to treatment outcome. *Drug and Alcohol Dependence*, *128*, 8–14.

Erol, A., & Karpyak, V. M. (2015). Sex and gender-related differences in alcohol use and its consequences: Contemporary knowledge and future research considerations. *Drug and Alcohol Dependence*, *156*, 1–13.

Forbes, D., Alkemade, N., Mitchell, D., Elhai, J. D., McHugh, T., Bates, G., et al. (2014). Utility of the dimensions of anger reactions—5 (DAR-5) scale as a brief anger measure. *Depression and Anxiety*, *31*, 166–173.

Grant, B. F., Goldstein, R. B., Saha, T. D., Chou, S. P., Jung, J., Zhang, H., et al. (2015). Epidemiology of DSM-V alcohol use disorder results from the National Epidemiologic Survey on alcohol and related conditions III. *The Journal of the American Medical Psychiatry*, *72*, 757–766.

Hazaleus, S. L., & Deffenbacher, J. L. (1986). Relaxation and cognitive treatments of anger. *Journal of Consulting and Clinical Psychology*, *54*(2), 222–226.

Hendershot, C. S., Witkiewitz, K., George, W. H., & Marlatt, G. A. (2011). Relapse prevention for addictive behaviors. *Substance Abuse Treatment, Prevention, and Policy*, *6*, 1–17.

Hook, J. N., Davis, D. E., Owen, J., Worthington, E. L., Jr., & Utsey, S. O. (2013). Cultural humility: Measuring openness to culturally diverse clients. *Journal of Counseling Psychology*, *60*(3), 353–366.

Humphreys, K., Wing, S., McCarthy, D., Chappel, J., Gallant, L., Haberle, B., et al. (2004). Self-help organizations for alcohol and drug problems: Toward evidence-based practice and policy. *Journal of Substance Abuse Treatment*, *26*, 151–158.

Kashdan, T. B., Goodman, F. R., Mallard, T. T., & DeWall, C. N. (2015). What triggers anger in everyday life? Links to the intensity, control, and regulation of these emotions, and personality traits. *Journal of Personality*, *84*(6), 737–749.

Kassinove, H., & Tafrate, R. C. (2002). *Anger management: The complete treatment guidebook for practitioners*. Atascadero, CA: Impact.

Kassinove, H., & Tafrate, R. C. (2006). *Anger management video program: An instructional guide for practitioners*. Atascadero, CA: Impact.

Kelly, J. F., Stout, R. L., Tonigan, J. S., Magill, M., & Pagano, M. E. (2010). Negative affect, relapse, and alcoholics anonymous (AA): Does AA work by reducing anger? *Journal of Studies on Alcohol and Drugs*, *71*, 434–444.

Kiluck, B. D., Dreifuss, J. A., Weiss, R. D., Morgenstern, J., & Carroll, K. M. (2013). The Short Inventory of Problems—Revised (SIP-R): Psychometric properties within a large, diverse sample of substance use disorder treatment seekers. *Psychology of Addictive Behaviors*, *27*, 307–314.

Kirshenbaum, A. P., Olsen, D. M., & Bickel, W. K. (2009). A quantitative review of the ubiquitous relapse curve. *Journal of Substance Abuse Treatment, 36*, 8–17.

Krenek, M., Prince, M. A., & Maisto, S. A. (2017). Life events and alcohol use disorder clinical course: Modeling the dynamic association. *Drug and Alcohol Dependence, 180*, 137–143.

Leibsohn, M. T., Oetting, E. R., & Deffenbacher, J. L. (1994). Effects of trait anger on alcohol consumption and consequences. *Journal of Child and Adolescent Substance Abuse, 3*, 17–32.

Lievaart, M., Franken, I. H., & Hovens, J. E. (2016). Anger assessment in clinical and nonclinical populations: Further validation of the State-Trait Anger Expression Inventory-2. *Journal of Clinical Psychology, 72*(3), 263–278.

Maurage, P., Campanella, S., Philippot, P., Vermeulen, N., Constant, E., Luminet, O., et al. (2008). Electrophysiological correlates of the disrupted processing of anger in alcoholism. *International Journal of Psychophysiology, 70*(1), 50–62.

McCloskey, M. S., Noblett, K. L., Deffenbacher, J. L., Gollan, J. K., & Coccaro, E. F. (2008). Cognitive-behavioral therapy for intermittent explosive disorder: A pilot randomized clinical trial. *Journal of Consulting and Clinical Psychology, 76*, 876–886.

McHugh, R. K., Fitzmaurice, G. M., Griffin, M. L., Anton, R. F., & Weiss, R. D. (2016). Association between a brief alcohol caving measure and drinking in the following week. *Addiction, 111*, 1004–1010.

Michie, S., Whittington, C., Hamoudi, Z., Zarnani, F., Tober, G., & West, R. (2012). Identification of behaviour change techniques to reduce excessive alcohol consumption. *Addiction, 107*, 1431–1440.

Miller, W. R., & Rollnick, S. (2013). *Motivational interviewing: Helping people change* (3rd ed.)). New York, NY: Guilford Press.

National Institute on Alcohol Abuse and Alcoholism. *Alcohol facts and statistics*. (2017). Downloaded from: https://pubs.niaaa.nih.gov/publications/AlcoholFacts&Stats/AlcoholFacts&Stats.pdf Accessed 16.04.18.

Novaco, R. W. (1975). *Anger control*. Lexington, MA: Heath.

Olson, R., Schmidt, S., Winkler, C., & Wipfli, B. (2011). The effects of target behavior choice and self-management skills training on compliance with behavioral self-monitoring. *American Journal of Health Promotion, 25*(5), 319–324.

Rath, M. S., Walitzer, K. S., & Deffenbacher, J. L. (2016). Anger management-based smoking cessation treatment: Three case studies. *Clinical Case Studies, 15*, 157–173.

Roos, C. R., & Witkiewitz, K. (2016). Adding tools to the toolbox: The role of coping repertoire in alcohol treatment. *Journal of Consulting and Clinical Psychology, 84*(7), 599–611.

Roy, M., Dum, M., Sobell, L. C., Sobell, M. B., Simco, E. R., Manor, H., et al. (2008). Comparison of the quick drinking screen and the alcohol timeline followback with outpatient alcohol abusers. *Substance Use & Misuse, 43*, 2116–2123.

Serafini, K., Malin-Mayor, B., Nich, C., Hunkele, K., & Carroll, K. M. (2016). Psychometric properties of the Positive and Negative Affect Schedule (PANAS) in a heterogeneous sample of substance users. *American Journal of Drug and Alcohol Abuse, 42*, 203–212.

Spielberger, C. D., Sydeman, S. J., Owen, A. E., & Marsh, B. J. (1999). Measuring anxiety and anger with the State-Trait Anxiety Inventory (STAI) and the State-Trait Anger Expression Inventory (STAXI. In M. E. Maruish (Ed.), *The use of psychological testing for treatment planning and outcomes assessment* (pp. 993–1021). Mahwah, NJ: Lawrence Erlbaum Associates Publishers.

Steckler, G., Witkiewitz, K., & Marlatt, G. A. (2013). Relapse and lapse. In P. Miller (Ed.), *Principles of addiction: Comprehensive addictive behaviors and disorders* (Vol. 1, pp. 125–132). New York, NY: Elsevier Press.

Substance Abuse and Mental Health Services Administration. *Trauma-informed approach and trauma-specific interventions.* (2015). Downloaded from: https://www.samhsa.gov/nctic/trauma-interventions (accessed on April 16, 2018).

Substance Abuse and Mental Health Services Administration, Key substance use and mental health indicators in the United States: Results from the 2016 National Survey on Drug Use and Health. In *HHS publication no. SMA 17-5044, NSDUH series H-52.* Rockville, MD: Center for Behavioral Health Statistics and Quality, Substance Abuse and Mental Health Services Administration; 2017. Retrieved from: https://www.samhsa.gov/data/.

Tafrate, R. C., Kassinove, H., & Dundin, L. (2002). Anger episodes in high and low trait anger community adults. *Journal of Clinical Psychology, 58*, 1573–1590.

van Achterberg, T., Huisman-de Waal, G. G., Ketelaar, N. A., Oostendorp, R. A., Jacobs, J. E., & Wollersheim, H. C. (2010). How to promote healthy behaviours in patients? An overview of evidence for behaviour change techniques. *Health Promotion International, 26*(2), 148–162.

Verissimo, A. D. O., & Grella, C. E. (2017). Influence of gender and race/ethnicity on perceived barriers to help-seeking for alcohol and drug problems. *Journal of Substance Abuse Treatment, 75*, 54–61.

Walitzer, K. S., Deffenbacher, J. L., & Shyhalla, K. (2015). Alcohol-adapted anger management treatment: A randomized controlled trial of an innovative therapy for alcohol dependence. *Journal of Substance Abuse Treatment, 59*, 83–93.

Witkiewitz, K., Donovan, D. M., & Hartzler, B. (2012). Drink refusal training as part of a combined behavioral intervention: Effectiveness and mechanisms of change. *Journal of Consulting and Clinical Psychology, 80*(3), 440–449.

Witkiewitz, K., & Marlatt, A. (2004). Relapse prevention for alcohol and drug problems: That was Zen, this is Tao. *American Psychologist, 59*(4), 224–235.

Witkiewitz, K., & Marlatt, G. A. (2007). Modeling the complexity of post-treatment drinking: It's a rocky road to relapse. *Clinical Psychology Review, 27*, 724–738.

Wurst, F. M., Thon, N., Yegles, M., Schrück, A., Preuss, U. W., & Weinmann, W. (2015). Ethanol metabolites: Their role in the assessment of alcohol intake. *Alcoholism: Clinical and Experimental Research, 39*, 2060–2072.

Index

Note: Page numbers followed by "*f*" and "*b*" refer to figures and boxes, respectively.

Kolibri 360 GmbH
Ferdinand-Jühlke-Straße 7
99095 Erfurt, Deutschland
produktsicherheit@kolibri360.de